Savage State

Savage State

Welfare Capitalism and Inequality

Edward J. Martin and Rodolfo D. Torres

ROWMAN & LITTLEFIELD PUBLISHERS, INC.
Lanham • Boulder • New York • Toronto • Oxford

ROWMAN & LITTLEFIELD PUBLISHERS, INC.

Published in the United States of America
by Rowman & Littlefield Publishers, Inc.
A wholly owned subsidiary of The Rowman & Littlefield Publishing Group, Inc.
4501 Forbes Boulevard, Suite 200, Lanham, Maryland 20706
www.rowmanlittlefield.com

PO Box 317
Oxford
OX2 9RU, UK

British Library Cataloguing in Publication Information Available

Library of Congress Cataloging-in-Publication Data

Martin, Edward J., 1957–
    Savage state : welfare capitalism and inequality / Edward J. Martin and
Rodolfo D. Torres.
        p. cm.
    Includes bibliographical references and index.
    ISBN 0-7425-2463-9 (cloth : alk. paper)
    1. Marxian school of sociology. 2. Social classes—Economic aspects.
    3. Capitalism. 4. Historical materialism. 5. Marxian economics. I.
    Torres, Rodolfo D., 1949– II. Title.

HM471 .M37 2004
301—dc22   2003024372

Printed in the United States of America

∞™ The paper used in this publication meets the minimum requirements of American
National Standard for Information Sciences—Permanence of Paper for Printed Library
Materials, ANSI/NISO Z39.48-1992.

In memory of Senator Paul Wellstone (1944–2002), a wise and visionary public intellectual who believed in a more democratic economy and humane future. Also dedicated to the memory of Paul Sweezy (1910–2004), the dean of radical economists. They will be missed.

Contents

Acknowledgments

This undertaking has been one of endurance. Indeed, the labor and toil involved in this project have manifested themselves late into the evening and wee hours of the morning. In this capacity I would like to thank my coauthor Rudy Torres who collaborated with me in composing and editing this manuscript. In so doing, we were equal partners in this project and the order of our names has no significance.

Special thanks are also extended to my colleagues at the Graduate Center for Public Policy and Administration at California State University, Long Beach—Michelle Saint Germain, John Ostrowski, Martha Dede, Bill Moore, Frank Baber, and David Powell—for their encouragement throughout the duration of this project. My former professors at Arizona State University—Dennis Palumbo, Nick Alozie, and Alvin Mushkatel—have also been more than generous with their time in providing feedback on various sections of this manuscript. I am also grateful for the invaluable comments from the following colleagues: Bob Bartlettt, Roger Karapin, Cheryl King, Lisa Zanetti, Camilla Stivers, Peter McLaren, Frances Fox Piven, Martin, Gillens, Ron Schmidt, Joel Handler, and Yeheskel Hasenfeld.

Finally, while many people have been influential in the construction of this book, none have been more so than my loving wife Sarah and our beautiful children, Ariana, Jeff, and Mike. Because of them I am reminded of the various levels of commitment we have to each other, specifically in crafting social policies that prioritize the poor. The overwhelming love and support they showed me during this time sustained me throughout. As a small token of my appreciation, two additions have been made to our household—Jake and Jeb—white Labrador puppies. *Con cariño!*

—Edward J. Martin

ix

A collaborative project of this kind is a long and arduous effort. I have a range of acknowledgments I wish to convey. Thanks to my new colleagues in Chicano–Latino studies, social ecology, and political science for their interest in and support of my work. I wish to thank Michael P. Clark and Katherine Tate for their advice and encouragement during a difficult and emotionally draining departmental move—I needed their all-important validation and support during that hellish year.

Many thanks to Bob Jessop and Martin Carnoy for their comments and suggestions on drafts of this book. Of course, any shortcomings in the final manuscript are the authors' own. I did some final work on this book while on sabbatical at the University of California Irvine Center for Research on Latinos in a Global Society, and I wish to thank Leo Chavez, the director of the center, for the support to complete this project. Portions of chapters 2–4 were written by and with Jonathan Aurthur in 1982–1983, with research support I received from Loyola Marymount University. In 2002, Ed Martin and I substantially revised, expanded, and updated this material; Jonathan's intellectual imprint remains, though, as well as selected passages of his on classical Marxism written over twenty years ago. Every effort was made to authenticate the paraphrasing or summarizing of work, sources, and citations, and to ensure the scholarly integrity of the 1982–1983 material presented in this book in accordance with conventional research protocol. The authors would be grateful to be notified of any omissions or irregularities and will make corrections in the next edition or reprint of this book.

I would like to acknowledge debts (in no particular order) to a host of friends and colleagues: Robert Miles, Antonia Darder, Mario Barrera, Gilbert Gonzalez, Darrell Y. Hamamoto, Linda Vo, Lou F. Miron, Zaragosa Vargas, Tim Tift, Lisa Garcia Bedolla, Mike Davis, Michele Knobel, Colin Lankshear, Vicki Ruiz, Fred Weaver, Noel Samaroo, Marlon Boarnet, Francisco Vazquez, Richard Brown, Peter Bohmer, Ann DeVaney, Raul A. Fernandez, Victor Valle, Juan F. Lara, and George Katsiaficas. Gracias to my seven Uni Hills homeboys—Victor Becerra, Mark Levine, Pat Farmer, Mike Arias, Diego Vigil, Richard Mathew, and Tahseen Mozaffar—for providing a source of distraction from the pettiness of academic life. To comrade Malaquias Montoya, I am grateful for his frontispiece art contribution "A Portrait of Poverty." Apologies to those I've missed; I will get you the next time around. Thanks to BhashaLeonard for her important technical and editorial assistance; her skill and attention to detail have enhanced this volume.

My work as associate editor of *New Political Science,* corresponding U.S. editor of *Ethnicities,* and as a member of the editorial board of the new and exciting journal *Radical Society* has put me in touch with a diverse group of progressive and activist scholars. These new friends and colleagues have been an important source of my intellectual and political renewal. I would like to express my appreciation to Dean Birkenkamp, a stellar editor who commissioned this project. I wish him continued success in his new publishing venture. Melissa McNitt and Alan McClare did a fine job of seeing this project into print. A big thank you to Edward Martin for being a stimulating and hard-working collaborator. All chapters were co-written and rewritten in a truly democratic and equal partnership and the authors listed alphabetically.

As always, I owe a great debt to my wife, Patricia Speier Torres, for her continued support of my work. I depend upon Patricia's love and support to get me through the day. Above all I draw my strength from two sources: the voices of dissent of the antiglobalization movement, and, especially, my five-year old son. I look at Jacob David Torres and see a more humane and democratic future.

— Rodolfo D. Torres

Introduction: Against Welfare Capitalism

> So I ask you now in the Congress and in the country to join with me in expressing and fulfilling that faith in working for a nation, a nation that is free from want and a world that is free from hate—a world of peace and justice, and freedom and abundance, for our time and for all time to come.
>
> —Lyndon B. Johnson, 1964 State of the Union Address

> The question of poverty today is a question of both reexamining the balance of power in our society and challenging a society that eviscerates its low-wage workers.
>
> —Beth Shulman, *The Betrayal of Work*

In 1964, during his State of the Union address, Lyndon B. Johnson declared an unconditional war on poverty in the United States. Programs such as Head Start, Medicare, and Medicaid, among others, were established. With this declaration the American Dream was renewed in public policy and political discourse. As we enter the twenty-first century, in the age of limited class mobility and the "Wal-Martization" of America, the lifetime "safety net" for welfare assistance in the United States has been removed at a time of greatest need. In the December 1, 2003, issue of *Business Week* an article entitled "Waking Up From the American Dream" reported a drastic increase in income and wealth inequality in the United States. America is increasingly looking like a society which Karl Marx would have described—a capitalist society of the haves and the have-nots in which poor people remain trapped in poverty jobs, no matter how hard they work. As we demonstrate in this book, in the area of welfare policy, the government is quickly removing itself from prior levels of intervention. The rationale for ending the welfare policy has nevertheless come about as the result of perceived failures in a welfare system that arguably has fostered dependency. This is an old argument. However, welfare policy has also been doomed with the onset of the new global market economy, which necessitates a competitive advantage on the global market. Social welfare spending undermines this new international economic arrangement of mass consumption within global markets.[1] The development known as "late capitalism," or as Jean Baudrillard and Fredric Jameson describe it, "postmodern capitalism," serves as a context for understanding the nuances of the production capacity of a mass culture's drive for commodity consumption and manufacturing.[2]

Welfare developed as a result of dysfunctions within the capitalist system during the Great Depression. The Great Depression, experienced by western Europe as well as the United States, forced industrialized countries to intervene for the economic well-being of their populations. The demand on the United States government to promote some form of redistribution of wealth to the poor was based on a liberal perspective of intervention in order to rescue the market and maintain secure democratic institutions. In Britain and Sweden, social democratic ideas were implemented along the lines of economic and social reform as "mixed" or "postcapitalist" measures.[3] The ruling wisdom since the Great Depression to the present has basically been that individuals and communities could best remedy the negative externalities that a capitalist system tended to embody. However, critics of this form of state welfare policy, on both the Left and Right, found little support in post–World War II society, since social programs were the preferred policies as opposed to none at all. Moreover, these critiques were virtually silenced since the dominant discourse at the time refused to include any discussion of "radical socialist" or feminist perspectives.

What ultimately shook the foundation of welfare policy was the result of a combination of profound social changes that took place in the industrialized world. With the emergence of the civil rights and peace movements of the 1960s and the simultaneous demise of the post–World War II economic boom in the United States, an explosion in the information and communication industry, primarily in computers, paved the way for a massive reorganization of both labor and capital on a global scale. This reorganization weakened the underlying assumption that an "industrialized" welfare state, which had faded to a large degree, is a necessary component in the new capitalist framework.[4] Missing from this analysis was a systematic understanding of the nature of capital and its tendencies toward contradiction and crisis, which was traditionally offered by the Left. The Right, for all intents and purposes, seized the intellectual high ground on the welfare policy debate by introducing neoliberal and public choice strategies.[5] This was highly effective in the 1980s during the Reagan and Thatcher years.

The theoretical differences between conservative welfare supporters who believed that state intervention was necessary to avoid social crisis, and neoliberals who rejected completely any intervention, was reconciled when the New Right reasserted the traditional liberal Enlightenment arguments in favor of market rationality and various economic forces that stood in contrast to the apparent irrationality of state intervention and bureaucratic largesse. The operative presupposition underlying this theory was that individual actors will act in their rational economic interests which, arguably, are superior to collective economic arrangements and the redistribution of private resources for public consumption. In addition to the demise of the welfare state came the transformation of Eastern European command economies into market economies in the late1980s and early 1990s. Coupled with China's inclusion of market measures, the global trend rapidly moved toward market strategies and away from collectivist and state welfare policies.

Modernity can best be described as the historical period in Western culture toward the later part of the eighteenth century that asserted the primacy of reason over intuition. This was known as the Age of Enlightenment. Modernity, or the Enlightenment, was perceived to be revolutionary in that it sought to replace unsophisticated notions of the universe with a more definitive truth: reason. Through the use of human reason and intellect, society, so it was argued, would then become emancipated from ignorance, which in turn would liberate the human community from ignorance, poverty, and sickness. As applications of modernity, both capitalism and socialism—understood as alternate versions of modernity—had promised human liberation: socialism as an economic and political theory, which in application has collapsed, and capitalism as a global system, which has never demonstrated any capacity to liberate on a global scale. Albeit, support for the ideological underpinnings of modernity can be identified in the neoliberal work of Lawrence Mead, Friedrich von Hayek, Milton Friedman, and George Gilder, and in the neo-Marxist works of Allen Buchanan, Samuel Bowles, Herbert Gintis, Thomas Bottomore, and Allen Wood.[6] However, the question facing modernity is whether it has been able to carry out the emancipatory strategy that it has claimed as its own, regardless of whether that strategy has been one of capital accumulation or revolutionary action. Regarding Jurgen Habermas' critique of modernism, Peter Leonard states:

Postmodernists argue that modernity has represented in practice, a Eurocentric, patriarchal and destructive triumphalism over populations and over nature itself. Modernity, it is maintained, represents the "triumph of the west" reflected in colonialism and post-colonial domination in which the interests of Western capitalism led to the attempted homogenization of a world of diverse cultures, beliefs and histories. In part to counteract these assertions, Habermas (1985, 1987) maintains that flawed and defective as it is, the modern project of emancipation retains its possibilities if we separate the universal claim to reason from the repression and domination [that] have historically accompanied it. The traditional modernist idea of autonomous rational individuality must be reworked, Habermas suggests, to emphasize a concept of reason based on egalitarian communication and the development of consensus amongst pluralities.[7]

While Habermas as a postmodernist arguably rescues modernity by differentiating theory from its flawed application, theorists such as Michel Foucault attempt to demonstrate how administrative control has resulted in "rules of exclusion," as Leonard puts it, "which ensure the invisibility of subordinate populations of the poor, of women and of oppressed and subjected masses of non-Europeans."[8] Moreover, the reflections of Jean-Francois Lyotard present an even more powerful critique of modernism as represented in Marxism and capitalism. Lyotard states:

Neither economic nor political liberalism, nor the various Marxisms, emerge from the sanguinary last two centuries free from the suspicion of crimes against humanity. . . . I use the name of Auschwitz to point out the irrelevance of empirical matter, the stuff of recent past history, in terms of the modern claim to help mankind to emancipate itself. What kind of thought is able to sublate Auschwitz in a general (either empirical or speculative) process towards universal emancipation?[9]

Thus, like Foucault, Lyotard argues that modernity's appeal to reason and scientific rationality empowers modernity to legitimize the power of authoritative bureaucracy and simultaneously delegitimize the power of those who make no appeal to reason and scientific management. As a result, the perspectives and voices of the oppressed and dispossessed are excluded from any dialogue or discourse on self-determination and well-being, a position that modernity claims to be its main focus.[10] The question of welfare policy can thus be addressed based upon whether welfare clients themselves have had significant input into the very policy that directly affects them. Consequently the thesis asserted in this book is that Marxism, specifically Marxist class analysis, has much to offer postmodernism in the way of a powerful social critique in relation to welfare policy and why certain sectors of society are not empowered to determine for themselves how welfare programs can best help them.

The reflections of Jameson and his work on late or postmodern capitalism can shed light on this purported synthesis between Marxist social analysis and postmodern deconstruction. Maintaining a Marxist orientation, Jameson identifies what he calls "the logic of late capitalism," in which culture (economic, social, political) has been organized around the driving force of commodity production and consumption. Mass media acts as the conduit by depicting superfluous wants as basic human needs. In fact, Jameson argues that this phenomena constitutes a form of hegemony and is as colonialistic in effect as any of the past colonial systems that once dominated the globe. Consequently, to unhinge the philosophical assumptions underneath this hegemony necessitates an ongoing assessment of the welfare state in a way that more clearly focuses on this principled philosophical discourse.[11]

Cultural conditioning will determine to some degree the understanding of what is generally considered to be "necessary" in terms of a meaningful material level of existence. These differences are connected to the economic and political elements of divergent social realities and must therefore factor into account a broad number of regulations—on both a local and international level, and inclusive of late or post capitalist cultures—the fabrication of economic desires as fundamental needs. Notwithstanding, the thesis put forth in this book further asserts the position that a thoroughgoing discourse on the various dimensions of social class, which postmodern critique has tended to dismiss, is the essential starting point for promoting awareness of the need for greater solidarity with respect to the needs of the poor and a more comprehensive understanding of social welfare policy. As the liberal welfare state witnesses its own demise, particularly within Western countries, a remnant of concerned peoples are attempting to combat its downfall. The issue remains as to whether this concern can be structured upon notions of solidarity between various individuals, coalitions, and factions. In essence this points to a return to Marxist analysis as a key theoretical construct for attempting to identify the causes in the demise of welfare policy and the lack of solidarity in support of retaining an adequate welfare policy agenda. By connecting postmodern concerns (diversity, ethnicity, multiculturalism, etc.) with radical analysis (root causes of class alienation and exploitation), the synthesis of both approaches in assessing social phenomena provides the optimal venue for social deconstruction and eventual reconstruction. When the discussion of poverty (whether marginal or absolute) is broached it is important to understand that the outcome of poverty is generally manifested in "populations whose material existence prevent their full expression as diverse moral agents."[12] And it is precisely in this discourse on poverty that the notion of social class is most apparent. In the present status of late capitalism it is paramount to identify class distinctions based on alienation and exploitation based upon the economic and political arrangements of international capital and its creation of new global markets. Thus reflections on social class on a domestic and global scale are constituent parts of any support for diversity issues in order to clarify and understand socially constructed forms of oppression that impinge on socioeconomic existence.

Class antagonism in and of itself does not necessarily mean that the class of exploited persons who struggle against the capitalist class reveals itself in the form of a vanguard of revolutionary proletariat. Rather, the struggle against oppression, as it becomes increasingly evident, is a form of conflict that has included diverse networks of people promoting an emancipatory project. This project necessarily includes diverse groups and coalitions with a broad range of social interests pitted against a perceived obstacle to their full liberation. We suggest that an emancipatory effort to reconstruct social welfare policy must be broached through multicultural dialogue and class analysis, as King and Stivers etal. have encouraged in their postmodern methods adumbrated in *Government Is Us*. Thus it is important to understand the major emphasis within capitalist societies that focuses on the accumulation of capital and all the numerous activities that constitute continued investment and profitability. Within this context, the activity of labor is viewed as a moral duty. In this sense individualism and capitalist beliefs merge into a type of religious belief, as Max Weber has noted in *The Protestant Ethic and the Spirit of Capitalism*.[13] Joel Handler and Yeheskel Hasenfeld have demonstrated in their studies on American welfare that meaningful work, according to the American ethos, is the responsibility of each individual. The authors state: "[T]hose who fail to find work, without a socially approved excuse, at a socially approved job are condemned. They are defined as deviant. The chronically unemployed, able-bodied malingerers, paupers, bums, tramps and those who work in socially disapproved jobs are considered threats to the ideology of labour discipline—hard work, thrift and reward through individual effort."[14]

Social approval of work in American society therefore emphasizes productive labor. The contrary is anathema in American society.[15] Weber argues that this unique distinction regarding labor is an integral part of modernity. In fact, during the early stages of capitalist development, the work ethic and capitalist accumulation emerged into what Thorstein Veblen has described as "conspicuous consumption."[16] Yet the activity of conspicuous consumption was not understood as a "moral virtue" in American society until late capitalism and its media-driven enterprise legitimated a consumer-based society. Indeed, as technological innovations take the place of labor, the demand for commodity consumption on a global basis becomes increasingly urgent in order to maintain markets and profitability. At one point in time, mass consumption was understood as the means to providing the basics, such as food, clothing, housing, transportation, etc, in order to sustain life. However, contemporary commodity consumption has taken on a new meaning in that "luxury" items, such as electronics, designer clothing, and other nonessential commodities, have now become marketed as "needs."

Zygmut Bauman refers to the marketing mechanism in late capitalism as the "weapon of seduction" in which individuals are seduced into becoming avaricious consumers.[17] Bauman further argues that individuals are "socialized" into this form of consciousness at early stages of their development. In other words, commodity consumption as the driving force of late capitalism becomes an uncritical and habitual form of economic interaction with others in society. This form of consumer seduction makes individuals dependent upon habitual consumption, which is equated with a new form of virtue. What emerges from this seduction is market dependency (which is essential to late capitalism), or what is otherwise known as postmodern capitalism. Jameson argues that postmodern capitalism subjugates individuals to the point where desire itself is commodified. For Jameson, the "cultural logic" of postmodern capitalism prevents any form of critical distance that would provide an essential critique for attempting any form of self-reflection on the entire system itself.[18] The capitalist system in its totality subordinates the individual to the logic of accumulation so much so that the individual then equates human value with commodity consumption. Jameson argues that it is virtually impossible to become disengaged in the dominant discourse of postmodern capitalism since the masses are immersed in a commodified culture that equates possessions with self-worth and autonomy. Here it is clear enough to comprehend the cultural demise of welfare subsistence in the face of postmodern capitalism. Arguments that welfare funding — at one point in time Aid to Families with Dependent Children (AFDC), now Temporary Assistance to Needy Families (TANF) provides a disincentive to leave welfare are otiose since the funding is hardly enough in the first place to act as an incentive to maintain a welfare lifestyle.

RECONSTRUCTING WELFARE POLICY

The emancipatory project associated with the struggle for social welfare demands a new theoretical focus that embraces both postmodern critique and Marxist analysis. While rejecting modernist Marxist theory, neo-Marxist and critical theory perspectives would be, nevertheless, essential tools of analysis in this emancipatory project. Along with postmodern deconstruction, Marxist analysis can act as an intellectual framework for assessing the structures of domination that perpetuate the injustice and oppression fabricated and marketed by late or postmodern capitalism. Leonard states, "the ethics [that] are counterposed to domination are culturally produced out of the material experience of oppression and injustice, a discourse of resistance which explicitly or implicitly assumes the possibility of the relative autonomy necessary to make moral choices."[19] Postmodern Marxist critique also provides an intellectual framework to assess the moral dimensions for promoting greater self-determination and well-being.

The welfare project we envision is one that, under the conditions of late or postmodern capitalism, eschews the old AFDC welfare state and its protagonists. It must not be structured on the old modernist version of welfare policy, complete with legitimated institutions and administrations. Reconstructing a new postmodern welfare culture will emphasize "process" rather than a grand scheme, and as Leonard insists, "a process based upon certain culturally produced assumptions [that] act as discursive signposts to assist us in the pursuit of welfare as an emancipatory idea. It is a process, furthermore, [that] stimulates us to imagine diverse ways of meeting human needs and to explore the possibilities open to people in furthering their own welfare, moving on from resistance to the creation of change."[20] Consequently, if the promotion of the human condition can in part be sustained through postmodern welfare, then it is incumbent upon both postmodern deconstruction and Marxist social analysis to reconstruct what is liberating in both traditions. Moreover, it is through this "praxis" methodology that more deeply committed efforts can be made to support antiracist and anticolonial realities. Nevertheless, based on the current welfare crisis and the breakdown of modern liberalism and support for welfare policy as embodied in old AFDC (now TANF) models, the modernist Keynesian welfare state for all intents and purposes has seen its day.

For a postmodern welfare policy to work it must include the recognition of social solidarity—that is, of "mutual interdependence," as Leonard contends. The evident challenge to any notion of solidarity is that mutual interdependence may slip into a modernist form of homogenization and domination that collectivist societies once, and still do, promulgate. However, mutual interdependence should not be viewed as an obstacle to human solidarity and responsibility to others in community. Leonard states that this form of "mutual interdependence is at the core of our subjectivity and that it therefore constitutes a foundation for any reconstructed welfare project [and] is a precondition for any effective ideological counter-move to the dominant, narcissistic individualism of the culture of late capitalism."[21] Thus the presupposition of a subjective mutual interdependence based on the notion of social solidarity provides the foundation for a reconstructed postmodern welfare policy. Any form of human solidarity that manifested itself with the liberal construction of the Keynesian welfare state basically has been eviscerated through the rhetoric of the neoconservative and libertarian discourse regarding welfare policy. This was accomplished by propagandizing society at large with a cult-like affection for individualism and individual responsibility based upon market competition and other social Darwinistic beliefs. Government intervention in market failures was perceived to be an enabling agent perpetuating dependency and obstructing market forces. Given this quasi-divine perspective on the market, the Right and postmodern capitalism were able to undermine liberal welfare schemes by pointing out that 80 percent of welfare funding went into the administration of the program itself. With this inefficiency constantly revealed to the public, coupled with the notion of welfare dependency, welfare policy was doomed in the United States.

In order to reverse the categorical demise of the liberal welfare state at the hands of Right-thinking detractors, the Left stands in a position to "resist" the emergence of postmodern capital and its destructive potential grounded in individualist ethos. By propagandizing the notion of social solidarity and mutual interdependence as a counter to the self-destructive tendencies of individualist pathologies, communities will be able to establish resistance to cultural domination and provide a clearer expression of what forms of welfare would be appropriate for themselves. What is being urged in this book is an emancipatory project in which mutual interdependence and social solidarity empower people and communities to define for themselves avenues with which to become subjects of their own destiny rather than objects of a welfare system. Having communities identify their own common and unique human needs is the intention of a newly constructed welfare policy. According to Leonard, welfare understood in the postmodern sense must act in an emancipatory manner in order to promote the greater human freedom necessary to provide the exact "preconditions for maximizing the opportunities for people to live their lives as moral agents."[22] The strategy for accomplishing this is to promote "communities of resistance" that in turn empower marginalized persons to secure and provide for their own fundamental human needs, especially in the wake of the devastation of welfare policy in the United States.

NOTES

1. Martin Carnoy, *The State and Political Theory* (Princeton, N.J.: Princeton University Press, 1984); David Schmidtz and Robert Goodin, *Social Welfare and Individual Responsibility* (New York: Cambridge University Press, 1988).

2. Fredric Jameson, *Postmodernism, or the Cultural Logic of Late Capitalism* (Durham, N.C.: Duke University Press, 1991); Jean Baudrillard, *The Consumer Society: Myths and Structures* (Thousand Oaks, Calif.: Sage Publications, 1997).

3. Michael Harrington, *Socialism: Past and Future* (New York: A Mentor Book, 1992).

4. David Ellwood, *Poor Support: Poverty in the American Family* (New York: Basic Books, 1988); Amartya Sen, "Justice: Means versus Freedoms," *Philosophy &*

Public Affairs 19, no. 2 (Spring 1990); Amartya Sen, *On Economic Inequality* (New York: Oxford, 1973); Samuel Bowles and Herbert Gintis, "Power and Wealth in a Competitive Capitalist Economy," *Philosophy & Public Affairs* 21, no. 4 (Fall 1992). Also see Amatai Etzioni, *The Spirit of Community: Rights, Responsibilities, and the Communitarian Agenda* (New York: Crown Publishers, 1993); Alisdair MacIntyre, *After Virtue: A Study in Moral Theory* (South Bend, Ind.: University of Notre Dame Press, 1981; William Sullivan, *Reconstructing Public Philosophy* (Berkeley: University of California Press, 1982).

5. Milton Friedman, *Capitalism and Freedom* (Chicago: University of Chicago Press, 1962); Gordon Tullock, *Private Wants, Public Means* (New York: Basic Books, 1970); George Gilder, *Wealth and Poverty* (New York: Bantam, 1982).

6. Lawrence Mead, *Beyond Entitlement: The Social Obligations of Citizenship* (New York: The Free Press, 1986); Friedrich von Hayek, *The Road to Serfdom* (Chicago: University of Chicago Press, 1976); Friedman, *Capitalism and Freedom*; Gilder, *Wealth and Poverty*; Bob Jessop, *The Future of the Capitalist State* (Cambridge, U.K.: Polity Press, 2003); Allen Buchanan, *Ethics, Efficiency and the Market* (Totowa, N.J.: Rowman and Allanheld, 1985); Samuel Bowles and Herbert Gintis, "Capitalism and Alienation," in *The Capitalist System: A Radical Analysis of American Society*, eds. Richard Edwards et al. (Englewood Cliffs, N.J.: Prentice-Hall, 1978); T. B. Bottomore, *Classes in Modern Society* (New York: Vintage Books, 1966); Allen Wood, "Historical Materialism and Functional Explanation," *Inquiry* 29 (March 1986).

7. Peter Leonard, *Postmodern Welfare: Reconstructing an Emancipatory Project* (Thousand Oaks, Calif.: Sage Publications, 1997).

8. Leonard, *Postmodern Welfare*. See Michel Foucault, *The Foucault Reader* (New York: Pantheon, 1984).

9. Jean-Francois Lyotard, "Defining the Postmodern," in *Postmodernism: ICA Documents,* ed. Lisa Appignanesi (London: Free Association Books, 1989).

10. Mary Jo Bane and David Ellwood, *Welfare Realities: From Rhetoric to Reform* (Cambridge, Mass.: Harvard University Press, 1994); Richard Arneson, "Liberalism, Distributive Subjectivism, and Equal Opportunity for Welfare," *Philosophy & Public Affairs* 19, no. 2 (Spring 1990): 158–194.

11. Fredric Jameson, "Marxism and Postmodernism," in *Postmodernism/ Jameson/Critique,* ed. Douglas Kellner (Washington, D.C.: Maisonneuve Press, 1989).

12. Leonard, *Postmodern Welfare*, 30.

13. Max Weber, *The Protestant Ethic and the Spirit of Capitalism* (London: Unwin, 1930).

14. Joel Handler and Yeheskel Hasenfeld, *The Moral Construction of Poverty* (Newbury Park, Calif.: Sage Publications, 1991).

15. Martin Gilens, *Why Americans Hate Welfare: Race, Media and the Politics of Antipoverty Policy* (Chicago: University of Chicago Press, 1999).

16. Thorstein Veblen, *The Theory of the Leisure Class* (New York: Random House, 1931).

17. Zygmut Bauman, *Intimations of Postmodernity* (London: Routledge, 1992).

18. Fredric Jameson, "Postmodernism, or the Cultural Logic of Late Capitalism," *New Left Review* 146 (1984): 53–92.

19. Leonard, *Postmodern Welfare*, 162.

20. Leonard, *Postmodern Welfare*, 163.

21. Leonard, *Postmodern Welfare*, 165.

22. Leonard, *Postmodern Welfare*, 169.

Chapter One

Marxist Social Theory Reconsidered

RECLAIMING MARX

We have a climate of opinion somewhat more conducive to a thoroughgoing critique of the neo-liberal version of capitalism in particular, if not capitalism in general. And signs of that critique abound. With all this fluttering going on in the wings, can that other spectre—the communist alternative—be far behind?

—David Harvey, *The Limits to Capital*

Cursory analyses have been all too common in academic discussions regarding the alleged demise of Marxist scholarship, especially in light of the political transformations of Eastern Europe and the catalytic drive of the globalization phenomena. Rational choice, public choice, and neoliberal devotees have assigned Marxism to anachronistic categories while identifying scholarship in this field as self-serving. To the contrary, leftist scholarship, especially that of Marxism, has much to offer by providing a conduit for enlightened criticism on issues ranging from the economy, government, policy and administration, to social welfare, health care, and other numerous topics in public affairs. As a conceptual framework within political economy, Marxism provides a rational vantage point for attempting to understand social phenomena and class relationships in society.

Marxist notions of historical materialism can indeed provide a dynamic model for public administrators and policy analysts in implementing and evaluating policy. Within the boundaries of qualitative research, critical theory has provided a dynamic and multifaceted venue for attempting to understand various forms of social construction. In turn, critical theories' use of Marxist methodology provides a context for deriving valuable information on

13

the systemic causes of social injustice and the subordination of fundamental human rights. The Marxist model of interpretation, along with other critical theory models, such as feminism, critical ethnography, or postmodern deconstruction, provides a unique tool for policy analysis. Suffice it to say, how theorists and practitioners conceptualize problems should not be limited to any one particular method of inquiry or analysis, including Marxist, neoliberal, or postmodern approaches.[1]

The crisis levels inherent within capitalism, coupled with the diminution of liberal social policy in the United States, set the stage for the potential intensification of class alienation. One of the major theses asserted in this corpus is that both neoliberal and postmodern theories, which currently dominate academic research and policy formulation, are theoretically flawed precisely because any critical and comprehensive understanding of class structure is lacking. A comprehensive dimension to understanding the nature of capital accumulation and the potential (but not necessarily deterministic) outcomes that are associated with this phenomenon also need urgent attention with respect to policy analysis and public administration. In this sense, the notion of providing merely symbolic support for those in more restricted social classes takes on greater significance in the ongoing discussion of the practical need to provide greater social solidarity, as argued by Kenneth Arrow.[2] Ultimately the test for utilizing a historical materialist approach to social analysis can be of significant benefit as a method for a more precise risk-management strategy in policy and planning.

The critical point of this book focuses on the insufficiency of neoliberal and postmodern thought with respect to class analysis and stratification. The argument throughout is the assertion that historical materialism provides the best (but not exclusive) and most comprehensive approach to understanding class dynamics, ethnic and gender politics, and the nature of capital accumulation. Historical materialism provides a heuristic method that identifies continued class antagonisms present on a domestic and global level. Thus a legitimate and timely argument in favor of Marxist methodology is being reintroduced to twenty-first-century scholarship, contrary to the specious rhetorical dismissals of historical materialism as "class warfare." Moreover, this book does not attempt to present Marxism as grand theory or some rigid form of reductionism. The fundamental assumptions of Marxism as grand and reductionistic theory have been thoroughly challenged, especially in the works of Frances Fox Piven, Richard Cloward, and Robert Heilbroner.[3] Thus the attempt to critique this work as vulgar Marxism will prove to be otiose. Likewise, the challenge to neoliberals is also to avoid identification as vulgar capitalists by questioning and restructuring the fundamental assumptions of capitalism as grand and reductionist theory, and challenge witless postmodernist assumptions regarding the absence of universal truths and the incompatibility of Marxist grand theory with respect to postmodern deconstruction of multicultural, racial, and gender politics. The contention here is that theories of capitalist accumulation and postmodern deconstruction will benefit from an ongoing dialogue by the necessary inclusion of Marxist historical materialism as a valid and necessary methodological construct for assessing social class. The accumulated benefits of historical materialism with respect to social policy and public administration provide a foundation for more meaningful political analysis. This is especially the case with the assessment of social class and class stratification.

FOUNDATIONS OF MARXIST THEORY

The Enlightenment witnessed a fundamental shift in the way social science and other academic disciplines viewed the world. In essence the Enlightenment rejected the rigid and fixed philosophical legacy of its classical Greek and medieval precursors. The new method for conducting research focused on causal relationships based on empirical evidence. One of the giants in this new method of inquiry was Karl Marx, who sought to analyze systematically the foundations of social arrangements. Social arrangements, Marx argued, were based on *economic* relationships, which provided the rationale for the social construction of a given society.[4] It was further argued by Marx that it was necessary to analyze economic forces and social arrangements that influence government institutions, cultural traditions, and so forth, that perpetuate class interests and obstruct change. Here, Marx believed that German religious traditions that reinforced fixed social stratifications and deference to authority played a key part in disallowing change. In the *Critique of Hegel's Philosophy of Right*,[5] Marx argues that this manifestation of religion is an "opiate" used to numb individual consciences with respect to contradictions and injustices in a given culture. Marx claimed that in order to alter social structures, individual traditions need to be questioned as a requirement for new ideas and beliefs to usher in social justice and progress.

One of the crucial developments in Marx's thought was that he believed the bourgeoisie and other elite members of society acted on ideas not because they were correct, but primarily on the basis of self-interest. This is because social interests determine precisely which ideas are to be adopted, specifically by the ruling class. In *The German Ideology* Marx argues that, "The ruling class having the means of material production has also control over the means of intellectual production, so that . . . the ruling ideas are nothing more than the ideal expression of the dominant [social class]."[6] In the *Economic and Philosophical Manuscripts*, Marx also argues that social interests are determined, to a large degree, by social position, particularly class status; the outcome of this for the working class and the poor results in what Marx terms "alienated labor." Marx believed that these ideas are grounded in social and structural conditions determined by the elite in society. Consequently, a critique of culture—the realm of ideas, values, meanings—is important precisely because it is connected to a critical analysis of the social conditions that sustain cultural meaning and symbols. Put another way, the economic substructure of a given society will invariably, for Marx, reveal the societal superstructure and its manifestations typical of bourgeois society. In so doing, Marx was distancing himself from idealist philosophy that was preoccupied with abstractions and metaphysical apriorisms. It was in *Capital* that Marx gravitated toward a "materialist" perspective that viewed the underlying source of social change and the struggle for social justice as a phenomenon related to the tensions and inequities resulting from economic social conditions. Thus, according to Marx, the economic self-interest of the capitalist class during the Industrial Revolution had a direct effect on the working class's alienation and exploitation, providing the setting for class antagonism and various forms of social conflict. Frederick Engels later termed this conflict "historical materialism," and in his *Anti-Durhing* further emphasizes the "scientific" character of Marxist socialism by labeling historical materialism as "dialectical materialism."

A starting point within Marxist theory examines how the labor of productive energies within an economic system is organized. Productive economic activities according to Marx mean economic labor or remunerated labor (in kind or money). Marxist theory seeks to initially explain the predominant means of a society's economic production. Generally this can be understood in the rational and methodological structuring of a society's economic labor and means of production (land, raw material, resources, technology, human labor power), which is predisposed usually in favor of the social class with the most affluence, power, and resources at their disposal. Marx rejects geographical and technological explanations for this rational structuring of economic influence since they are unable to account for social variations in socioeconomic systems. However, Marx does focus on the class dynamics that shape the organization of socioeconomic systems. These class dynamics then shape the structure and direction of the society at large, and as Marx and Engels state in *The Communist Manifesto*, "[T]he history of all hitherto existing society is the history of class struggles. Freeman and slave, patrician and plebeian, lord and serf, guild-master and journeyman, in a word, oppressor and oppressed, stood in contrast opposition to one another."[7] Thus Marx and Engels formulate the conceptual starting point for the basis of historical materialism.

Marxist historical materialism is not the only valid explanation for social phenomena. While social theorists such as Emile Durkheim concur with Marx's descriptions of the underlying causes of class conflict, Durkheim nevertheless believed that rigid and unjust class systems would disappear as society became more democratized.[8] This would result in an evolutionary pattern where different forms of political rationality would emerge within social milieus, replacing outdated ones. In contrast to both Marx and Durkheim, Max Weber addressed multiple levels of stratification (class, status, party) in which property and class were no longer construed as a "social base," but simply one axis of social formation.[9] Culture and politics, as Weber conceptualized them, were not necessarily derived, ipso facto, from the economic substructure of society. These notions could be explained as parallel dimensions of any social organization.[10] Talcott Parsons argued, in opposition to Marxism and utilitarian neoliberalism, that society is constructed of individuals fabricating shared meaning through various forms of social solidarity. Nonetheless, while agreeing with certain dimensions of Marxist thought, even Ralf Dahrendorf disputed the central Marxian claim that social dynamics are explained best by analyzing the underlying class structure of society. The reason for this, according to Dahrendorf, is that, "the remarkable spread of social equality in the past century [within industrial society] has rendered class struggle and revolutionary changes utterly impossible."[11]

In contrast to Dahrendorf, social critics such as C. Wright Mills argued that the very nature of class structure does indeed promote social inequity. With the deepening drift of United States' culture into a mass society, political power increasingly concentrates among elites. Mills asserts in *The Power Elite* the existence of an elite in the United States that exercises power with little social accountability over a fragmented and atomized social mass.[12] Thus Mills concluded that a power elite had been formed in postwar America composed predominantly of white males who held power in either the corporate, political, or military sector. While power elites do not necessarily act in a deliberate, concerted way, they share similar interests and pursue a common social agenda. The interlocking character of the power elite, for the most part, reflects the interconnecting nature of economic, political, and military institutions. Elite decision makers in any one institutional sphere cannot avoid consulting and cooperating with like-minded policy makers in other spheres. Further, there are personal ties binding elites and separating them from the social masses. In this capacity elites stand apart from the blue-collar and white-collar Americans primarily by their accrued wealth. Suffice it to say, wealth translates into an entire series of benchmarks that divide the elite from the masses—for example, education, property, and social opportunities. It becomes axiomatic in this sense that elites share similar interests, in particular an

interest in maintaining the current unequal distribution of wealth, prestige, and
power, which is of course to their advantage. To reinforce this position according to Mills they can, and do, act in concert to implement and enforce their
social will and related policies. Mills, though sympathetic to liberal and Marxist theory, nonetheless rejected both indulgent liberalism and authoritative
Marxism as a remedy to social inequities. Neither did Mills completely agree
with Marx's notion of class conflict resulting from economic relationships.
However, Mills believed that elitist theory was, for all intents and purposes,
narrowly self-serving precisely because elitist theory in its extreme turned
away from current realities to serve narrow ideological interests. What was
needed, according to Mills, was a public intellectual discourse that was critical, yet addressed complex social realities in terms of the practical possibilities for democratic renewal.

As a result of these theoretical developments, Marxists were forced to re-
assess their own methodology in response to these significant criticisms. In
fact, as claimed by Marxist interpreters, not all social phenomena could be assessed in terms of historical materialism. Moreover, the absence of working
class radicalism, reinforced by the rise of social movements among students
and marginal groups (women, gays, ethnic minorities), became sufficient
enough proof that social unrest and contentious political encounters could not
be interpreted definitively according to Marxist social analysis as the result
of, or lack of, social and economic injustice. Hence, neo-Marxists began to
reinterpret Marx in much less rigid and analytic categories.

An example of this revisionist agenda can be identified in neo-Marxists
such as Jurgen Habermas, who developed a unique theoretical perspective
synthesizing various forms of social theory with Marxist critique. As part of
the Frankfurt School, Habermas and others developed a new Marxist methodology known as "critical theory." This critical stance embraced a combination
of social analysis that included more subjective, psychoanalytic methods,
with a less deterministic interpretation of historical materialism and class
conflict. Based on this perspective, various social arrangements can be analyzed with respect to the distribution of power, which Habermas and the
Frankfurt School argue inhibits personal freedom and social liberation.
Notwithstanding, through the use of critical self-reflection, which identifies
societal and interpersonal contradictions, the unification of theory and practice (praxis) is sought in order to transform and promote social and economic
justice. Thus the foundations of praxis methodology can be derived from
Marx's famous dictum in the *Thesis on Feuerbach* that "the philosophers have
interpreted the world in various ways; the point is, to change it."[13]

Habermas, as a result of his reformulations of Marxist theory, sought to integrate philosophy and empirical science for the purpose of moral critique

and social change.[14] In so doing, he reoriented neo-Marxists and critical theorists to a less rigid and deterministic emphasis on economic exploitation and class conflict by analyzing the shift from competitive to corporate, state-managed capitalism. Three reasons for reconstructing Marxism in this capacity were thus proposed. First, Marxism was dismissed far too readily as mere ideology; accordingly, its social criticisms and political intent lacked legitimacy and credibility. In response to this, Habermas took on the unique challenge of providing an epistemological justification for critical theory that would provide Marxism with greater legitimacy. In other terms, he intended to make the case that critical theory is an expression of reason, and not a result of reactive militancy. Second, Habermas argued that the conceptual framework of Marxism was flawed because its fundamental principles could not be generalized universally, at least for those who interpreted Marx in rigid scientific or dogmatic categories. For example, Marxism's failure to explain the absence of revolution in the West and its occurrence in the East, the rise of fascism, and, in the postwar years, the rise of the new social movements, indicates defects in Marxism's most basic premises and categories—historical materialism. Third, Habermas claimed that while the theoretical shortcomings of Marxism rendered Marxist critiques of capitalism as inadequate, he nevertheless held the position that Marxist social analysis provided one of the better systematic methodologies for critiquing capitalism and simultaneously clarifying the major dynamics of social construction.

Habermas portrayed his reconstruction of Marxism as a critical social science committed to promoting human freedom and solidarity. His critical theory methodology "praxis" was constructed in order to reveal various dimensions of conflict between theory and action and the prospects for social transformation. In identifying these "contradictions," social and economic justice would be promoted in a given society through enlightened policy. The support for this methodology, Habermas argues, can be found in Marx's *Capital*, which critiques capitalism by claiming that the ideals of liberty, equality, and justice, invoked as the foundation of liberal capitalist culture, are: (1) contradicted by the exploitation of human labor, and (2) contradicted by the accumulation of capitalist wealth, which further perpetuates class domination. Marx, as Habermas asserts, intended to foster a critical attitude on the part of laborers toward capitalism. Indeed, he argues that Marx's intention was to transform blue-collar laborers into a politicized working class whose personal discontents would translate into a struggle against capitalism. In this sense Marxism was to provide the theoretical foundation for change that the oppressed and working class would implement in order to bridge the distance between theory and practice. In exactly this process the ideal of justice versus the reality of oppression would be addressed and reconciled in what Habermas describes as "immanent critique."

The Frankfurt School welcomed Habermas's formulation of immanent critique as a model for analyzing the underlying values behind the legitimization of capitalist institutions and structures. The theory of immanent critique purported to expose or awaken individuals to the contradictions between exploitive relationships and the social ideals of justice and fairness. In the process, Habermas initiated what has become known within Marxist social theory as "critical consciousness." As the Frankfurt School conceived it, critical consciousness (social critique) is a force for social change to the extent that it challenges the dominant social ideologies that present the existing society as a rational and just social construct. The new critical theorists sought to: (1) clarify the socially constructed character of society, (2) reveal the existence of ruling social groups whose world views justified an unequal and unfair social arrangement; and (3) identify social agents who have an interest in enacting just social change.[15] This form of critical analysis for Habermas and the Frankfurt School focused not only on the apparent contradictions within a capitalist framework, but also on identifying the unquestioned assumptions of social construction within any social configuration that legitimize any authoritative order. The intent of this methodology is not simply to critique, but to remedy those underlying contradictions.[16] The critical point that must be noted is that this very methodology is, nonetheless, based on a neo-Marxist reconfiguration of historical materialism.

In this resulting methodology, Habermas and critical theorists argued that the major site of social crisis and conflict could not be located entirely in capitalist economic policies (monetary policies, price supports, inflation, etc.), but also in cultural and political spheres. Nevertheless, he insisted that a capitalist culture possesses sufficient inherent contradictions and that the risk of human exploitation was still an intricate component of the capitalist state since that very state must fulfill the *contradictory demands* of ensuring capitalist growth while maintaining mass public support. The former imperative demands that the state favor particular interests of property owners, elites, and their administrators; the latter imperative demands that the state act as if it represents the interests of all segments of society, including the working class and poor. This "legitimation crisis," as Habermas termed it, is driven by a critical awareness of the realities of contradictions within society. Consequently, it is to the advantage of those maintaining such a social order to in fact conceal capitalist or authoritative social arrangements. Furthermore, while the inherent role of this methodology is to expose the implicit contradictions within a capitalist society, the very same methodology can be applied to any situation that legitimizes the status quo—for example, authoritative, totalitarian, or religious social and political arrangements. Thus the universal nature of praxis methodology provides a systematic critique of any "unjust" social construction. It is important once again, then, to reinforce the concept that within the field of critical theory, revised notions of historical material- ism continue to provide an essential critique in attempting to remedy societal contradictions that perpetuate injustice.[17]

CRITICAL THEORY, AN ALTERNATIVE

A critical theory perspective examines social phenomena from various purviews. At times it can be used to focus on isolated issues, such as un- employment, inflation, or hunger. In other contexts it focuses on the poli- cies that address these issues, such as job training, fiscal policy, nutrition programs, and social welfare policy in general. This approach examines the broad structures of economic, political, social, and cultural institutions from which such issues arise and to which policies are addressed. Yet there is a danger that the significance of neo-Marxist critical theory could be inter- preted as a panacea for social ills. Other methodological approaches pro- vide a venue for social critique. Positivist, interpretive, discourse, and post- modern theories provide a variety of analytical tools. Positivism attempts to acquire knowledge about the human condition that can be used to explain, predict, and control human behavior. Positivist explanations are generally defined in terms of describing functional behavior and proposing a general rule or law that allows for the prediction of behavior. This method is de- signed to ensure the "objective" validity or "truth" of a researcher's find- ings. The weakness of this method, however, is that the perspective of the theorist is generally a considerable distance from the perspective and inter- ests of the subject under study. In contrast, interpretive or hermeneutic the- ory aims to enhance intersubjective forms of understanding that positivism cannot adequately provide.[18] The goal within this methodological frame- work is to promote greater mutual- and self-understanding by facilitating meaningful dialogue between participants. Interpretive theory requires that individuals come to a consensus with one another in the context of human interaction.

Diverse methods for conducting social analysis present unique challenges. In positivist and interpretive theories, there is no immediate need to bridge ex- isting gaps between theory and practice. Discourse and postmodern theories as analytic devices agree on issues of human interdependence and the attempt to promote sincere dialogue. Still, these methods remain aloof from social prac- tice, thus limiting the possibilities for change in social structures and ideolo- gies. As such, critical theory as a social analytic tool arguably provides a more comprehensive approach to assessing social phenomena precisely because

critical theory seeks not only to analyze social contradictions, but to simultaneously implement fundamental changes in society. The task of critical theory
is therefore the promotion of human liberation and the securing of fundamental human rights and needs that are the basis of any social justice theory.[19]

An application of this methodology can be found in the work of Brazilian
educator Paulo Freire. Heavily influenced by the Frankfurt School, Freire asserts that the relationship between persons and their culture is not a static one,
but rather a dynamic alternating current in which people and communities
shape their culture and color individual perspectives of the world. The culture
into which people are born in Western society is nevertheless all pervading
with respect to networks of inherent beliefs regarding society and philosophy.
However, to be "critically conscious" of this world, Freire argues that persons
need to assume a questioning stance of all social phenomena by inspecting
what society has inculcated as the "truth." Here Freire emphasizes the need
to target individual and societal "self-consciousness" (an examination of individual and societal contradictions), so that it becomes a habit of "critical
consciousness" to question all underlying assumptions regarding authority
and the construction of society.[20]

Freire argues that critical consciousness methodology has met with resistance by elites in any given social setting. Generally the attempt to silence an
individual or a collective capacity for critical consciousness thinking is more
commonly done when elites censor particular questions regarding structures
within society. But, for Freire, to restrict critical consciousness—a distinctly
human achievement—means that fundamental human rights are violated in the
process. Consequently, to deny or limit critical consciousness is to simultaneously *dehumanize* that person or society.[21] The cultural oppression of persons
is discovered whenever individual capacity to think freely is denied or hin-
dered, and whenever individuals and cultures are reduced to submissiveness,
passivity, and silence. Freire argues that this form of oppression is most acute
in the poorest areas of the world where people have no access to the various
levers of power that the middle class and rich take for granted, via money, influence, status, legal access, and finance. For these reasons, he believes that
people in marginal settings consequently tend to see themselves in a defeatist
light, as objects of others' decisions, powerless to change their social setting.
Freire argues that in order for persons to liberate themselves from any defeatist
mindset and dehumanizing oppression it is essential to encourage critical consciousness. This provides the context for those living in oppressive settings to
emerge as fully conscious subjects who are in control of their own destiny.
This can be contrasted to the uncritical masses who, for Freire, remain objects
of historical conditions, unable to effectively implement change to bring about
greater justice. The goal of this methodology is to encourage people to con-

front systemic contradictions, both societally and interpersonally, in order to provide for greater autonomy and self-actualization. In both senses critical consciousness is important with respect to praxis. Thus, within the critical theory tradition, Freire argues that self-consciousness (awareness) needs to be explicitly understood when critically analyzing social phenomena.[22] Self-consciousness gives human life its distinctive character precisely because it promotes changes in consciousness which lead to action.[23] According to Freire, by critically analyzing the fundamental assumptions that are at the core of a culture's values and beliefs, people become liberated. But liberation takes place when it becomes clear that the strategy of the oppressor is to keep the oppressed from knowing that they are oppressed in the first place.

MODERNITY AND ITS DISCONTENTS

Modernity, understood as a significant intellectual movement within Western culture, is derived from eighteenth-century Enlightenment philosophy. The intellectual foundation of modernism is based on the notion that human "reason" and "scientific truth" are superior forms of understanding, as compared to any metaphysical and/or religious speculation with regard to discovering order in the universe. Naturally, modernist theory questioned any rational basis for cosmological speculations while conjointly seeking to improve the conditions of society through scientific advancements and technological applications. This modernist perspective translated into a belief in the liberation of the human person from ignorance, poverty, and oppression. In so doing, it sought to free the world from human ignorance and suffering.

At the same time, modernism asserts that underlying universal principles can be discovered in nature, innate human capacities, and social arrangements. Based on this new form of rationalism, both capitalism and socialism have emerged as the preeminent applications of modernist thinking. Still, both modernist perspectives have yet to reveal their comprehensive liberating capacities according to postmodernists. Zygmut Bauman and Steven Seidman, twenty-first-century postmodernists, argue that while socialism as an economic and political system has failed (given the collapse of Eastern Europe and the radical market restructuring of China in the late twentieth century), international capitalism has also failed to demonstrate its liberating capacity. Because of its inherent contradictions (boom–bust cycles), crises (market failures), and labor tensions (downward pressure on wages), capitalism has yet to provide a stable and coherent strategy in meeting human needs on a global scale.[24] This can be assessed with respect to domestic economies and the phenomena of globalization.

As a result of the apparent crisis in modernism—that is, the question of whether modernism presents itself as a universal and efficient mechanism for human liberation based on either individual or collective rights—postmodernists argue that modernity has, for all intents and purposes, signified an application of Eurocentric paternalism and triumphalism over indigenous populations, women, and for that matter, the entire ecosystem.[25] The manifestation of modernity, it is argued, reveals the superiority of the Western world in its colonial, postcolonial, imperial, neo-imperial, and now globalized politico-economic world. Both capitalist and socialist systems have therefore attempted to homogenize conquered regions of the world through their domination of indigenous cultures, histories, and beliefs. Consequently postmodernists, on the one hand, reject the modernist universal tendencies of individual actors in capitalism, and on the other hand, reject the purely collectivist strategies within socialist remedies. Suffice it to say, postmodernism rejects what is known as "grand theory" speculations, which attempt to provide the foundations for ameliorating the human condition based upon the rational foundations of capitalism and socialism.

Using postmodernism as a starting point for analysis, Michel Foucault attempted to identify some of the more subtle premises of modernism.[26] Foucault did this by examining the social mores within Western culture that addressed issues such as madness, delinquency, and sexuality. At the heart of these studies, Foucault discovered that modernity utilized a number of linguistic tools that legitimized the modernist methodological domination of scientific and methodological truth. This coincided with the phenomena of emerging nation-states during the eighteenth and nineteenth centuries, which in turn gave birth to related notions of bureaucracy and administration. This new modernist development emphasized a distinct notion of "the truth" contrasted with a clear and definitive notion of "the false." Consequently, modernism according to Foucault promoted a rigid dichotomy between what it considered to be true or false. Subsequent discourses asserted by Foucault are conditioned by regulations and the nomenclature of exclusion, which in turn perpetuate the marginal value and worth of subordinate truth statements. It is precisely through such regulations and nomenclature that the Enlightenment and modernist approaches systematically excluded from dialogue alternative perspectives of marginalized populations, the poor, women (predominantly poor and non-European), and indigenous persons.

Yet one of the most cogent and formidable critiques of modernism offered by postmodernists can be identified in the work of Jean-Francois Lyotard. Marxists, according to Lyotard, have the tendency to critique modernity in similar fashion to the way Marx analyzed capitalism—that is, by identifying the inherent contradictions within society based on the developing notion of what was later to be described by Engels as historical materialism. Lyotard's powerful condemnation of modernity, as manifested primarily in capitalist and Marxist theory, is so stated:

> Neither economic nor political liberalism, nor the various Marxisms, emerge from the sanguinary last two centuries free from the suspicion of crimes against humanity. . . . I use the name of Auschwitz to point out the irrelevance of empirical matter, the stuff of recent past history, in terms of the modern claim to help mankind to emancipate itself. What kind of thought is able to sublate Auschwitz in a general (either empirical or speculative) process towards universal emancipation?[27]

Here Lyotard associates the modernist agenda with fundamental violations of human rights and an assortment of crimes against humanity. While Lyotard agrees that democratic institutions have ameliorated the condition of some populations within liberal democracies, he nevertheless argues that modernism is responsible for injustices such as Auschwitz, Nagasaki, Soviet gulags, and the "killing fields" of Cambodia. These crimes, argues Lyotard, are derived from modernist concepts that invariably lead to the so-called betterment of the world. Consequently, liberal capitalism, fascism, and Marxism are, for all intents and purposes, part of the same byproduct of modernism rooted in the Age of Reason. For Lyotard, such "grand narratives of legitimization are no longer credible."[28]

However, in a concerted effort to address Lyotard's and Foucault's postmodern critiques of Marxism, Habermas argued that postmodern critiques of Marxist theory were quite valid. He argued, nevertheless, that modernity can maintain its project of emancipation by severing the universalist claims to reason from actual domination and oppression of marginalized people. Claims to a universal truth based on reason and the actual fact of historical injustice are not mutually inclusive concepts for Habermas; the core principles of modernity—individual autonomy and reason as underlying truths—need to be reformulated into a notion of rational thought and discourse grounded on egalitarian communication and consensus within a pluralistic setting.[29] But what remains a constant challenge to both postmodernists and neoliberals—in fact one that both theoretical positions have been unable to significantly discredit—is that Marxist historical materialism, reassessed and reformulated within a post-capital, globalized world, still provides an efficient and effective tool in attempting to analyze class antagonisms.[30] This challenge reasserts the thesis that Marxist historical materialism provides one of the most cogent and comprehensive interpretations for identifying the roots of injustice and exploitation. Although it is dominated by the Left, postmodernism has come under increasing criticism for its insufficient and inadequate attention to class analysis and corresponding complicity with capitalist social construction.[31] Thus the relevance of social critique based on Marxist historical materialism (as opposed to modernist ideology) arguably maintains its preeminence as radical social critique with the onset of the twenty-first century.

EMPIRE AND SOCIAL WELFARE

The emancipatory project of the Enlightenment and its modernist progenitor have also influenced the development of international capital and neoliberal apologists such as Freidrich von Hayek and Milton Friedman.[32] Neoliberals in general argue that economic growth, with the most limited or nonexistent forms of government regulation, is the ultimate measure of the success of market systems. The liberal motivation for self-interest and profit, rooted in Adam Smith's *Wealth of Nations*, provides the rational motivating force for the economic structuring of society in Western culture.[33] But a different nuance to this application has emerged in the latter part of the twentieth century and has consequently taken on a quite different dimension in the phenomenon of globalization.

The theory of capitalism has become the predominant modernist economic orthodoxy not only in Western culture, but now is manifested in a new global market arena. This is nothing particularly new from a Marxist perspective since capitalist ventures have continually perpetuated the dynamic of globalization in their compulsion for market expansion and increased profits in a competitive international community. Vladimir Lenin noted this unique phenomenon in the late nineteenth century in his study of imperialism as a concomitant dimension of capitalism.[34] Harry Magdoff and Paul Sweezy, in the late twentieth century, identify similar "imperialistic" dimensions with respect to international capital as well.[35] The premises underlying the phenomena of globalization assume that capitalism as the dominant mode of production is driven by continual economic growth and reinvestment. This is the fundamental precondition that drives accumulation, consumption, and profitability, without which the economy recedes.

Over the last twenty years the logic of capitalist advancement has been refashioned and catalyzed as a result of several developments. The most significant development has been in the increased number of capitalist economies in non-Western societies such as Japan, Indonesia, Malaysia, Taiwan, and South Korea. And with the market innovations in China's economy, most Asian economies are now connected structurally with Western capitalist countries through consumption, production, and investment. Transnational corporations are able, with great dexterity, to redirect capital investment in these nations by taking advantage of cheap labor, no inkling of organized labor, and minimal government regulation in order to maximize profits.[36] Moreover, with the disintegration of state socialist economies such as those of the former Soviet Union and Eastern Europe, international capital has been establishing economic inroads into these sectors in like manner. In fact, with the Cold War now at an end, international capital has expanded to a global dimension meeting no recognizable political opposition precisely because no viable alternative economic system exists.

A second development in the phenomena of globalization has been in the technical and organizational development of information systems.[37] By obtaining the latest sophisticated innovations in technology, international corporations are able to be more competitive in the international arena. In point, both knowledge and information become powerful tools or *commodities* in the new global market. Postmodernists such as Fredric Jameson and Jean Baudrillard argue that information and knowledge in the new global market is a form of commodification indicative of the relationship between economic and political power.[38] This process has translated into an international competitive struggle where information and knowledge are produced and marketed for corporate profit. The venue for this commodification is found in marketing strategies worldwide (i.e., Nestlé's powdered milk formula marketing strategies in the developing countries) and in popular culture influenced by the media, cable television, sporting events, rock and pop concerts, superstar endorsements. Notwithstanding, popular culture serves as a conduit to not only create market needs, whether real or imagined, but to also reinforce dependency and consumer fetishism. Furthermore, this form of global commodification reinforces and maintains corporate public relations, most acutely through sponsoring athletic events.

Another facet in the development of globalization has been the reconfiguration of international financial institutions that are able to coordinate their business affairs at multinational levels. This phenomenon can be understood, according to David Harvey, in terms of a "dual movement," which includes the development of international conglomerates at one dimension, and swift creation and decentralization of financial programs through innovative financial speculations at another.[39] The deregulation and restructuring of international financial systems is critical with respect to the life and profitability of financial hubs within the context of an international market where distance, time, communication, currency, and geographic setting no longer provide barriers to trade. With respect to capital accumulation, and as impediments to international trade are inevitably lowered, capital itself can be more quickly deployed with greater dexterity, larger investment, and higher profitability in markets. The high yield profitability of this economic activity results precisely because these financial arrangements permit the accelerated transaction of capital to the most lucrative investments while eschewing marginal or failing ones. Consequently, various sectors of the global market function at more profitable levels of investment through decreased labor costs, deregulated industries, and minimal overhead production.[40] In contrast, relatively high wages and union support, increasing expenses for overhead costs, and stiff government regulation are witnessing the withdrawal of investment and capital from "First World" countries to more attractive investments in the "Third World."

The emergence of international capital within corresponding institutions has promoted the insecurity of domestic First World enterprises currently experiencing vulnerability regarding investment decisions of financiers. Distant reaches of the global market are viewed as prime investment for capital speculation and corresponding investments. Yet nations are finding it increasingly problematic to direct their financial affairs as national borders become less significant in the development of international capital. Naturally this juxtaposition produces inherent conflict between domestic governmental affairs and international corporations, and as Swank concludes, the nation-state, "is called upon to regulate the activities of corporate capital in the national interest at the same time as it is forced, also in the national interest, to create a 'good business climate' to act as an inducement to trans-national and global finance capital, and to deter (by other than exchange controls) capital flight to greener and more profitable pastures."[41]

The emergence of international capital and its global financial satellites, coupled with innovations in technology, have arguably influenced the atrophy of nation-states and corporate capitalism. This is precisely because the nation-state itself no longer possesses the same type of domination and control that it once had over domestic and international economic affairs. The outcome of this, according to Peter Leonard, has been "a major consequence of globalization . . . argued as the central issue in the fiscal crisis of the welfare state: the discourse on the contradiction between the market and social investment."

> Western governments are faced with the problem of managing the social consequences of globalization—unemployment, increasing deficits, the widespread growth of uncertainty and apprehension—factors which progressively polarize incomes and substantially affect class relations and are part and parcel of the dynamic of the new capitalist world economy. Apart from the obvious effects of large-scale, long-term unemployment on income levels and therefore consumer spending, the ruthless and near frantic search for ever higher levels of profits has a direct impact on production methods, skills and the wage levels of those who are employed.[42]

This development within international capital—generally rationalized by market competition, leaner overhead expenditures, and job creation in "Third World" settings—has nevertheless counterproductively generated its share of increased global poverty, especially the increased disparity in wealth between those countries of the Northern and Southern Hemispheres.[43] The disproportionate economic relationship that continues to be perpetuated between the hemispheres has not been remedied through neoliberal "development" policies (Argentina currently is one case in point). These policies, generally based on World Bank and International Monetary Fund (IMF) strategies, call for debt restructuring, devaluation of currency, wage concessions, export production, and reduction of domestic infrastructure development in an attempt to provide a favorable domestic climate for economic growth and investment. This strategy has yet to provide substantial economic growth for the vast majority of people in the "Third World."

These recent innovations in global capital brought about greater dexterity in financial institutions, modes of operation, and labor organization, all of which translated into mobile capital and market consumption around the world. Here within the new global phenomena of capital, labor was once again subordinated to the priorities of capital accumulation and profit maximization. It is at this point that postmodern critiques are best understood within this new global context of capital accumulation, most significantly the postmodern critique that incorporates Marxist analyses. Postmodern Marxist analysis focuses on the struggle between labor and capital—profits prioritized to people—which necessitates the continuation in fostering ever new cohorts of workers and consumers at significantly lower wages and escalating profits.[44] This form of late capitalism, or what has become known as "post-Fordism" in some circles, has been constructed by Michael Rustin into a model that provides a venue for assessing the interrelation between economic and social relations.[45] The post-Fordist (post-assembly-line production) model attempts to establish a Marxist rationale for change, yet attempts to eschew the more deterministic characterizations of Marxist orthodoxy. Still, what remains consistent in this postmodern Marxist venue is the fact that inherent contradictions based on the theoretical construct of historical materialism, relative to the phenomena of capital production and labor conflict, is reaffirmed as the sine qua non of radical social analysis.

In the effort to delineate a number of changes in class structure, which have been to a large extent the result of a post-Fordist economy, the observation of increasing poverty, inequality, and unemployment has been noted on a domestic and international level. With the strategy of aggressive international capital and the retreat from domestic capital investment, most notably in the United States, the welfare state has been viewed as expendable and subordinate to the priorities of the new global market.[46] The material settings in which an increasing number of people work and live under these conditions initiates intense pressure on social welfare expenditures in spite of the 1996 Personal Responsibility and Work Opportunity Reconciliation Act (PRWORA) enacted by the United States Congress, which limits a recipient's lifetime benefits to a five-year period. The apparent inconsistency that the welfare state faces is that during a period of economic transition or recession, a demand is elicited for increased welfare spending while political power is leveraged against further social expenditures. The perceived welfare crisis—derived from a new service economy, low wage jobs, and unstable hiring and employment patterns—produces a change in class forces that in turn increases stress on other related services (health) and may result in negative externalities (crime). And with the reality of market failures and the need for public goods, the welfare state, understood as an essential safety net within a capitalist economy, may need to be reexamined with respect to a five-year limitation on supplemental income. A renewed vision of obligation to the poor has emerged in response to the welfare demise in the United States.[47]

While capitalism has established itself as a transformative force throughout history, it nevertheless remains vulnerable to various market imperfections. Its lack of predictability at times may also effect the ability of the social welfare state to intervene in the case of market failures. The various crises that come from the inability to moderate the maximization of profits may tend to jeopardize the context of meaningful social relationships. This is because the premise of capitalist endeavors is based upon the maximization of profits that has produced its share of successes and failures. What is quite difficult to achieve is a consistent and sustainable level of growth. With various economic choices come inevitable outcomes and externalities. In order to better manage the negative externalities that emerge from market relationships, social welfare institutions take on greater significance with respect to managing conflict and crises in the market system. Consequently, with increased poverty, declining incomes and purchasing power, and the general population left to the whims of the market, the state and capital are confronted with irreconcilable differences that may negatively impact the lives of people.

To deal with this market complexity evidenced during the Great Depression, the United States adopted Keynesian strategies designed to intervene and regulate the precariousness of the market.[48] Simultaneously the emergence of the welfare state and the support by organized labor brought about significant changes in the structural management of the market. The welfare state was able to provide some form of work and sustenance for a large segment of the United States population. As a result of this strategy, full employment became a policy that was virtually synonymous with the emerging understanding of economic rights. This new direction acted as a risk management approach that softened the devastation of social and economic misfortunes existing in capitalist economies in both U.S. and European market economies. However, toward the end of the 1970s, Keynesian strategies aimed at market intervention were no longer perceived to be viable, especially in a post-Fordist market system. Any discussion, let alone attempt, to mitigate the crisis tendencies of the market was stridently argued to be unacceptable. The excesses of Keynesian strategies and social welfare policy were argued by neoliberals, such as Friedman and Hayek, to be in violation of market efficiency, since it was argued by neoliberals that market equilibrium would be restored on its own and thereby establish a unique form of social well-being and justice.[49]

This notion was seized upon by neoliberal strategists and business corporations who sought significant decreases in corporate taxation that would then lead to capital reinvestment, increasing dividends, and thus provide a more favorable environment for investment and profit. The global force of capital and the inevitable elimination of social welfare have yet to stimulate the imagination of welfare policy theorists to focus enthusiastically on discussions centered around the developing notion of "social capital." Nevertheless, this was the "good news" of the so-called Reagan revolution. According to neoliberal devotees, this revolution initiated massive fortunes for the country as a whole, and especially for the upper 5 percent of the population in the United States; the remainder of wealth "trickled down" to the remaining population. Deregulation of industries and the devolution of social welfare to the local level were encouraged. The negative attributes of neoliberal economic strategies would unquestionably lead to reductions in public expenditures, which could potentially lead to crises in public health and other social programs that benefit the public at large. During the 1980s this practice led to a "legitimation crisis," in which the United States experienced sharp increases in poverty, inequality, unemployment, falling incomes, and labor unrest. The post-Fordist approach to this form of crisis was to "develop" new economic sectors in the global market, especially in developing Third World countries, where U.S. corporations would financially profit.

With the collapse of state socialist regimes, opportunities emerged for multinational corporations to capitalize on new investments, production, consumption, and significantly cheaper labor costs. Coupled with "free trade" and virtually nonexistent tariffs and taxes, transnational corporations were aggressively pursuing globalized strategies in the face of competitive market structures. Nevertheless, the permanent solution to the crisis tendencies of a capitalistic system remains a significant issue for both domestic and global economic policies. To date, neoliberal and postmodern critiques have been unable to provide a comprehensive analysis to remedy inherent crises in capitalism, especially where capital and profit are pitted against labor. What this situation requires in the way of analysis is a reassessment of the fundamental principles of Marxist theory relevant to the new post–Cold War era in a globalized international economy.

NOTES

1. Randy Martin, *On Your Marx: Rethinking Socialism and the Left* (Minneapolis: University of Minnesota Press, 2002); J. K. Gibson-Graham, Stephen Resnick, and Richard Wolff, eds., "Toward a Poststructuralist Political Economy," *Re/Presenting Class: Essays in Postmodern Marxism* (Durham, N.C.: Duke University Press, 2001).

2. Kenneth Arrow, "Redistribution to the Poor: A Collective Expression of Individual Altruism," in *Poverty and Social Justice: Critical Perspectives*, ed. Francisco Jimenez (Tempe, Ariz.: Bilingual Press, 1987).

3. Frances Fox Piven and Richard Cloward, *The Class War: Reagan's Attack on the Welfare State and Its Consequences* (New York: Pantheon, 1982); Robert Heilbroner, *Twenty-First-Century Capitalism* (New York: Norton, 1993).

4. Karl Marx, *Capital*, vol. 1. (1867; London: Penguin Books, 1976).

5. T. B. Bottomore, trans., *Karl Marx: Early Writings* (1844; New York: McGraw-Hill, 1964).

5. Karl Marx, "The German Ideology," in *Karl Marx: Selected Writings*, ed. Lawrence H. Simon (1845; Indianapolis, Ind.: Hackett Publishing Co., 1994), 129.

6. Karl Marx and Friedrich Engels, 1848, "The Communist Manifesto," in *Karl Marx: Selected Writings*, 158–159.

7. Emile Durkheim, *The Division of Labor in Society* (New York: Free Press, 1933).

8. Max Weber, *The Theory of Economic and Social Organization*, eds. Alexander Morell Henderson and Talcott Parsons, trans. Talcott Parsons (New York: Oxford University Press, 1947).

9. Talcott Parsons, *The Social System* (Glencoe, Ill.: Free Press, 1951).

10. Ralf Dahrendorf, *Class and Class Conflict in Industrial Society* (Stanford, Calif.: Stanford University Press, 1959), 61.

11. C. Wright Mills, *The Power Elite* (New York: Oxford University Press, 1959).

12. Marx, "Thesis on Feuerbach," in *Karl Marx: Selected Writings*, 101.

13. Jürgen Habermas, *Communication and the Evolution of Society* (Boston: Beacon Press, 1979).

14. Jürgen Habermas, *Knowledge and Human Interests* (Boston: Beacon Press, 1971).

15. Jürgen Habermas, *Legitimation Crisis* (Boston: Beacon Press, 1975).

16. Habermas, *Legitimation Crisis*.

17. Hans-Georg Gadamer, *Truth and Method* (New York: Seabury Press, 1975). Also see Hans-Georg Gadamer, *Philosophical Hermeneutics* (Berkeley: University of California Press, 1976).

18. Jay White, "On the Growth of Knowledge in Public Administration," *Public Administration Review* 46 (January/February 1986): 15–24. Also see Robert Denhardt, "Toward a Critical Theory of Public Organization," *Public Administration Review* 41 (November/December 1981): 628–636.

19. Paulo Freire, *Pedagogy of the Oppressed* (New York: Continuum Publishers, 1970).

20. Paulo Freire, *Education for Critical Consciousness* (New York: Sheed & Ward, 1974); Paulo Freire, *Cultural Action for Freedom* (New York: Penguin Books, 1972); Neil Postman and Carl Weingartner, *Teaching as a Subversive Activity* (New York: Penguin Books, 1971).

21. Freire, *Cultural Action*.

22. By engaging in critical social analysis, an implicit set of values are employed that will prompt controversy. Social critique based on critical theory methodology is implicitly linked to an implied deontology or objective moral order. See Rodney G. Peffer, *Marxism, Morality, and Social Justice* (Princeton, N.J.: Princeton University Press, 1990).

23. Zygmut Bauman, *Intimations of Postmodernity* (London: Routledge, 1992); Steven Seidman, *Postmodernism and Social Theory* (Oxford: Blackwell, 1992).

24. Mary Daly, *Gyn/Ecology* (London: The Women's Press, 1979); Adrien Katherine Wing, ed., *Critical Race Feminism* (New York: New York University Press, 1997).

25. Michel Foucault, *Politics, Philosophy, Culture*, ed., Lawrence Kritzman (New York: Routledge, 1988); Michel Foucault, *The Foucault Reader* (New York: Pantheon, 1984).

26. Jean-Francois Lyotard, "Defining the Postmodern," in *Postmodernism: ICA Documents,* ed. Lisa Appignancsi (London: Free Association Books, 1989).

27. Lyotard, *Postmodernism.*

28. Jürgen Habermas, *The Philosophical Discourse of Modernity* (Cambridge, Mass.: MIT Press, 1987); Jurgen Habermas, "Questions and Counter-Questions," in *Habermas and Modernity*, ed. Richard Bernstein (Cambridge: Polity Press, 1985).

29. Walden Bello, *Dark Victory: The United States, Structural Adjustment and Global Poverty* (Oakland: Institute for Food and Development Policy, 1994).

30. John McGowan, *Postmodernism and Its Critics* (Ithaca, N.Y.: Cornell University Press, 1991); Peter McLaren and Peter Leonard, eds., *Paulo Freire: A Critical Encounter* (London: Routledge, 1993); Peter Leonard, *Postmodern Welfare: Reconstructing an Emancipatory Project* (Thousand Oaks, Calif.: Sage Publications, 1997); Robert Miles and Rodolfo Torres, "Does 'Race' Matter? Transatlantic Perspectives on Racism after 'Race' Relations," in *Race, Identity, and Citizenship: A Reader*, eds. Rodolfo Torres, Louis Miron, and Jon Xavier Inda (Oxford: Blackwell Publishers, 1999); Edward Martin, *Welfare Policy, the Market, and Community* (Tempe, Ariz.: Arizona State University, 2000).

31. Friedrich von Hayek, *The Road to Serfdom* (Chicago: University of Chicago Press, 1976); Friedrich von Hayek, *Rules and Order* (London: Routledge, 1973); Milton Friedman, *Capitalism and Freedom* (Chicago: University of Chicago Press, 1962).

32. Adam Smith, *An Inquiry Into the Nature and Causes of the Wealth of Nations*, 1776 (Chicago: Encyclopedia Britannica, 1952).

33. Vladimir I. Lenin, "Imperialism: The Highest Stage of Capitalism," in *Selected Works* (New York: International Publishers, 1967).

34. Harry Magdoff, *The Age of Imperialism: The Economics of United States Foreign Policy* (New York: Monthly Review Press, 1969); Paul Sweezy, "Capitalism and Democracy," *Monthly Review* 32, no. 2 (June 1980).

35. Bob Jessop, *The Future of the Capitalist State* (Oxford: Blackwell, 2003).

36. Malcolm Waters, *Globalization* (New York: Routledge, 1995).

37. Fredric Jameson, "Marxism and Postmodernism," in *Postmodernism/Jameson/Critique,* ed. Douglas Kellner (Washington, D.C.: Maisonneuve Press, 1989); Jameson, "Postmodernism, or the Cultural Logic of Late Capitalism," *New Left Review* 146 (1984): 56–92; Jean Baudrillard, *Simulations* (New York: Semiotext, 1983).

38. David Harvey, *The Condition of Postmodernity: An Enquiry into the Origins of Cultural Change* (Oxford: Blackwell, 1990).

39. Duane Swank, *Global Capital, Political Institutions, and Policy Change in Developed Welfare States*(New York: Cambridge University Press, 2002).

40. Swank, *Global Capital*, 170.

41. Leonard, *Postmodern Welfare*, 117.

42. George Soros, *Open Society: Reforming Global Capitalism* (New York: Public Affairs, 2000).

43. Jameson, "Marxism and Postmodernism."

44. Michael Rustin, "The Politics of Post-Fordism: Or, the Trouble with 'New Times,'" *New Left Review* 175: 54–78.

45. William Kymlicka, *Contemporary Political Philosophy* (New York: Oxford University Press, 2001).

46. Alexander Kaufman, *Welfare in the Kantian State* (New York: Oxford University Press, 1999).

47. John Maynard Keynes, *The General Theory of Employment, Interest, and Money* (New York: Harcourt, Brace & Ward, 1964).

48. Keynes, *The General Theory of Employment, Invests, and Money*.

49. Von Hayek, *The Road to Serfdom*; Von Hayek, *Rules and Order*; Friedman, *Capitalism and Freedom*.

Chapter Two

Marx and the Marxist Method

MARX FOR OUR TIMES

The reasons why a Marxist school of political scientists has not yet emerged, despite what appear to be favorable conditions, are rooted chiefly in the historical peculiarities of both Marxism and political science.

—Bertell Ollman, *Dance of the Dialectic*

Marx is generally recognized as the foremost radical thinker of the modern era. To date, Marxism has enjoyed prominence as an intellectual methodology, in spite of its utilization by many as a political vanguard within revolutionary settings over the past ninety years. Even with the demise of totalitarian Marxism in Eastern Europe, leftist political parties have been able to maintain sufficient political representation in fledgling democracies in Eastern Europe and to some lesser degree in Western democratic societies. In the United States, Mexico, and Costa Rica, leftist political parties have been insulated from democratic participation for one reason or another. And while certain market measures have been introduced to China, North Korea, Vietnam, Angola, and Cuba, liberalization of totalitarian Marxism has not radically changed it. Suffice it to say, Cuba, Angola, and North Korea have maintained their rigid adherence to militant revolutionary visions of monolithic and reductionistic Marxism. Still, for those who are opposed to radical economic and social transformation, Marxism and its political expression, communism, are without question the preeminent danger to the old world order. The "specter" haunting Europe in 1848, communism, has, in the period since that time, become inextricably bound to its most elaborate and consistent expression, Marxism.[1]

With its intense and openly political and partisan nature, Marxism has not enjoyed a smooth and unhindered development.[2] Such a philosophy is acceptable

35

to the present revolutionary class in which dialectical materialism is the theoretical reflection of the proletarian revolution. Nonetheless, Marxism has been bitterly and voluminously attacked by antisocialists of every stripe and from every point of view outside the socialist movement on the grounds that it is not what it claims to be—namely, scientific and objective—but is instead tendentious, sectarian, and simply incorrect in its main philosophical, economic, and political projections.[3] From within the socialist movement, and even from within Marxism, sharp disagreements have existed almost from the time of the original development of the doctrine, to the point where even today there is no universal agreement even among Marxists on what "Marxism" is. For example, is Marxism economic determinism? Is it a "system" as opposed to an open-ended methodology? Is it an integral whole of a collection of more or less discrete "structures" (economics, history, sociology, philosophy, etc.)? The point of this book, albeit, is not to offer an exhaustive exposition of all the questions and issues that have been raised and points of view that exist toward them. Instead, this analysis is simply an attempt to offer a summary of the main principles of Marxist methodology as expressed by "orthodox" proponents and simultaneously present new methodological perspectives from recent developments in this theory that would also point to the future direction of historical materialism in the twenty-first century.[4]

In order to better understand Marxist methodology it is best to examine the foundations upon which Marxist theory is based—that is, the economic theory that Marx and Engels termed Communism. In brief, Marx and Engels believed in the state ownership of major industries and transportation rather than the private ownership of these sectors. In the *Communist Manifesto* Marx and Engels mapped out their strategy for attaining the Communist state: a classless society arrived at through the common ownership of the means of production, distribution, and exchange. As a materialist philosophy—that is, one that does not refer to extraneous phenomena or metaphysical assumptions to explain temporal events—Marxism seeks to understand the nature of social relationships, transform unjust social arrangements in the present historical setting, and thus create a more egalitarian society.

Marxist critiques of capitalism focus on the exploitation of the working class by the capitalist class. The tension within this relationship generally results in the increased hostility between capital and labor. That is, under capitalism, which advocates liberal autonomy, workers are relegated to the status of slaves if they seek to maintain a wage relationship with capital. This form of alienation is what Marxists term *reification*. Reification takes place when the worker is perceived to be part of the labor force precisely because the concerns of capitalism—its profit and loss margin—take priority over all other social and economic considerations in capital ventures. As a result, workers become no more than "cogs in the machine" and are simultaneously dehumanized precisely because they are relegated to the demeaning level of capital. Here, the notion of reification implies that under any given capitalist system, capital and profit ultimately take priority over labor. Marxists conclude that this rational design inherent within capitalism promotes increasing class antagonisms and stratification.

Marxist thought is constructed upon a specific model of society in which the base (material means of production, distribution, and exchange) is the driving force of society. The superstructure within Marxist thought (the cultural world of ideas, art, religion, and law) is in turn shaped by the base or what is otherwise known as the economic substructure. Based on this notion of economic determinism, Marxist literary criticism, for example, would maintain that a writer's social class and prevailing ideology (outlook, values) clearly have a major bearing on what s/he writes. The nature of literature is understood as being influenced by the social and political circumstances within which it is produced, and vice versa. The same holds true for religion, law, education, etc. Notwithstanding, traditional Marxist critique attempts to identify inherent conflicts between social classes and the systemic causes of the very ideological dictates that foment crude forms of class conflict. The Marxist remedy to unjust social arrangements (either through social reconstruction or variant forms of upheaval and revolution) will invariably lead to liberation, or as Marx describes, a "new Man." This new socialized milieu is one that promotes greater democratic rights within the work environment.

RETHINKING, ONCE AGAIN, WHAT IS MARXISM?

According to its intellectual founders (Marx, Engels, Lenin), Marxism is fundamentally a materialist philosophy. It is *not*, as all previous philosophical doctrines had been prior to Marx, a self-contained, closed, and finite set of explanations and principles designed to answer all past, present, and future questions. All philosophers from the time of Plato to the nineteenth century had felt the necessity to set forth their ideas of constructing systems—that is, models of reality (nature, society, ethics, aesthetics, etc.). The necessity of doing so came, essentially, from the nonhistorical nature of classical philosophy with its interpretation of the world as a closed, limited structure rather than an open-ended, evolving process. Whether this structure was cyclical or teleological didn't matter. The point was that it was limited and, as such, demanded an explanation that would embrace its totality.

Arguably, the last great "systematic" philosopher was Georg Hegel, who attempted, in his body of work (*The Phenomenology of Mind, Science of Logic, Philosophy of History, Philosophy of Right*, etc.), to explain all phenomena in a finalized form. As Engels states, "[Hegel] was compelled to make a system, and, in accordance with all the traditional requirements, a system of philosophy must conclude with some sort of Absolute Truth."[5] However, during the period in which Hegel wrote, events in both science and philosophy itself were undermining the traditional, historical view of nature and human development. Engels further states that Immanuel Kant, a contemporary of Hegel, "began his career by resolving the stable solar system of Newton and its eternal permanence—after the initial impulse had once been given—into a historical process: the formation of the sun and of all the planets out of a rotating nebulous mass."[6] In the realm of politics, the sudden and violent bourgeois revolutions of the late eighteenth centuries, particularly in France, exploded the "eternal" verities of social estate, the divine right of kings, and all feudal obligation. The epoch-making development of industrialization and world trade, characteristic of modern capitalism, modified all former notions of profession, civilization, human wants and needs, money, and "civil" life in general.

As "one of the finest intellectuals of all time,"[7] Hegel, according to Engels, incorporated these new deterministic philosophical developments into his system of thought, giving it an inherent dynamism and a core of reality that contradicted the dominant "systematic" methods of the scholastic tradition. As Engels states, "[W]hat distinguishes Hegel's mode of thought from that of all other philosophers was the enormous historical sense upon which it was based. Abstract and idealist though it was in form, yet the development of his thoughts always proceeded in line with the development of world history, and the latter was really meant to be only the test of the former."[8]

Because he possessed not only "creative genius" but also "encyclopedic erudition," Hegel was able to describe the underlying laws of motion (social as well as natural), the laws of dialectics, and in essence, the law of development through contradiction.[9] On the one hand, this approach leads to what is termed a "forced construction"—a metaphysical need to explain everything, even what is not yet known.[10] On the other hand, it necessitates a "teleology" —the notion of an inherent goal within the workings of history, a goal ordained according to Hegel by God. Hegel states:

> Philosophy would teach us that the real world is as it ought to be—that the truly good, the universal divine reason, is not a mere abstraction, but a vital principle capable of realizing itself. This *Good*, this *Reason*, in its most concrete form, is God. God governs the world: the actual working of his government—the carrying out of his plan—in the History of the World. This plan philosophy strives to comprehend; for only that which has been developed as the result of it possesses bona fide reality. That which does not accord with it is negative, worthless existence.[11]

While understood to be erroneous from the standpoint of modern science, these notions in no way detract from Hegel's basic discovery of the laws of development, which serve as both the apex of eighteenth century rationalism and its limit or "negation." "With Hegel," Engels states, "philosophy comes to an end: on the one hand, because in his system he comprehended its whole development in the most splendid fashion; and, on the other hand, because, even if unconsciously, he showed us the way out of the labyrinth of 'systems' to real positive knowledge."[12]

Although the "wild speculation" of Hegel, and its antithesis, the "sober philosophy" of English and French materialism of the Enlightenment, are at first blush irreconcilable, they are in reality cut from the same cloth: the ideology of the eighteenth century revolutionary bourgeoisie.[13] Despite its mystical, religious veneer, Hegelianism shares with English and French materialism a belief in the possibility and inevitability of human progress, the perfectibility of man, and the rationality and knowledge of the universe, typical of idealist suppositions.[14] It was the first great task of Marx and Engels, via Ludwig Feuerbach, to uncover the link between these two traditions, cleanse each of its philosophical dross (idealism in Hegelianism, a mechanistic and atomistic view of society in French and English rationalism), and reestablish them in a new, integral whole—the *new* materialism. Furthermore, in the *Essence of Christianity*, Feuerbach "exploded" the moribund Hegelian "system" and "liberated" the young generation of German intellectuals to which Marx and Engels belonged. Engels thus summarizes Feuerbach: "Nature exists independently of all philosophy. It is the foundation upon which human beings, as products of nature, have grown up. Nothing exists outside nature and the human condition, and the higher beings as religious fantasies have created are only the fantastic reflection of our own essence."[15] However, according to Engels, Feuerbach did not defeat the Hegelian system in the sense of disproving it:

> [Feuerbach] broke through the system and simply discarded it. But a philosophy is not disposed of by the mere assertion that it is false. And so powerful a work as Hegelian philosophy, which had exercised so enormous an influence on the intellectual development of the nation, did not allow itself to be disposed of by simply being ignored. It had to be "sublated" in its own sense, that is, in the sense that while its form had to be annihilated through criticism, the new content which had been won through it had to be saved.[16]

This "sublation" was accomplished by Marx and Engels in a series of works written in the first half of the 1840s, which include Marx's *Economic and Philosophic Manuscripts of 1844*, his *Critique of Hegel's Philosophy of Right, Thesis on Feuerbach, The German Ideology, The Holy Family, The*

Poverty of Philosophy (1846–1847), and others. In these, rather than simply being denied, the Hegelian system is criticized in terms of its own internal contradictions and failures, particularly its failure to explain the polarization of society (rather than its unity "in the Idea") coming about through the alienation of the human person's labor, the separation of labor and property. As Engels argues, Hegel's system, which demands unity and reconciliation in the interests of consistency and "overcoming all contradictions," crashes on the rock of *real contradiction*, the real alienation of man from the product of his labor expressed in the estrangement of a man from his mental processes (abstract thinking).[17] Because he transforms a material contradiction—the alienation of man from his product (labor)—into a philosophical problem, Hegel cannot resolve this problem except through philosophical claims that have no objective validity. Rather, they are in the end "uncritical positivism" and "uncritical idealism"—purported solutions that leave the essential problem untouched. Hegel's *Encyclopaedia*, according to Marx, "is in its entirety nothing but the *display*, the self-objectification, of the *essence* of the philosophic mind, and the philosophic mind is nothing but the estranged mind of the world thinking within its self-estrangement, i.e., comprehending itself abstractly."[18]

As for Feuerbach, Marx demonstrates through a series of insights (of which the *Theses on Feuerbach* is the summation) that the weakness of the "old materialism" (basically that of the English and French Enlightenment) lies, first, in its failure to understand the relationship between matter and mind, in its serving of the two in a sort of dualism, and, second, in its reification of the individual "species being," the abstract man divorced from society, as the starting point of social investigation.[19] The solution to both these problems lies in a transformed consciousness of society. Society is not an aggregate or arithmetical sum of discrete and autonomous "abstract individuals." Rather, it is a complex organism that creates the human person, without which the human person's essence—"the ensemble of social relations"—does not exist. In a very real way, society exists prior to and creates the human person more than the human person as an individual creates society.[20] Human nature, far from being an unchanging, abstract notion, is changing and dynamic. In this sense, humanity creates itself through collective action. Similarly, rather than being the isolated creations of individuals, ideas become part of the social activity of people and thus, at least potentially, a material force when they are acted upon by masses of people.

For Feuerbach, existence is individual and salvation is a question of the satisfaction of the individual "essence." This position is consistent with the modern bourgeois conception of "enlightened self-interest" summarized by Jeremy Bentham: "The interests of the individual should give way to public interests. But . . . what does that mean? Is not every individual as much a part of the public as any other? This public interest, which you personify, is only an abstract expression: it represents only the mass of individual interests. . . . Individual interests are the only real interests."[21]

Consequently Marx interprets Feuerbach:

[T]he conditions of existence, the mode of life and activity of an animal or human individual are those in which its "essence" feels itself satisfied. Here, every exception is expressly conceived as an unhappy chance, as an abnormality which cannot be altered. Thus, if millions of proletarians feel by no means contented with their living conditions, if their "existence" does not in the least correspond to their "essence," then, according to the passage quoted, this is an unavoidable misfortune, which must be borne quietly. The millions of proletarians and communists, however, think differently and will prove this in time, when they bring their "existence" into harmony with their "essence" in a practical way, by means of a revolution. Feuerbach, therefore, never speaks of the world of man in such cases but always takes refuge in external nature and, moreover, in *nature* which has not yet been subdued by men. But every new invention, every advance made by industry, detaches another piece from this domain so that the ground which produces examples illustrating such Feuerbachian propositions is steadily shrinking.[22]

By placing "man" within society, Marx is able to bridge the gap between the individual and the masses. In doing this, Marx demonstrates the internal logic of history as the self-creation of human beings according to definite and knowable social laws; he is able to bridge the gap between activity and contemplation. He states: "[A]ll social life is essentially *practical*. All mysteries which lead theory to mysticism find their rational solution in human practice and in the comprehension of this practice."[23] According to Marx, the "mysteries" confounding theory can be solved not by speculation, but by examination of human practice itself, and not human practice as an abstraction—since such a thing does not exist in the minds of the Robinson Crusoe-ists of bourgeois political economy and their spawn—but human practice as it exists historically, as it actually exists, and has existed in the real world.[24]

And how can this historical practice be characterized? Marx states:

We must begin by stating the first premise of all human existence and, therefore, of all history, the premise, namely, that men must be in a position to live in order to be able to "make history." But life evolved before everything else, eating and drinking, a habitation, clothing, and many other things. The first historical act is thus the production of the means to satisfy these needs, the production of material life itself. . . . Therefore, in any interpretation of history one has first of all to observe this fundamental fact in all its significance and all its implications and to accord it its due importance. It is well known that the Germans have never done this, and they have never, therefore, had an earthly basis for history and consequently never an historian.[25]

After defining how the production of material life takes place and develops through history (through cooperation, division of labor, etc.), Marx concludes:

> It follows from this that all struggles within the State, the struggle between democracy, aristocracy, and monarchy, the struggle for the franchise, etc., etc., are merely the illusory forms in which the real struggles of the different classes are fought out among one another. . . . Further, it follows that every class which is struggling for mastery, even when its domination, as is the case with the proletariat, postulates the abolition of the old form of society in its entirety and of domination itself, must first conquer for itself political power in order to represent its interest in turn as the general interest, which immediately it is forced to do.[26]

Thus, the *ideas* of individuals, which the old materialism cannot link to the material world because it views them abstractly, become the reflections of class interests and find their material manifestation in political activity, the struggle of classes, and the political parties that represent them. Such, in its main outlines, is the "new materialism"[27] of Marx and Engels. For the first time, it uncovers the unity of the human person (previously an abstract, idealized "species being"[28]) and nature and thus is able to place social development within the framework of the material world without, however, reducing that development and accompanying ideas to purely mechanistic phenomena.[29] The person's unity with nature allows her/him not only to understand, but to change this nature. Engels states, "the real unity of the world consists in its materiality, and this is proved not by juggling a few phrases," (about "being," the "Idea," etc.) "but by a long and protracted development of philosophy and natural science."[30]

The "ontology" of Marxism (a word not used in Marxist literature itself), then, is materialism. It is a new materialism that takes into account the actual laws of motion, the *dialectic* of matter itself and its products—namely, human society and thought. Its "epistemology"—that is, its notion of the origin of ideas and knowledge, is the theory of reflection: ideas are the reflections of real material processes in the minds of people, transmitted through sense perceptions. Ideas have their basis in, and are predicated upon, the material world, and come from nowhere else (neither God nor innate qualities of the subjective mind). In Marx's words, "to Hegel, the life-process of the human brain, i.e., the process of thinking, which, under the name of 'the Idea,' he even transforms into an independent subject, is the demiurge of the real world, and the real world is only the external, phenomenal form of 'the Idea.'" Consequently, just as materialism changes in the treatment of Marx and Engels, the Hegelian dialectic changes, also, from a mystified, idealistic conception to one that is clear and straightforward: "dialectics is nothing more than the science of the general laws of motion and development of nature, human society and thought."[31]

There is no substantial evidence in the writing of Marx and Engels, however, that in transforming the Hegelian dialectic they deny the basic validity of the actual dialectical laws that Hegel discovered— the law of contradiction, the law of quantitative leading to qualitative change, and the law of the negation of the negation. Yet, all signs point to Marx and Engles having accepted Hegel's exposition of those laws as valid, only not in the form in which he presents them. In the same afterword quoted above, Engels states:

> My dialectic method is not only different from the Hegelian, but is its direct opposite. . . . The mystifying side of Hegelian dialectic I criticized nearly thirty years ago, at a time when it was still in fashion. But just as I was working at the first volume of "Das Kapital," it was the good pleasure of the peevish, arrogant, mediocre (Epigono Ettyovol) who now talk large in cultural Germany, to treat Hegel in the same way as the brave Moses Mendelssohn in Lessing's time treated Spinoza, i.e., as a "dead dog." I therefore openly avowed myself the pupil of that mighty thinker, and even here and there, in the chapter on the theory of value, coquetted with the modes of expression peculiar to him. *The mystification which dialectic suffers in Hegel's hands, by no means prevents him from being the first to present its general form of working in a comprehensive and conscious manner.* With him it is standing on its head. It must be turned right side up again, if you would discover the rational kernel within the mystical shell.[32]

Marxism represents the "sublation" of all previous attempts to explain phenomena and is the end point of traditional philosophy. Engels states:

> Modern materialism is essentially dialectic and no longer needs any philosophy standing above the other sciences. As soon as each separate science is required to get clarity as to its position in the great totality of things and of our knowledge of things, a special science dealing with this totality is superfluous. What still independently survives of all former philosophy is the science of thought and its laws—formal logic and dialectics. Everything else is merged in the positive science of nature and history.[33]

Or in the words of Marx:

> Where real speculation ends—in real life—there real, positive science begins: the representation of the practical activity of the practical process of development of men. Empty talk about consciousness ceases, and real knowledge has to

take its place. When reality is depicted, philosophy as an independent branch of knowledge loses its medium of existence. At the best its place can only be taken by a summing-up of the most general results, abstractions which arise from the observation of the historical development of men. Viewed apart from real history, these abstractions have in themselves no value whatsoever. They can only serve to facilitate the arrangements of historical material, to indicate the sequence of its separate strata. But they by no means afford a recipe or schema, as does philosophy, for neatly trimming the epochs of history.[34]

As demonstrated, the Marxist "negation" of previous philosophy does not mean denial or destruction of its real content, only of its unreal, speculative, "systemic" form. The positive content is sublated—that is, destroyed in its form while preserved in its content, the latter being nothing more nor less than the long attempt by human intellect to comprehend itself and its environment. Engels states:

This modern materialism, the negation of the negation, is not the mere reestablishment of the old, but adds to the permanent foundations of this old materialism the whole thought content of two thousand years of development of philosophy and natural science, as well as of the historical development of these two thousand years. It is in fact no longer a philosophy, but a simple world outlook which has to establish its validity and be applied not in a science of sciences standing apart, but with the positive science. In this development philosophy is therefore "subjected," that is "both overcome and preserved"; overcome as regards its form, and preserved as regards its real content.[35]

Far from being a rejection of the past, Marxism is in the finest tradition of world culture. Lenin states:

The history of philosophy and the history of social science show with perfect clarity that there is nothing resembling "sectarianism" in Marxism, in the sense of development of world civilization. On the contrary, the genius of Marx consists precisely in his having furnished answers to questions already raised by the foremost minds of mankind. His doctrine emerged as the direct and immediate *continuation* of the teachings of the greatest representatives of philosophy, political economy and socialism. The Marxist doctrine is omnipotent because it is true. It is comprehensive and harmonious, and provides men with an integral world outlook irreconcilable with any form of superstition, reaction, or defense of bourgeois oppression.[36]

Thus, concludes Marx, "we see far because we stand on the shoulders of giants": the Hegels, Feuerbachs, Pettys, Diderots, Spinozas, Aristotles, and so on. If individual persons see farther than they, it is not so much because intellects are superior, but because the human person lives in a time in which history itself has provided the human condition with the raw material—both in scientific research and in the sharpening and amplification of the class struggle—with which to solve the questions that earlier intellects could only pose.

The notion of Marxism's sublation of the past—its simultaneous overcoming and preservation of it—must be stressed because one of the avenues of attack on Marxism has been the claim that it denies or rejects the past. For example, a current critique states that, whereas Hegel's concept of history was one of continual summation, Harry Boyte states: "[F]or Marx, the past was simply dead weight or, as he described it in the *Eighteenth Brumaire*—a nightmare on the brain of the living. Indeed both Marx and Engels held that class consciousness meant a kind of radical disconnection from existing structures and traditions as part of its definition. It derives from disconnection."[37] But for Marx, the "past" was *not* "simply dead weight." In a society based on thousands of years of class struggle—in the political sense in which Marx is speaking in the *Eighteenth Brumaire*—tradition and history play an important role precisely because the context of class struggle has been connected to a tradition of slavery, oppression, greed, self-delusion, and hypocrisy. It is the bourgeois wish to maintain the "hallowed" traditions of chattel slavery, the eighteen-hour workday, poverty, and the degradation of the working people for the "cultured" aggrandizement of a small elite. Marx and Engels themselves mock those who accuse them of attempting to destroy tradition and family. In "Abolition of the Family" Marx and Engels state:

> On what foundation is the present family, the bourgeois family, based? On capital, on private gain. In its completely developed form this family exists only among the bourgeoisie. But this state of things finds its complement in the practical absence of the family among the proletarians, and in public prostitution. The bourgeois family will vanish as a matter of course when its complement vanishes; and both will vanish with the vanishing of capital. Do you charge us with wanting to stop the exploitation of children by their parents? To this crime we plead guilty.[38]

The proletariat, according to Marx and Engels, is the only class that has *no stake* in all the "traditions" of slavery and oppression because it owns no property and has no relations of production that favor it and are worth preserving. But this means that the proletariat is the only heir to the *positive* aspect of the past, the millennia-old struggle of humanity to emerge from prehistory into real history, from necessity into freedom. The proletariat is the only class capable of *saving* culture. But it can do so only by demystifying it, by demystifying the past and all the hallowed ghosts—the (bourgeois) family based on exploitation and inheritance and the "idiocy of rural life," small-scale production based on semistarvation of the producers and the narrowness of the guild, the "culture" of a few based on the toil of the many, etc.—that strangle its intellectual and political development. This is a contradiction, but it is a real contradiction. The proletariat can preserve all that is great in human history only by moving beyond it.

MARXISM AS METHOD

In response to the "false positivism" of Hegel's economic and political apologetic for the Prussian monarchy of Frederick William III,[39] Marxist critique came into being in the attempt to refute the narrow reasoning of Hegel's own theory. While Hegel provided an authoritarian justification within his dialectical theory, he somehow failed to identify the inherently revolutionary nature of his own interpretation of dialectics. For whatever reason, Hegel was unable to assess how the premises of his own theory of dialectics opened the way for a truly revolutionary critique of society as Marxism was able to do. Marxism as materialism was able to take into account not only the primacy of the material world vis-à-vis ideas, but also the real laws of motion through dialectical analysis. Still, Engels makes it clear that Marxist materialism is not a dogma designed to truncate or discourage the expansion of research and knowledge through other avenues, but rather, it is a guide to investigation in the ever-widening spheres of the sciences, natural and social.[40] In fact, Marx did not arrive at his conclusions about the inevitability of the socialist transformation of society (summarized in the last section of volume one of *Capital*) by starting explicitly with the dialectical principle of the "negation of the negation" and then imposing it upon the subject matter at hand, as Eugen Duhring and subsequent critics contend. Nevertheless, only on the basis of the most exhaustive study of capital accumulation is Marx able to "uncover" its dialectical workings.

In classical Marxist literature, perhaps the clearest examples of dialectics can be found in the works of Lenin, particularly *Imperialism, The Highest Stage of Capitalism,* and *Materialism and Empirico-Criticism.* As a theoretical foundation for these works, Lenin utilizes physics as a model, particularly atomic theory, to defend the Marxist materialist "ontology." In this interpretation, Lenin includes and revises virtually every major tenet of Marxist materialism, from the materialist outlook itself, to the theory of reflection and action, to the laws of dialectics, to the theory of the state, to the theory of value, and beyond. While as a method Marxism is flexible and able to adapt to every real advance in social development and scientific knowledge, its basic outlook and tools of analysis, insofar as they have been proven correct in practice, do not change. As an "integral world outlook," materialism, according to Lenin, is not an eclectic hodgepodge of discrete, autonomous elements. "From this Marxist philosophy," Lenin states, "which is cast from a single piece of steel, you cannot eliminate one basic premise, one essential part, without departing from objective truth, without falling prey to bourgeois-reactionary falsehood."[41] Because "the real unity of the world consists in its materiality,"[42] and because that materiality includes the dialectic as an objective process, any departure from a dialectical materialist outlook in any area of Marxist investigation (namely, the "three component parts": philosophy, political economy, and socialism[43]) is bound to affect the entire body of Marxist science. Thus one cannot "disprove" the labor theory of value or the validity of the dialectics of nature without destroying the whole, any more than one can remove one of the body's vital organs without killing the entire body, and, in the process, "departing from objective truth."

The difference between "orthodox" and "nonorthodox" Marxism is that the latter, sooner or later, must openly call into question one or more of the essential principles of dialectical and historical materialism. In doing so, it ceases to be Marxism. This is not to say that nonorthodox Marxism may not be correct, of course, but only that it is not the outlook of Marx, Engels, and Lenin—it is something else. For example, when Antonio Gramsci asserts that "the concept of objectivity which exists even outside of man . . . is either to state a metaphor or to fall into a form of mysticism,"[44] to Lenin, this statement is a departure from the Marxist outlook, which *does* assert the objective existence of the material world, and not as a "metaphor." Gramsci here is falling into a subjectivism that is inconsistent with Marx and Engels, as Lenin describes in *Materialism and Empirico-Criticism*. Similarly, when E. P. Thompson criticizes "reflection theory,"[45] he is not being sufficiently Marxist, since reflection theory, for good or ill, is indubitably part of Marxism. And even Louis Althusser does likewise, calling the "category of reflection" derogatorily "empiricist,"[46] or when he modestly proposes to cleanse *capital* of its "Hegelian influence,"[47] he, too, is not being true to Marxist theory.

TOWARD A MARXIST POLITICS

In "Marxism and Revisionism," Lenin discusses how, by the 1890s, Marxist socialism had defeated all other brands, intellectually and practically, in the workers' movement (anarchism, Proudhonism, Lassalleanism, etc.). With the founding of the Second International, Lenin states:

> [T]he revived international, organization of the labour movement—in the shape of periodical international congresses—from the outset, and almost without a

struggle, adopted the Marxist standpoint in all essentials. But after Marxism had
ousted all the more or less integral doctrines hostile to it, the tendencies expressed in those doctrines began to seek other channels. The forms and causes
of the struggle changed, but the struggle continued. And the second half-century
of the existence of Marxism began (in the nineties) with the struggle of a trend
hostile to Marxism within Marxism itself.[48]

This trend, revisionism, has its roots in the "middle strata" and "small producers" who are, with the centralization and concentration of capital, continually
being thrust into the proletariat and its political movement.[49] The intellectual
representatives of these groups, the "petty proprietors" of the intellect, turn the
strivings and vacillations of these groups into theory. They seek to transform the
thoroughly revolutionary and proletarian science of Marxism into something
acceptable to the middle strata. Thus, those who consider themselves to be orthodox Marxists tend to view revisionism as bourgeois liberalism disguised as
Marxism, although its forms may vary widely. Jean-Paul Sartre, for instance,
claims Marxism as the only "living philosophy" of our time, but then proceeds
to try to steer it in *his* direction of existentialism. Similarly, with structuralists
such as C. Wright Mills, Marxism's tremendous intellectual and *practical*
power draws these essentially non-Marxist elements to it, but then they attempt
to remold it in line with their way of thinking, introducing into it unsolicited
"clarifications," "improvements," "purifications," "amendments," etc.

The consequence of all these revisions, according to the so-called orthodox
Marxists, is, nevertheless, liberalism. The hallmark of liberalism is the desire
to overcome all contradictions, to reconcile all differences. These would include the differences between the bourgeoisie and proletariat, between materialism and idealism, between science and religion, between socialism and
capitalism, between the state as an instrument of violence and the state as a
"mediating structure," and between Marxism and traditional bourgeois ag-
nosticism. Historically, liberalism as a theory is a form of "afterbirth" of the
Enlightenment, the radical ideas of English and French rationalism (including
materialism) domesticated by the pressures of having to represent the real interests of the modern and grand bourgeoisie. Economically, it is a reflection
of the bourgeoisie's struggle against feudalism, which necessitated the abolition of "unnatural" inequalities of estate, constraints on free economic development of capital, etc. As such its call word is "free trade"—that is, unhindered economic production and commodity exchange. Politically, liberalism
reflects the antifeudal bourgeoisie's enlistment of the proletariat as the actual
fighting force in the war against the old order under the banner of *"liberté"*
(of the bourgeoisie from feudal fetters, and wage labor from guild restrictions), *"égalité"* (of capitalist and worker in the political realm, leaving only
the "minor matter" of property ownership and wealth as the differential), and

"fraternité" (of capitalist and worker in the common fight against the common enemy, feudalism, until the struggle is won through blood shed by the proletariat, at which time the bourgeoisie refocuses its attention from the aristocracy back on the proletariat, its erstwhile *"frère"*).[50]

The essence of liberalism as a social and political philosophy is the overcoming of contradictions through gradual reform. In describing "bourgeois socialism" in the *Manifesto*, Marx and Engels describe its more leftist form:

> The socialistic bourgeois want all the advantages of modern social conditions without the struggles and dangers necessarily resulting therefrom. They desire the existing state of society minus its revolutionary and disintegrating elements. They wish for a bourgeoisie without a proletariat. The bourgeoisie socialism develops this comfortable conception into various more or less complete systems. In requiring the proletariat to carry out such a system and thereby to march straightway into the social New Jerusalem, it requires in reality that the proletariat should remain within the bounds of existing society, but should cast away all its hateful ideas concerning the bourgeoisie.[51]

Such a philosophy, obviously, is the opposite of Marxism, which bases itself upon the irreconcilability of contradictions between classes. Liberalism, representing the bourgeoisie, which is either seeking power or is in power over the proletariat, naturally attempts to do away with the latter's "contradictoriness" toward it. Marxism, representing the proletariat, has no need to paper over or ameliorate the antagonism between labor and capital, since any such amelioration can only put off the day of the proletariat's victory.[52]

"The Marxist doctrine," Lenin states, "is omnipotent because it is true." He states elsewhere, "We do not regard Marxist theory as something completed and inviolable; on the contrary, we are convinced that it has only laid the cornerstone of the science which Socialists *must* further advance in all directions if they wish to keep pace with life."[53] These two formulations are by no means contradictory, more precisely they form a dynamic contradiction in line with the Marxist understanding of the development of knowledge from the lower to the higher, from the less to the more perfect, but a development that never achieves absolute perfection of absolute knowledge because such a thing does not exist *practically*. The basic truth of Marxism as an outlook and method drives its practitioners forward to deepen their understanding of nature and society; this deepening, in turn, makes the "truth" ever more (but never completely) whole. Expressing the essential *unity* between the material world and man's perception of it, Lenin states:

> [H]uman thought then by its nature is capable of giving, and does give, absolute truth, which is compounded of a sum total of relative truths. Each step in the development of science adds new grains to the sum of absolute truth, but

the limits of the truth of each scientific proposition are relative, now expanding, now shrinking with the growth of knowledge . . . for dialectical materialism there is no impassable boundary between relative and absolute truth. . . . From the standpoint of modern materialism, i.e., Marxism, the *limits* of approximation of our knowledge to objective, absolute truth are historically conditional, but the existence of such truth is *unconditional*, and the fact that we are approaching nearer to it is also unconditional.[54]

The criterion for knowing what is true is not based on speculation or subjectivity; it is the human person's ability to *produce* reality in line with their thinking. Marx points this out in the second *Theses on Feuerbach*: "The question whether objective truth can be attributed to human thinking is not a question of theory but is a *practical question*. Man must prove the truth, i.e., the reality and power, the this-sidedness of his thinking in practice. The dispute over the reality or non-reality of thinking that is isolated from practice is a purely *scholastic* question."[55]

Engels adds to this, refuting the agnostics who deny the knowledge of the world:

The most telling refuting of this as of all other philosophical fancies is practice, viz., experiment and industry. If we are able to prove the correctness of our conception of a natural process by making it ourselves, bringing it into being out of its conditions and using it for our own purposes into the bargain, then there is an end of the Kantian incomprehensible "thing-in-itself". . . . For three hundred years the Copernican solar system was an hypothesis with a hundred, a thousand or ten thousand chances to one in its favor, but still always an hypothesis. But when Leverrier, by means of the data provided by this system, not only deduced the necessity of the existence of an unknown planet, [he] also calculated the position in the heavens which this planet must necessarily occupy, and when Galle really found this planet, the Copernican system was proved.[56]

Marxism as a whole must be judged according to this criterion of its practical applicability in the material world, both natural and social. Has it effectively analyzed modern society and pointed accurately to the direction of its inevitable development? Now here again, obviously, there is fierce partisan debate with historians and ideologists calling into question the very historical facts of, for example, the Russian or Chinese revolutions, in the effort either to confirm or deny Marxism's applicability in those instances. But debate is to be expected and should not constitute a diversion from understanding the actual historical process as being the only legitimate or possible "court of appeal" for or against Marxism or, for that matter, any theory of history or science.[57] Although there are various trends in contemporary Marxism, one particular trend, the structuralist school of Louis Althusser, Nicos Poulantzas, and others, centering on Poulantzas' *Political Power and Social Classes*, represents a major attempt to develop Marxism from at least an *avowedly* orthodox standpoint.

Poulantzas's major contribution to political theory is his effort to deal, from a Marxist standpoint, with the various non-Marxist trends in political science and sociology represented by such theoreticians as C. Wright Mills, Max Weber, Herbert Marcuse, and others. Using primarily the political writings of Marx (namely, *The Eighteenth Brumaire of Louis Bonaparte* and *Class Struggles in France*), Poulantzas critiques the concepts of the welfare state, "elites," "zero-sum power," and other concepts of current political thought. His basic orientation is the fact that although society in the twentieth century is extremely complex and offers phenomena (state monopoly capitalism, new forms of "legitimacy," etc.) that could not have been foreseen by Marx, the nature of politics and the state as forms of struggle and domination has not changed. Poulantzas thus argues against those political scientists who either reject Marxism (as a theory of the class struggle) out of hand as simply wrong, or else as a nineteenth-century ideology that, while perhaps relevant to the period of the Industrial Revolution, is no longer valid in the era of the "welfare state."[58]

The main effort of these political thinkers, in keeping with their liberal approach (that is, in reconciling contradictions), is to deny class antagonisms entirely (or to at least minimize the risk of antagonisms) or to separate the question of economic classes from that of political power,[59] predicating the latter on the practices not of social classes, but of "elites." The existence and power of these elites are explained differently by various schools of thought. "Their unity," Poulantzas states:

> is sometimes based . . . on the mere fact of their relation (in terms of influence or participation) with institutionalized political power. This power, without any possible foundation, is considered as a simple place whose very existence unifies the various elites, with the heights of the bureaucracy constituting simply one elite among others. Subsequently, this school attempts to discover *parallel* sources of political power, considering the economic itself as one source of power and the state as another. The elites, including the bureaucracy, though they are reduced to their relations to these various sources, are nonetheless unified, according to Wright Mills, by the fact that the "heads of economic corporations," the "political leaders" (including the heights of the bureaucracy) and the "military leaders," that is to say all the elites, belong to what he calls the "corporate rich." In this case, this conception, which wanted to supersede so-called Marxist economic determinism and examine the autonomous functioning of the bureaucracy, appears to reduce the problem precisely to an economic over-determinism. . . . Finally, as in Burnham, this unity is sometimes explained

by the fact that the various elites belong to the new technico-bureaucratic "class" of managers, which controls production in large enterprises through the so-called separation of ownership from control and in the nationalized sector through its membership of the state apparatus. . . . The major defect of these theories consists in the fact that they do not provide any *explanation* of the foundation of political power. In addition, they acknowledge a plurality of courses for political power but can offer no explanation of their relation.[60]

Poulantzas uncovers the various non-Marxist and semi-Marxist political theories of classes and the state by examining the "effect of isolation" of the capitalist mode of production on, among other things, the ideology of its members. The effect of isolation, according to Poulantzas,

consists of the fact that the *juridical and ideological structures* (determined in the last instance by the structure of the labour process), which set up at their level agents of production distributed in social classes as juridico-ideological subjects, produce the following effect on the economic class struggle: the effect of concealing from these agents in a particular way the fact that their relations are class relations.[61]

This isolation of individuals, or "atomization" as it has been termed, into individual commodity-owners (the capitalists of the means of production and the social product, the proletarians of their labor-power), manifested through the "terrifyingly real" competition among the workers and among the capitalists, masks class relations at all levels. Even the capitalists find it difficult (if not impossible) to unite in their own class interests, and the bourgeois state, far from being a simple "class instrument" or tool of the capitalists,[62] is "the organizing agent of their class struggle," with its own autonomy over the various factions of the capitalist class and a capability of acting in contradiction to the interests of some or all of them at various times, or at least in contradiction to their immediate interests as they see them. Poulantzas continues:

In the case of the capitalist state, the autonomy of the political can allow the satisfaction of the economic interests of certain dominated classes, even to the extent of occasionally limiting the economic power of the dominant classes, restraining, where necessary, their capacity to realize their short-term interests; but on the one condition, which has become *possible* in the case of capitalist states, that their political power and the state apparatus remain intact.[63]

Elsewhere, Poulantzas critiques the various attempts ("neo-liberal," "neo-corporatist," etc.) of current social scientists to reduce power relationships in modern capitalist society to struggles of "interest groups," "pluralism," and so on.[64] At this point it is important to note that theoretical differences exist with respect to the precepts of structural Marxism, and its self-description as orthodox Marxism is by no means universally accepted. E. P. Thompson, for example, in a polemic entitled *The Poverty of Theory*,[65] has called into serious question the work of Althusser: Thompson accuses him and Poulantzas of committing the very errors of which they (namely, Poulantzas in *Political Power*) accuse bourgeois social scientists. E. P. Thompson states:

> Class is a category which, in Althusser's major work, goes unexamined. And the classes which do make an entrance from time to time, and march up and down the pages—the bourgeoisie, the proletariat—are exceedingly crude projections of *Theory*, like primeval urges with iron heads, since "politics," "law," etc., etc., have been taken out of their heads and put at different levels, and since consciousness, values, and culture have been excluded from the vocabulary.[66]

Thus Thompson accuses them of

> the de-historicising of process, and . . . reducing class, ideology, social formations, and almost everything else, to categorical states. The sociological section: the elaborate differential rotations within the closure of the orrery; the self-extrapolating programmed developmental series; the mildly disequilibrated equilibrium models, in which dissensus strays unhappily down strange corridors, searching for a reconciliation with consensus; the systems-analyses and structuralisms, with their torques and their combinatories; the counterfactual fictions; the enconometric and cleometric groovers—all of these theories hobble along programmed routes from one static category to the next.[67]

Since E. P. Thompson's credentials as a Marxist are equal to those of Althusser, Poulantzas, et al., it is clear that at the present time there is no consensus on many basic questions of Marxist theory, even among those within the tradition. As previously discussed, the sole criterion of the validity of the ideas of the various schools of thought, as of that of Marxism as a whole, is and will continue to be its efficacy in the *practical* movement of society—the working-class movement, the development of science, etc. At the present time, the final "verdict" has not yet been delivered on the numerous issues facing Marxism, especially in light of post-Eastern European communism and the revisions of classical Marxism it is attempting to undertake concerning the modern state.[68] Thus the "crisis" in Marxism and the world communist movement in general—a crisis caused, among other things, by the extremely complex international situation brought about by World War II's physical devastation of the socialist camp and the enormous strengthening of the capitalist camp led by the United States—brought about the complicated but inevitable process of decolonization, etc.

MARXISM AS MODEL

The question of whether Marxism is a workable model with respect to welfare policy is a pertinent question, especially as postmodern and neoliberal models attempt to evaluate welfare policy from their diverse perspectives. Moreover, it is important to understand that Marxism, too, can play an important part in assessing welfare policy. As a method within critical theory, Marxist and neo-Marxist perspectives need not be understood as anachronistic, but rather as important methodological investigations of the causes and effects of poverty. "The materialistic outlook on nature," according to Engels, "means no more than simply conceiving nature just as it exists without any foreign admixture."[69] In practical terms, however, the usefulness of such an outlook can exist only in the context of real examination of real processes, as we attempted to indicate earlier in showing that the Marxist "view" is not a substitute for actual investigation. Theory is the summation of practical experience, and without practical experience (whether in the social or scientific realm) there can be no theory; without the continual gathering of new experience, theory cannot develop.

To illustrate this point, Marx himself describes his perception of the difference between practical knowledge and grand theory. In a letter to a Russian periodical regarding an article that it had published on *Capital*, Marx states:

> The chapter on primitive accumulation does not claim to do more than trace the path by which, in Western Europe, the capitalist economic system emerged from the womb of the feudal economic system. . . . Now what application to Russia could my critic make of this historical sketch? Simply this: If Russia wants to become a capitalist nation after the example of the West-European countries—and during the last few years she has been taking a lot of trouble in this direction—she will not succeed without having first transformed a good part of her peasants into proletarians; and then, once drawn into the whirlpool of the capitalist economy, she will have to endure its inexorable laws like other profane nations. That is all. But that is too little for my critic. He insists on transforming my historical sketch of the genesis of capitalism in Western Europe into an historico-philosophic theory of the general path of development prescribed by fate to all nations whatever the historical circumstances in which they find themselves, in order that they may ultimately arrive at the economic system which ensures, together with the greatest expansion of the productive powers of social labour, the most complete development of man. But I beg his pardon. (He is doing me too much honour and at the same time slandering me too much.) Let us take an example. . . . In several parts of *Kapital* I allude to the fate which overtook the plebeians of ancient Rome. They were originally free peasants, each cultivating his own piece of land on his own account. In the course of Roman history they were expropriated. The same movement

which divorced them from their means of production and subsistence involved the formation not only of big landed property but also of big money capital. Thus one fine morning there were to be found on the one hand free men, stripped of everything except their labour power, and on the other, the owners of all the acquired wealth ready to exploit this labour. What happened? The Roman proletarians became not wage labourers but a mob of do-nothings more abject than those known as "poor whites" in the South of the United States, and alongside them there developed a mode of production that was not capitalist but based on slavery. Thus events strikingly analogous but taking place in different historical surroundings led to totally different results. *But by studying each of these forms of evolution separately and then comparing them one can easily find the clue to this phenomenon. But one will never arrive there by using as one's master key a general historico-philosophical theory the supreme virtue of which consists in being supra-historical.*[70]

Aside from having a general idea of Russia's fate if it embraces the capitalist path (a general idea stemming from the existing theory of capitalist development, itself a summation of the historical practice of different countries), one can know little about the actual process without investigating it per se. In Lenin's *The Development of Capitalism in Russia*, such an investigation is evident, beginning with "the basic theoretical propositions of abstract political economy," then going on to actual investigation of the "factual" material on Russia's economy itself.[71]

NOTES

1. Karl Marx and Frederick Engels, "Manifesto of the Communist Party," in *Collected Works* (Moscow: Progress Publishers, 1971).

2. See Victor Adoratsky, *Dialectical Materialism* (New York: International Publishers, 1932), 44.

3. See Vladimir I. Lenin, "The Three Sources and Three Component Parts of Marxism," in *Collected Works*, vol. 19 (Moscow: Progress Publishers, 1967).

4. Antonio Gramsci, *Selections from the Prison Notebooks* (New York: International Publishers, 1971).

5. Frederick Engels, *Ludwig Feuerbach and the Outcome of Classical German Philosophy* (New York: International Publishers, 1978), 13.

6. Frederick Engels, *Anti-Duhring* (New York: International Publishers, 1965), 29.

7. Engels, *Ludwig Feuerbach*, 77 (appendix, review of Marx's *Critique of Political Economy*, written in 1859).

8. Engels, *Ludwig Feuerbach*, 77.

9. Lenin, "Philosophical Notebooks," in *Collected Works*, vol. 38 (Moscow: Progress Publishers, 1967), 222.

10. Engels, *Ludwig Feuerbach*, 14.

11. George Wilhelm Fredrich Hegel, *The Philosophy of History* (New York: Dover Press, 1956), 36.

12. Engels, *Ludwig Feuerbach*, 15.

13. Karl Marx and Frederick Engels, "The Holy Family: Or Critique of Critical Critique," in *Collected Works* (New York: International Publishers, 1975), 125.

14. It is no accident that Hegel "always speaks with the greatest enthusiasm" of the French Revolution, the political offspring of the French Enlightenment. (See Engels, *Ludwig Feuerbach*, 10).

15. Engels, *Ludwig Feuerbach*, 18.

16. Engels, *Ludwig Feuerbach*, 19.

17. Engels, *Ludwig Feuerbach*, 13.

18. Karl Marx, *Economic and Philosophic Manuscripts of 1844* (New York: International Publishers, 1974), 174, emphasis added.

19. In particular, see the First and Sixth Theses. Karl Marx, *The German Ideology* (New York: International Publishers, 1970), 120–121. Vis-à-vis the first problem: "The chief defect of all hitherto existing materialism (that of Feuerbach included) is that the thing, reality, sensuousness, is conceived only in the form of the *object of contemplation*, but not as *sensuous human activity*, *practice*, not subjectively. Hence, in contradistinction to materialism, the *active* side was developed abstractly by idealism. . . ." Vis-à-vis the second problem: "Feuerbach resolves the religious essence into the *human* essence. But the human essence is no abstraction inherent in each single individual. In its reality it is the ensemble of social relations." [italics added]

20. The view of the "abstract man" is the philosophical reflection of the classical bourgeois political economy's notion of the independent commodity producer, and very much a product of modern capitalist society's creation of "atomized" individuals, connected to each other only in the act of commodities' exchange. The reductionism of much of modern social (and even some natural) science to theories of "human nature" find their classical expression in what Marx calls the "Robinson Crusoe-isms" of vulgar political economy (See, e.g., Engels's *Anti-Dühring*, 172).

21. Jeremy Bentham, "Theory of Rewards and Punishments," quoted in Engels, *Ludwig Feuerbach*, 90.

22. Marx, *German Ideology*, 61, emphasis added.

23. Karl Marx, "Theses on Feuerbach," in *Karl Marx: Selected Writings*, ed. Lawrence H. Simon (1845; Indianapolis, Ind.: Hackett Publishing Co., 1994), 84.

24. See the notion "system-creating" (Eügen Dühring) in Frederick Engels, *Anti-Duhring*, 171.

25. Marx, *The German Ideology*, 48–49.

26. Marx, *German Ideology*, 54. The best-known expression of the material basis of human activity is in Marx's *A Contribution to the Critique of Political Economy* (New York: International Publishers, 1976), 188–93. In volume one of *Capital* (New York: International Publishers, 1974, 82), Marx makes fun of those modern economists who, while admitting that the modern era is based on "economics," see earlier eras as being based on other things: religion, politics, etc.: "This much, however, is clear, that the middles ages could not live on Catholicism,

nor the ancient world on politics. On the contrary, it is the mode in which they gained a livelihood that explains why here politics, and there Catholicism, played the chief part. For the rest, it requires but a slight acquaintance with the history of the Roman Republic, for example, to be aware that its secret history is the history of its landed property."

27. Marx, *Thesis on Feuerbach*, 122.

28. See Engels, *Ludwig Feuerbach*, 33–41, for a discussion of his "real idealism," the dualism between his materialist conception of nature and physical man and the idealism of his social and ethical ideas.

29. We can indicate here only the nonmechanistic and nondeterministic nature of Marxism's understanding of the relation of thinking to being, an understanding that has been consistently misunderstood, consciously or unconsciously, by its critics and even some friends. Engels, in his often-quoted letter to Joseph Bloch (Marx and Engels, *Selected Correspondence*, Moscow: Progress Publications, 1965, 394–395) deals with this, but it is a theme running throughout his and Marx's writings. The *Thesis Feuerbach* itself is a theme running throughout the passive, quietistic, contemplative character of the old materialism: "The question whether objective truth can be attributed to human thinking is not a question of theory but is a *practical question*. Man must prove the truth, i.e., the reality and power, the this-sidedness of his thinking in practice. . . . And, the coincidence of the changing of circumstances and of human activity or self-changing can be conceived and rationally understood only as *revolutionary practice*." (Marx, *Thesis on Feuerbach*, 120, emphasis added).

30. Engels, *Anti-Dühring*, 51.

31. Engels, *Anti-Dühring*, 155.

32. Engels, *Anti-Dühring*, 19–20, emphasis added.

33. Engels, *Anti-Dühring*, 31.

34. Marx, *The German Ideology*, 48.

35. Engels, *Anti-Dühring*, 152.

36. Vladimir I. Lenin, "The Three Sources and Three Component Parts of Marxism," in Marx, *The German Ideology*, 23 (emphasis Lenin's).

37. Harry Boyte, "A Democratic Awakening," *Social Policy* (September/October 1979): 11.

38. Marx and Engels, *Collected Works*, 223.

39. Engels, *Ludwig Feuerbach*, 13–14.

40. See Engels's discussion of the negation of the negation, *Anti-Dühring*, 154–155.

41. Lenin, "Materialism and Empirico-Criticism," in *Collected Works*, vol. 14, 326.

42. Lenin, "Materialism and Empirico-Criticism," 236.

43. See Lenin, *Collected Works*, vol. 19, 23.

44. Antonio Gramsci, "Critical Notes on an Attempt at a Popular Presentation of Marxism by Bakharin," in *The Modern Prince and Other Writings* (New York: International Publishers, 1978), 107.

45. Edward P. Thompson, *The Poverty of Theory and Other Essays* (New York: International Publishers, 1978).

46. Louis Althusser, "Lenin and Philosophy," in *Lenin and Philosophy and Other Essays* (New York: MR Press, 1971), 52.

47. Althusser, "Preface to *Capital*," *Lenin and Philosophy*, 95.

48. Lenin, *Collected Works*, vol. 19, 32.

49. Lenin, *Collected Works*, vol. 19, 39.

50. See, for example, Marx's "Address of the Central Authority to the League, March 1850," in Marx and Engels, *Collected Works*, vol. 10 (New York: International Publishers, 1978), 277–287, for a discussion of bourgeois liberalism as a political phenomenon vis-à-vis the proletariat. Marx makes the distinction between the liberalism of the big bourgeoisie and the petty bourgeoisie owing to their different material interests at different periods of the class struggle. However, their contempt and attitude toward the working class movement is in essence the same. Marx speaks of the treachery of the liberal bourgeois opposition in Germany after 1848, when they "immediately took possession of the state power and used this power at once to force back the workers, their allies in the struggle, into their former oppressed position. . . . And the role, this so treacherous role, which the German liberal bourgeois of 1848 have played against the people, will in the coming revolution be taken over by the democratic petty bourgeois, who at present occupy the same position in the opposition as the liberal bourgeois before 1848 " (p 179). Marx then differentiates between those sections of the new liberal opposition "which pursue the aim of the immediate, complete overthrow of feudalism and absolutism" ("the most advanced sections of the big bourgeoisie"), those "republican petty bourgeois" who "cherish the pious desire of abolishing the pressure, of big capital on small, of the big bourgeois etc" (p. 279). The political aims of all the liberal opposition groups, however, are the same: preservation of capital through the use of the workers as the "battering ram" against feudal remnants and the financial aristocracy.

51. Lenin, *Collected Works*, vol. 19, 236.

52. See "Address of the Central Authority of the League," in Marx and Engels, *Collected Works*, 281–285, for a discussion of the necessity of the proletariat's rejection of unity with the liberal opposition even when they are fighting a common enemy.

53. Vladimir I. Lenin, "Our Program," in *Marx, Engels, Marxism* (Moscow: Foreign Languages Publishing House, 1951), 126.

54. Lenin, "Materialism and Empirico-Criticism," in *Collected Works*, vol. 14, 135–136, emphasis added.

55. Lenin, *Marx, Engels, Marxism*, 121, emphasis added.

56. Engels, *Ludwig Feuerbach*, 22–23.

57. It is no accident that the most bitter anticommunists, understanding this intuitively if not intellectually, deny not only Marxism as a doctrine, but also its historical predecessor, the Enlightenment, and rationalism in general, as well. (See, e.g., Victor Navasky, *Naming Names*, New York: Viking Press, 1980, 17).

58. Nicos Poulantzas, *Political Power and Social Classes* (London: New Left Books, 1973), 51. Also see, Nicos Poulantzas, *Classes in Contemporary Capitalism* (London: New Left Books, 1975).

59. Poulantzas, *Political Power*, 103.

60. Poulantzas, *Political Power*, 329–30, emphasis added.

61. Poulantzas, *Political Power*, 130.

62. Poulantzas, *Political Power*, 191.

63. Poulantzas, *Political Power*, 191–192.

64. Poulantzas, *Political Power*, 266ff.

65. Thompson, *Poverty of Theory.*

66. Thompson, *Poverty of Theory*, 106.

67. Thompson, *Poverty of Theory*, 108.

68. Gil Eyal, Ivan Szelenyi, and Eleanor Townsley, "The Theory of Post-Communist Managerialism," *New Left Review* 222 (March/April 1997): 60–92; James Petras, "Latin America: The Resurgence of the Left," *New Left Review* 223 (May/June 1997): 17–47; Ann Phillips, "From Inequality to Difference: A Severe Case of Displacement," *New Left Review* 224 (July/August 1997): 143–153.

69. Engels, *Ludwig Feuerbach*, 68.

70. Karl Marx and Frederick Engels, *Selected Correspondence* (New York: International Publications, 1942), 294, emphasis added.

71. Lenin, *Collected Works*, vol. 3, 26.

Chapter Three

On Class

CLASS MATTERS

It is when people act in society as members of a class, Marx believed, that they have their greatest effect on what that society is, does, and becomes, particularly as regards the "big" questions and at the most crucial moments of its development.

— Bertell Ollman, *Dance of the Dialectic*

"The history of all hitherto existing society is the history of class struggles,"[1] as Marx and Engels state. Thus begins the most basic of all the texts of Marxism, the 150 year old *Manifesto of the Communist Party*. The modern reader might expect this thesis to be accompanied by a definition of the term "class," which is certainly the key concept expressed above. However, this is not what happens. Instead, what follows is an enumeration of examples of such class struggles: "freeman and slave, patrician and plebeian, lord and serf, guildmaster and journeyman—in a word, oppressor and oppressed—stood in constant opposition to one another, [and] carries on an uninterrupted, now hidden, now open fight, a fight that each time ended . . . either in a revolutionary re-construction of society at large, or in the common ruin of the contending classes."[2] Rather than a general definition of "class," what is important to understand here is a historical treatment of the development of the two great modern classes, the bourgeoisie and the proletariat, as well as ancillary social groupings.

The writings of Marx and Engels do not provide for any one single definition of "class." The only exception is a fragment, tantalizingly brief, at the very end of volume 3 of *Capital*, a chapter entitled "Classes."[3] After barely a page it breaks off. Brief as it is, however, it gives an indication of how

61

Marx treats the question of class *and also of how he does not treat it*, and thus it might serve as a point of departure for our investigation. Although the concept of "class" is apparent in Marxist literature, the notion itself is not present in any sophisticated way within the work of Marx. The idea first appears in *Capital* when Marx states, "The first question to be answered is this: What constitutes a class?—and the reply to this follows naturally from the reply to another question, namely: What makes wage-labourers, capitalists and landlords constitute the three great social classes?"[4] Marx also implies that "a class" does not exist except in relation to other classes. There is no such thing in the Marxist outlook as "one hand clapping." Marx states:

> There are three great social groups whose members, the individuals forming them, live on wages, profit and ground-rent respectively, on the realization of their landed property. . . . However, from this standpoint, physicians and officials, e.g., would also constitute two classes, for they belong to two distinct groups, the members of each of these groups receiving their revenue from one and the same source. The same would also be true of the infinite fragmentation of interest and rank into which the division of social labour splits labourers as well as capitalists and landlords—the latter, e.g., into owners of vineyards, farm owners, owners of forests, mine owners and owners of fisheries.[5]

Based on these rudimentary notions of class, it can be understood that a common source of revenue alone does not determine a class. For example, a landowner and capitalist (in Marx's scheme of three major classes) are not members of the same class merely because the income of each is $100,000 per year. Nevertheless, Marx identifies class, and so states: "In England, modern society is indisputably most highly and classically developed in economic structure. Nevertheless, even here the stratification of classes does not appear in its pure form. Middle and intermediate strata even here obliterate lines of demarcation everywhere although incomparably less in rural districts than in the cities."[6]

For a more developed definition of class, it is important to focus on the words of Lenin:

> Classes are large groups of people differing from each other by the *place* they occupy in a historically determined system of social production, by their *relation* (in most cases fixed and formulated in law) to the *means of production*, by their role in the social organization and labor and, consequently, by the *dimensions of the share of social wealth* of which they dispose and the mode of acquiring it. Classes are groups of people, one of which can appropriate the labor of another owing to the different places they occupy in a definite system of social economy.[7]

Here Lenin puts into secondary place the two factors mentioned (as the "at first glance" criteria for classes) by Marx at the beginning of his truncated discussion of what determines classes, namely, "dimensions of the share of social wealth" (corresponding to Marx's "identity of revenues"), and "the mode of acquiring it" (corresponding to Marx's "sources of revenue"). It is not that these considerations are unimportant, only that they are the *consequences*, rather than the determiners, of something more basic: people's relation to each other (their place in a historically determined system of social production) and to "the means of production"—that is, their relation to *property*.[8]

The existence of classes thus assumes, first, a division of labor—differing functions in the production of the social product or means of subsistence, culture, tools of production, etc. However, a mere division of labor does not suffice for the existence of classes. There must be, second, differing *property relations*, that is, differing types of ownership of the means of production. In primitive communal society there is a division of labor corresponding, broadly, to sexual differentiation—between hunting and gathering, on the one hand, and domestic horticulture and handicraft, on the other. However, classes did not arise as a direct result of these inevitable contradictions. It was only with the development of techniques of production of the means of subsistence that the division of labor led to class divisions. Engels explains why this is so:

> The increase of production in all branches—cattle raising, agriculture, domestic handicrafts—gave human labor-power the capacity to produce a larger product than was necessary for its maintenance. At the same time it increased the daily amount of work to be done by each member. . . . It was now desirable to bring in new labor forces. War provided them; prisoners of war were turned into slaves. With its increase of productivity of labor, and therefore of wealth, and its extension of the field of production, the first great social division of labor was bound, in the general historical conditions prevailing, to bring slavery in its train. From the first great social division of labor arose the first great cleavage of society into classes: masters and slaves, exploiters and exploited.[9]

Class division, therefore, historically means not simply a division of labor in terms of functions in production but a division between exploiter and exploited, between the one who owns the conditions of production and thus the product from those conditions of production (the laborers together with means of production—land, implements, raw materials, etc.), and the one who *is part of* the conditions of production themselves.[10] This division implies that the productivity of labor is such that the laborer can produce a surplus above what is needed to sustain him as a laborer, and which can thus sustain a section of society, or class of persons, who consume that surplus rather than produce means of subsistence themselves. This division into producing and nonproducing classes corresponds to the division between manual and mental labor, and leads, historically, to a great advance in both production, at one pole, and nonproductive activity (broadly, the social superstructure of politics, law, philosophy, religion, art, etc.) at the other.

This first great division into classes—masters and slaves—gives rise, in turn, to the further development of society, namely, the development of trade, and with it, towns. Marx states:

> The greatest division of material labour is the separation of town and country. The antagonism between town and country begins with the transition from barbarism to civilization, from tribe to state, from locality to nation, and runs through the whole history of civilization to the present day. . . . The existence of the town implies, at the same time, the necessity of administration, police, taxes, etc., in short, of the municipality, and thus of politics in general. Here first became manifest the division of population into two great classes, which is directly based on the division of labour and on the instruments of production. The town already is in actual fact the concentration of the population, of the instruments of production, of capital, of pleasures, of need, while the country demonstrated just the opposite fact, their isolation and separation. The antagonism of town and country can only exist as a result of private property. It is the most crass expression of the subjection of the individual under the division of labour, under a definite activity forced on him—a subjection which makes one man into a restricted town-animal, and daily creates anew the conflict between their interests. . . . Labour is here again the chief thing, power *over* individuals, and as long as the latter exists, private property must exist.[11]

Here it is important to return to the final part of the definition of classes given by Lenin above: "Classes are groups of people one of which can appropriate the labour of another owing to the different places they occupy in a definite system of social economy." Class divisions are based, historically, on exploitation, the development of owning and nonowning sections of society—in short on private property—ownership and the control of one section of the conditions of production, which allows it to appropriate the product of labor. Marx states: "What we have here as an essential relation of appropriation is the *relationship of domination*. Appropriation can create no such relation to animals, the soil, etc., even though the animal serves its master. The appropriation of another's *will* is presupposed in the relationship of domination."[12]

In summary, classes develop historically from the division of labor in primitive society. At the beginning this division of labor is based on communal property and is thus nonantagonistic, but eventually it tears the communalism asunder and creates a situation of polarization, of antagonism, in which one class dominates the other (or others) through control of the means of production—land, tools, raw materials, etc.—and thus of the laborers themselves. Classes exist on the basis of exploitation. They come into being through antagonism and violence and are in no sense the result of "social contracts," or "agreements," among different individuals or groups for the "maximization of resource usage," or any other rationalist schema. The antagonism inherent in the relationship of the exploiting and exploited class is based in their polarity, the fact that one lives only from the impoverishment or destruction of the other, and that the exploited class can free itself only by the destruction of its nemesis. In the words of the *Manifesto*, quoted above, each class struggle "ended . . . either in a revolutionary re-constitution of society at large, or in the common ruin of the contending classes"—that is, in either case, freedom comes with the destruction of the particular antagonism.

This is to state the problem historically. To state it in its philosophical reflection, antagonistic classes—freeman and slave, patrician and plebeian, capitalist and proletarian—exist as a *unity of opposites*, as mutually exclusive, antagonistic, but inextricably linked and interdependent aspects of a totality, the given *mode of production*. There is no slave without a slavemaster, no slavemaster without a slave; no bourgeois without proletarian, no proletarian without a bourgeois. In each case the antagonism is based, again, on the other. Thus the Marxist concept of classes is essentially dialectical—based on contradiction and struggle—rather than static and exclusively "structural." It is also *material* rather than mental or moral. Classes are not ideological categories, or states of mind, or moral concepts, or subjective in any way; they are material entities based in real social relationships and defined, in most cases, in terms of property.

What is important to note here is that the dialectical or "relational" essence of the Marxist view of classes is the fact that their existence implies antagonism and that modern society in particular, with all its heights of "civilization," rests on the most brutal slavery. Marx mercilessly ridicules those petty-bourgeois socialists who wish to maintain bourgeois existences while doing away with exploitation. In the *Manifesto*, Marx and Engels state: "[T]he Socialistic bourgeois want all the advantages of modern social conditions without the struggles and dangers necessarily resulting [from the] reform. They desire the existing state of society minus its revolutionary and disintegrating elements. They wish for a bourgeoisie without a proletariat."[13] This ideology in Marx's view inevitably degenerates into the most petty and hypocritical reformism, the attempt to get rid of the worst abuses of capitalism while maintaining (and even glorifying) the very conditions that continually regenerate those abuses. Marx rejects such a one-sided approach to dealing with social antagonisms. The proletariat cannot be abolished, or more correctly, abolish itself, without abolishing its antagonistic "opposite number." And since the modern bourgeoisie exists, like all previous exploiting classes, on the basis of private property, it can only be abolished through "the abolition of private property" —the definition, in the *Manifesto*, of Communism.[14]

MODERNITY, CLASSES,
AND CLASS CONSCIOUSNESS

In order to understand the class structure of modern society from the Marxist perspective, and particularly the role of class and welfare, it is important to identify the starting point for this discussion in the *Communist Manifesto*. Marx and Engels state:

> In the earlier epochs of history, we find almost everywhere a complicated arrangement of society into various orders, a manifold gradation of social rank. In ancient Rome we have patricians, knights, plebeians, slaves; in the Middle Ages, feudal lords, vassals, guildmasters, journeymen, apprentices, serfs, in almost all of these classes again, subordinate gradations. . . . The modern bourgeois society that has sprouted from the ruins of feudal society has not done away with class antagonisms. It has but established new classes, new conditions of oppression, new forms of struggle in place of the old ones. . . . Our epoch, the epoch of the bourgeoisie, possesses, however, this distinctive feature: it has simplified the class antagonisms. Society as a whole is more and more splitting up into great hostile camps, into two great classes directly facing each other: Bourgeoisie and Proletariat.[15]

Several enumerations are in order here:

1. Precapitalist forms of society, based on relatively backward productive forces, were, in comparison with the modern era, static, and their development took place very slowly. ("Conservation of the old modes of production in unaltered form, was . . . the first condition of existence of all earlier industrial classes.")[16] The scattered and dwarfed nature of production and exchange manifested itself in the existence of many different classes and strata existing side by side in the same societies. Intellectual life, culture, science, and other aspects of the "superstructure" were, as a result of the backward economic situation, also scattered, localized, relatively static, and parochial.
2. Owing to the backward state of production in precapitalist societies, different forms of economy and different types of class antagonisms could

exist within the same social frameworks. For example, in the feudal period one class antagonism (between lord and serf, or lord and vassal) could exist in the countryside and another (between guildmaster and journeyman) in the town, with neither polarity having direct bearing on the other.[17]

3. Because of this, it is impossible to speak of former societies as unities based on any one fundamental class antagonism. This lack of unity was reflected both within the old societies and among different regions and states in a lack of any one, all-pervading class ideology such as has existed, historically, in countries like the United States.

4. Although class struggles constantly took place between the different antagonistic "sides" within the old modes of production (lord versus serf, guildmaster versus apprentice, etc.), these antagonisms were not, on the whole, the levers of social transformation in the historical sense. Slavery did not end with the overthrow of the slavemasters by the slaves; feudalism did not end with the overthrow of the feudal lords by serfs, or the overthrow of guildmasters by the apprentices. The backward material and social conditions of the times made victorious rebellions of the oppressed classes impossible. In *Pre-Capitalist Economic Formations*, Marx discusses one such period, the late Middle Ages:

> The flight of the serfs into the towns went on without interruption right through the Middle Ages. These serfs, persecuted by their lords in the country, came separately into the towns, where they found an organized community, against which they were powerless, in which they had to subject themselves to the station assigned to them by the demand for their labour and the interest of their organized competitors. These workers, entering separately, were never able to attain to any power, since if their labour was not such as had to be learned, and therefore not of the guild type, they became day-labourers and never managed to organize, remaining an unorganized rabble. These towns were true associations, called forth by the direct need of providing for the protection of property, and multiplying the means of production and defense of the separate members. The rabble of these towns was devoid of any power, composed as it was of individuals strange to one another who had entered separately, and who stood unorganized against an organized power, armed for war, and jealously watching over them. . . . While, therefore, the rabble which remained completely ineffective because of their powerlessness, the journeymen never got further than small acts of insubordination within separate guilds, such as belong to the very nature of the guild. The great risings of the Middle Ages all radiated from the country, but equally remained totally ineffective because of the isolation and consequent crudity of the peasants.[18]

Feudalism (as other social formations existing before it) did not end with the victory of the exploited, producing classes, but with that of a new exploiting class, the bourgeoisie, which sought, as Marx says above, "to fortify their already acquired status by subjecting society at large to their conditions of appropriation." While revolutionary with respect to the feudal powers (landowners, church, and guildmasters) and representing a far more advanced and dynamic mode of production than them, the bourgeois were conservative with respect to "their already acquired status"—that of property owners and appropriators of the labor of the classes working for them. Thus two points are salient here: (1) the bourgeoisie grew up, as did capitalism itself, *within* feudalism as a foreign body that could and did coexist with the old economic and political structure for a long time. The bourgeoisie as a class did not evolve out of the feudal ruling classes. From the very beginning the "third estate" (as opposed to the two original estates—landed aristocracy and the clergy—the bastions of the feudal power) existed as a unique, truly new force in the old society. However, its growth did not immediately signify the end of feudalism. Capitalism grew alongside feudalism economically; political antagonism on a class basis, while existing embryonically in conflicts over feudal jurisdiction over the cities, relations of merchants and guilds, etc., developed *after* the economic development had reached a relatively high level. This was reflected in the fact that (2) the bourgeoisie's class consciousness, its intellectual understanding of itself as a section of society with political interests antagonistic to the feudal order, developed *out of* its economic interests. Politics followed economics. First developed capitalist relations of production; only then, after the bourgeoisie *had something to lose*, had "an acquired status," in the words of Marx, "to fortify," did it develop a political understanding, manifesting itself in political parties, whose aim was to transform the social superstructure (the state apparatus and intellectual and cultural life in general) in the interests of the bourgeoisie as a class.[19] In sum, the bourgeoisie's relation to the feudal mode of production allowed the two to coexist because they were not directly antagonistic to each other in the economic sense of exploiter versus exploited—they were both exploiters of *other* groups. These were over the questions of dividing the spoils. The new bourgeoisie was like a new gang moving into the territory of an older gang. No one questioned the propriety of crime and extortion themselves; the battle was over the methodology and who would gain the most.

Further, the bourgeoisie's class consciousness grew "organically," so to speak, out of its economic conditions of appropriation. In struggling politically against the old order it was simply reflecting its *already existing* economic interests—freedom from feudal land tenure and obligations, from guild restrictions on the development of industry, from church laws against usury and in favor of "the divine right of kings," and the rest. The bourgeoisie did not have to invent new theories—its appeals to the masses ("liberty, equality, and fraternity," "the rights of man") were simply universalizations of existing economic laws of capital, particularly the law of economic equality among independent commodity producers; they were idealizations of bourgeois relations already in existence in the realm of private property and "free enterprise." The modern proletariat and its political movement, which had developed over a period of hundreds of years from the naive egalitarianism and "leveling" of the earliest proletarians to the movement of scientific socialism begun in the 1840s, developed in a different way. In order to understand the unique ideological position of the modern working-class movement, it is important to examine how and why it developed differently.

First, capitalist production, unlike earlier forms, is inherently dynamic. The bourgeoisie cannot for any period of time leave the old forms of production as they are. Marx and Engels state:

> The bourgeoisie cannot exist without constantly revolutionizing the instruments of production and thereby the relations of production, and with them the whole relations of society. Conservation of the old modes of production in unaltered form, was, on the contrary, the first condition of existence for all earlier industrial classes. Constant revolutionizing of production, uninterrupted disturbance of all social conditions, everlasting uncertainty and agitation distinguish the bourgeois epoch from all earlier ones.[20]

The inherent dynamism of capitalism is based subsequently on the development of production for a world market rather than production for use or for a small, restricted, local market. The fundamental law of capitalism, according to Marx, is the maximization of profit. This necessitates the cheapening of commodities (and particularly labor power), of capital, etc. The rapid growth of modern production techniques and world trade undermine *all* the old modes of production and the old classes. Again, as stated in the *Manifesto*:

> The bourgeoisie, wherever it has got the upper hand, has put an end to all feudal, patriarchal, idyllic relations. It has pitilessly torn asunder the motley feudal ties that bound man to his "natural superiors," and has left remaining no other nexus between man and man than naked self-interest, than callous "cash payment". . . . All fixed fast-frozen relations, with their train of ancient and venerable prejudices and opinions, are swept away, all new-formed ones become antiquated before they can ossify. All that is solid melts into air, all that is holy is profaned, and man is at least compelled to face, with sober senses, his real conditions of life, and his relations with his kind.[21]

Marx and Engels continue:

> In proportion as the bourgeoisie, i.e., capital, is developed, in the same proportion is the proletariat, the modern working class, developed—a class of labourers, who

live only as their labour increases capital. . . . Modern industry has converted the little workshop of the patriarchal master into the great factory of the industrial capitalist. Masses of labourers, crowded into the factory, are organized like soldiers. . . . Differences of age and sex have no longer any distinctive social validity for the working class. . . . The lower strata of the middle class—the small tradespeople, shopkeepers, and retired tradesmen generally, the handicraftsmen and peasants—all these sink gradually into the proletariat, partly because their diminutive capital does not suffice for the scale on which Modern Industry is carried on, and is swamped in the competition with the large capitalists, partly because their specialized skill is rendered worthless by new methods of production. Thus the proletariat is recruited from all classes of the population.[22]

Thus the growth of capital destroys the old forms of production (e.g., medieval guilds), and with them the old classes. With it the proletariat comes into existence side-by-side with the bourgeoisie in basic, irreconcilable antagonism. They are symbiotically joined, with a common set of organs and a common system of blood circulation, but, withal, inexorably hostile to each other owing to the immanent laws of capitalism itself with its basis in exploitation, the necessity of reducing the value of labor power (the standard of living of the worker) to maximize profit, etc. In Marx there is no romanticization of free enterprise or anything of the kind. Neither is there any description that capitalism developed peacefully and that the differences between capitalist and proletarian evolved out of harmony. In *Capital*, one of Marx's critique's of Adam Smith's *Wealth of Nations* is that capitalism developed on the basis of the slave trade and colonial domination in order to increase the very wealth of dominant nations. In fact, according to Marx, the destruction of aboriginal peoples in the New World and the elimination of European peasantry from titleship to generations of family-owned land during the prehistory of capital (primitive accumulation), was simply a natural outcome of Smith's "rational" model. And for Marx, Smith's rational model manifested itself in the hedonistic–utilitarian models in which the most brutal overwork of people, and particularly women, in the "dark Satanic mills" of England's and the continent's Industrial Revolution, took place. The subjugation of the older producing classes, particularly the peasantry, and their transformation into modern proletarians, was in no sense a natural or peaceful process. Marx states:

> The historical movement which changes the producers into wage-workers, appears, on the one hand, as their emancipation from serfdom and from the fetters of the guilds and this side alone exists for our bourgeois historians. But, on the other hand, these new freedmen became sellers of themselves only after they had been robbed of all their own means of production, and of all the guarantees of existence afforded by the old feudal arrangements. And the history of this, their expropriation, is written in the annals of mankind in letters of blood and fire.[23]

Marx thus concludes, "if money, according to Augier, 'comes into the world with a congenital blood-stain on one cheek,' capital comes dripping from head to foot, from every pore, with blood and dirt."[24]

Thus, the inherent dynamism and universal quality of capitalist production rapidly does away with all old forms of production.[25] And with its historical victory in the economic realm, the bourgeois gains universal victory in the intellectual or ideological realm. Again Marx states:

> The bourgeoisie has through its exploitation of the world market given a cosmopolitan character to production and consumption in every country. . . . And as in material, so also in intellectual production. The intellectual creations of individual nations become common property. National one-sidedness and narrowmindedness become more and more impossible, and from the numerous national and local literatures, there arises a world literature.[26]

The entire world, in short, becomes intellectually, as well as economically, *bourgeoisified*. Engels is only half-joking when he describes the situation in England in 1858 as follows: "The English proletariat is actually becoming more and more bourgeois, so that this most bourgeois of all nations is apparently aiming ultimately at the possession of a bourgeois aristocracy and a bourgeois proletariat *alongside* the bourgeoisie. For a nation which exploits the whole this is of course to a certain extent justifiable."[27]

The degree to which the bourgeoisie is able to universalize its ideology and make it seem as if capitalism were "the natural order of things" is partly predicated on its ability to "bribe" the working class into acquiescence by material and social privileges. Hence, in Engels' remarks above, the "class peace" within England, at least as far as the upper strata of workers were concerned, was largely a result of England's monopoly on world production, trade, and colonies. But this is only part of the story. The other part leads to the second reason (the first being capital's inherent dynamism)—for the uniqueness of the ideological struggle between bourgeoisie and the proletariat. The universalization of bourgeoisie production destroys all previous modes of production and *prohibits the development of any new ones*. Capitalist production excludes the possibility of the proletariat's developing its own mode of production within capitalist society, as the nascent bourgeoisie, on the contrary, was able to do within feudalism. The proletariat is unable to develop, within capitalism, a mode of production (socialism) corresponding to its social interests. The "conditions of appropriation" it has "acquired," based on the sale of its labor power for means of subsistence (in turn based on nonownership of the product of its own labor) enslave it to capital rather than liberate it. Thus socialism, based on common property—that is, the unification of the laborers with their means of production—is rendered impossible by the

economic as well as political dictates of capital. The proletariat cannot develop its own ideology based on an *already existing mode of production
within capitalism*. Whereas the bourgeois relations of production already existed under feudalism, the proletariat has no such social relations of production on which to develop, "organically," a new ideology.

What are the consequences of this state of affairs? A paradox, namely, that
whereas the bourgeoisie and the proletariat come into existence together in a
state of extreme antagonism on the economic level (much more extreme than
the state of conflict between the feudal ruling classes and the nascent bourgeoisie), on the political level the proletariat has no "organic" class consciousness of its own with which to represent itself against its class enemy; it
has no independent ideology counterposed to that of capital. Although from
its birth the proletariat struggles militantly against the employers, and raises
naive cries of (social *as well as* political) "equality for all," politically it remains for a long time the extreme left wing of the bourgeoisie, the enemy itself.[28] During this stage of capitalist development, any political unity the
workers achieve is at the behest of the bourgeoisie. Marx and Engels state:

> If anywhere they unite to form more compact bodies, this is not yet the conse-
> quence of their own active union, but of the union of the bourgeoisie, which . . .
> in order to attain its own political ends, is compelled to set the whole proletariat
> in motion, and is moreover yet, for a time, able to do so. At this state, therefore,
> the proletarians do not fight their enemies, the remnants of absolute monarchy,
> the landowners, the non-industrial bourgeois, the petty bourgeoisie. Thus the
> whole historical movement is concentrated in the hands of the bourgeoisie; every
> victory so obtained is a victory for the bourgeoisie.

Marx and Engels further state:

> Altogether collisions between the classes of the old society further, in many
> ways, the course of development of the proletariat. The bourgeoisie finds itself
> involved in a constant battle, at first with the aristocracy, later on with those por-
> tions of the bourgeoisie whose interests have become antagonistic to the
> progress of industry, and at all times with the bourgeoisie of foreign countries.
> In all these battles it sees itself compelled to appeal to the proletariat, to ask for
> its help, and thus to drag it into the political arena. The bourgeoisie itself, there-
> fore, supplies the proletariat with its own elements of political and general edu-
> cation; in other words, it furnishes the proletariat with weapons for fighting the
> bourgeoisie. . . . Further, as we have already seen, entire sections of the ruling
> classes are, by advance of industry, precipitated into the proletariat, or are at
> least threatened in their conditions of existence. These also supply the proletariat
> with fresh elements of enlightenment and progress. . . . Finally, in times when
> the class struggle nears the decisive hour . . . a portion of the bourgeoisie goes

over to the proletariat and, in particular, a portion of the bourgeois ideologists, who have raised themselves to the level of comprehending theoretically the historical movements as a whole.[29]

Proletarian class consciousness, then, does not develop "organically" or spontaneously within the proletariat as such because there is no "proletarian mode of production" serving as a material basis for such a consciousness. The only material existence the workers have is the immediate reality of exploitation, and this material life does give rise, spontaneously, to an ideology: trade unionism. Hence, Lenin, in a famous passage of *What Is To Be Done?*[30] counterposes the ideology that arises spontaneously within the working class—trade union consciousness—true *socialist* consciousness, which must be brought to the working class from without, precisely by the aforementioned "bourgeoisie ideologists . . . who have raised themselves to the level of comprehending theoretically the historical movement as a whole." On its own, says Lenin, the proletariat can advance in its consciousness only as far as its material conditions allow, that is, to the level of uniting as workers of various separate industries into trade unions, whose function is to defend their members from attacks by the employers on their wages, working conditions, etc.

However, trade unions and even strikes in themselves do not call into question the property relations from which they spring—the polarization between capital on one end and labor power on the other. The most militant labor struggles, then, leave the essential problem, the cause of those struggles, untouched: the existence of an exploiting and an exploited class, the existence of private property. Trade unionism does not question this polarity. At best, the workers as workers can only develop a naive, mystical, embryonic ideal of a society without polarization, such as has been the dream of virtually every oppressed class in history. In the words of Marx and Engels:

> The first direct attempts of the proletariat to attain its own ends, made in times of universal excitement, when feudal society was being overthrown, these attempts necessarily failed, owing to the then undeveloped state of the proletariat, as well as to the absence of the economic conditions for its emancipation, conditions that had yet to be produced, and could be produced by the impending bourgeois epoch alone. The revolutionary literature that accompanied these first movements of the proletariat had necessarily a reactionary character. It included universal asceticism and social leveling in its crudest form.[31]

Thus, capitalism, as a mode of production, universalizes itself with a rapidity and completeness unknown in previous history. The entire world becomes "bourgeoisified" and the bourgeoisie's antagonistic opposite, the proletariat, is able to develop within the capitalist mode of production neither its own alternative mode of production[32] nor an "organic" class ideology representing such a mode. At best it develops a radical and militant ideology of "fightback," a mixture of extreme left-wing bourgeois ideology on the one hand, and trade union solidarity on the other.

Socialist consciousness is the result of highly developed intellectual activity by persons versed in history, philosophy, economics, and political theory. In its finished Marxist form, it points to a mode of production *that does not exist yet* (at least when Marx and Engels were writing), and which could be predicted or foreseen only on the basis of the most profound analysis of historical trends, not on the basis of daily struggles on the assembly line. The theory of modern or scientific socialism is thus the result not of the reflection in thought of already existing relations of production, but of the most thorough and inclusive understanding of history in motion. Proletarian class consciousness—that is, the working class' understanding of its historical role— is not a product of its own spontaneous intellectual activity, but that of thinkers from the educated strata trained by capitalist society.[33]

Because Marxism taught the impossibility of the proletariat's spontaneously achieving class consciousness, it has been accused of elitism, of positing the necessity of a group of intellectuals leading the workers. However, Marx specifically says, also, that "the emancipation of the working class must be the act of the working class itself."[34] In contrast, the proletariat cannot discover from its own economic struggles a way out of the polarization in which it finds itself and which threatens to destroy it physically and mentally. Yet no other section of society is equipped, either numerically or organizationally, to do the job, least of all the "declasse" sections of the intelligentsia. No "condescending savior" exists to lift the workers out of their misery; they must do so themselves.

The contradiction exists, and it is real. The solution can only be, according to Marx, the creation of a force that embodies or *comprehends* two contradictory things—the proletariat as a social class *and* the theoretical understanding of the most advanced political thought of scientific socialism. Such a force is a political party of the working class that represents the unity of the *objective* motion or development of the proletariat in its inevitable struggles with the bourgeoisie on a national and international scale, and the *subjective* reflection of the objective motion in the minds of revolutionary intellectuals who either come from the working class itself or else from the intelligentsia and put their understanding, intellectual training, etc., at the disposal of the workers.

Such a party is inevitably different from previous parties of earlier classes fighting for power. Again, the reason lies in the fact that the proletariat's struggle is not to defend and expand on existing property relations but construct entirely new ones. Thus the party of the proletariat (the modern Communist Party) cannot be satisfied simply with representing the workers in the struggles they necessarily carry on from day to day over wages, working conditions, for political representation, etc. Such struggles, according to Marx, will not and cannot in themselves lead to fundamental improvement in the lives of the workers. As Marx and Engels themselves point out:

> In the various stages of development which the struggle of the working class against the bourgeoisie has to pass through, they (the Communists) always and everywhere represent the interests of the movement as a whole. . . . The Communists, therefore, are on the one hand, practically, the most advanced and resolute section of the working-class parties of every country, that section which pushes forward all others; on the other hand, theoretically, they have over the great mass of the proletariat the advantage of clearly understanding the line of march, the conditions and the ultimate general results of the proletariat movement.[35]

And again: "The Communists fight for the attainment of the immediate aims for the enforcement of the momentary interests of the working class; but in the movement of the present, they also represent and take care of the future of that movement."[36]

In short, the proletariat, like every class in history, must develop a political force to represent it in its struggle for power. This force must be strong and disciplined enough to combat the inevitable tendency of capitalist society to divide the workers among themselves, drive them into demoralization and self-brutalization, destroy them mentally, physically, and morally, and generally render them powerless and apolitical. "The Communist revolution," according to Marx and Engels, "is the most radical rupture with traditional property relations; no wonder that its development involves the most radical rupture with traditional ideas."[37] Although the development of capitalism, by creating a proletariat, produced the conditions for socialist revolution, it also created divisions, demoralization, and ignorance among the workers themselves. Thus there is, in a sense, nothing "natural" about the socialist revolution; it truly means a "most radical rupture" with tradition. The proletarian party must be able to embrace the contradiction between the spontaneous movement of the workers against the employers and toward unity among themselves and the very unspontaneous understanding of the direction the movement must take, but which it will not take if left to its own devices. Class consciousness, in other words, must comprehend both these contradictory aspects: the spontaneous militancy, heroism, "instinctive" decency and morality of the working people *and* the most intellectually developed scientific understanding, not only of the daily ebbs and flows of the working class movement, but its necessary and (once it becomes a conscious movement) its inevitable result—the abolition of the polarity between property (dead labor) and labor power (living labor). Notwithstanding, the aim of the modern Communist Party is to transform the proletariat from a merely *objective* class— that is, a class that exists as such for capital, an economic entity—into a *subjective* class, a class *aware of itself* as such, a class that is a class not only for capital, but for itself. Philosophically, this has been expressed by Mao Zedong as a class "*in* itself" becoming a class "*for* itself."

BETWEEN LABOR AND CAPITAL: CLASSES IN MODERN SOCIETY

With respect to social class, Marx discusses the presence of "middle and intermediate strata" even in England—the most ostensibly developed capitalist country at the time he is writing. In other writings, such as the *Manifesto,* he discusses these other classes and who comprises them: the petty bourgeoisie, lumpen proletariat, landowners (in those areas where capitalism has not completely revolutionized the countryside), and so on. He also discusses the various strata within the working class, and the groupings of people who do not seem to fit well into any category. Some commentators have become confused and upset about Marx and Engels's seeming vagueness or contradictoriness in how they define the class nature of different professions. For example, a passage from the *Manifesto* states: "The bourgeoisie has stripped of its halo every occupation hitherto honoured and looked up to with reverent awe. It has converted the physician, the lawyer, the priest, the poet, the man of science into its paid wage-labourers."[38] Does this mean that teachers, doctors, etc., are proletarians or part of the working classes?

That such questions are asked testifies to the misunderstandings that have arisen in the conscious or unconscious attempt to reduce Marxism to a series of formulas, into separate and isolated logical categories or "factors" (the economic Marx, the historical Marx, the sociological Marx, and so forth). Marxism is "holistic" in the sense that, at least according to its adherents, it accurately reflects a "holistic" world, a dynamic, constantly changing process of many different interconnected forms of activity whose unity lies in their materiality. Although these different forms must be, to a certain extent, isolated and studied (as physics, chemistry, history, etc.) in order to understand them, any *absolutization* of the results inevitably leads to greater errors and distortions. Similarly, a society is not a discrete series of "factors," that is, economics, politics, religion, psychology, etc. Thus Marxism, reflecting society as it really is, is not sociology. Any substantive discussion of *actual* class relations must take into account *all* the aspects of groups in society in their relations with each other. A discussion of class only has real meaning in the context of an understanding of polarization in bourgeois society. Consequently, it is this inevitable polarization that Marx and Engels are expressing when they discuss the transformation of doctors, priests, poets, celebrities, etc., into "wage labourers."

The history of the United States has given rise to several peculiarities of which we need to take note in rounding out our discussion of classes and class consciousness, and which are outlined by Engels in his correspondence with socialists in the United States, of anything but a bourgeois tradition, and the mitigating effect this absence has had in the development of class antagonisms on the level of material life and particularly of ideology. In a letter to Florence Kelly-Wischnewetzky, 3 June 1886, Engels discusses the outbreak of sharp class struggles in the United States (the eight-hour movement, the Haymarket Massacre, etc.) and the effect of these on the world's bourgeoisie:

> For America after all was the ideal of all bourgeois; a country rich, vast, expanding, with purely bourgeois institutions unleavened by feudal remnants or monarchical traditions and without a permanent and hereditary proletariat. Here everyone could become, if not a capitalist, at all events an independent man, producing or trading, with his own means, for his own account. And because there were not, *as yet*, classes with opposing interest, our—and—bourgeois thought that America stood *above* class antagonisms and struggles. That delusion has now broken down, the last Bourgeois Paradise on earth is fast changing into a Purgatorio, and can only be prevented from becoming, like Europe, an Inferno by the go-ahead pace at which the development of the newly fledged proletariat of America will take place.[39]

In a subsequent letter of 31 December 1892, to Friedrich Sorge, who was then working in the United States, Engels writes:

> Here in old Europe things are livelier than in your "youthful" country, which still doesn't quite want to get out of its hobble-de-hoy stage. It is remarkable but wholly natural how firmly rooted bourgeois prejudices are even in the working class in such a young country, which has never known feudalism and has grown up on a bourgeois foundation from the beginning. Out of his opposition to the mother country—which is still garbed in its feudal disguise—the American worker imagines that the traditional bourgeois regime he inherited is something progressive and superior by nature and for all time, a *non plus ultra*. . . . The Americans may strain and struggle as much as they like, but they simply cannot discount their future—colossally great as it is—like a bill of exchange; they must wait for the date on which it falls due; and just *because* their future is so great, their present must occupy itself mainly with preparatory work for that future, and this is, as in every young country, of a predominantly material nature

and involves a certain backwardness of thought, a clinging to the traditions connected with the foundation of a new nationality. The Anglo-Saxon race—these
damned Schleswig-Holsteiners, as Marx always called them—is slow-witted
anyhow, and its history, both in Europe and America (economic success and predominantly peaceful political development), has encouraged this still more. . . .
The class struggles here in England too, were more turbulent during the period
of development of large-scale industry and died down just in the period of England's undisputed industrial domination of the world.[40]

The United States developed historically on the basis of capitalism from
the very outset. The colonial power that settled the original colonies, Britain,
was already a rapidly developing capitalist country. Even the slavery of the
southern colonies was capitalist slavery.[41] Two things resulted from this:
First, the workers in the thirteen colonies, and later the United States as a
whole, *had nothing which they could compare capitalism.* Second, the bourgeoisie themselves, as the only "class for itself," in the young country, inevitably achieved leadership in the revolutionary struggles of the day (the war
against England and later the Civil War), and gained undisputed "hegemony"
in the ideological sphere as well. If we add to these historical factors the
tremendous expansiveness of U.S. capitalism, its great strength relative to the
older, smaller European powers, which brought untold riches to the country
as a whole, including even large sections of the proletariat, a situation results
in which: (1) class antagonisms have been blunted, and (2) even when they
have not been thoroughly blunted, the ideological prejudices in the minds of
the working class, with its bourgeois preconceptions, have served to keep the
workers from understanding, even when socialist ideas were present, the nature of class struggle and the necessity of transforming property relations. In
a word, the universalization of bourgeoisie ideology has been more profound
in the United States, for historical reasons, than in perhaps any other country.
Whereas the European workers were very early in the game embroiled in a
fight between feudalism and capitalism, and had a chance to see that capitalism has not existed, and perhaps will not exist, eternally, the U.S. workers
have not had that perspective.

Thus, bourgeois ideology is more deeply ingrained in American society
than in virtually any other country. This has led, among other things, to severe problems within the socialist or Marxist movement itself, which, one
could argue, has fallen victim to the ideology of "American Exceptionalism,"
the form that U.S. bourgeois prejudice has taken within the ranks of the Marxist intelligentsia. And it certainly makes particularly difficult the task of those
who, in the Marxist tradition, see the need for helping transform the U.S. proletariat from a "class in itself"—a class that exists objectively but not yet self-
consciously—into a "class for itself"—a class that has internalized its objec-

tive existence as a class in irreconcilable antagonism to capital (the bourgeoisie) and thus is able to act consciously in its own interest.

NOTES

1. Karl Marx and Frederick Engels, *Selected Correspondence* (Moscow: Progress Publishers, 1965), 32.

2. Marx and Engels, *Selected Correspondence*, 32.

3. Karl Marx, *Capital*, vol. 3 (New York: International Publishers, 1967), 885–886.

4. Marx, *Capital*, 885–886.

5. Marx, *Capital*, 885–886.

6. Marx, *Capital*, 885.

7. Vladimir I. Lenin, "A Great Beginning," in *Collected Works*, vol. 29 (Moscow: Progress Publishers, Volume, 1965), 421, emphasis added.

8. People's relationship to property is merely a "reified" form of their relationship to each other. As a materialist philosophy that does not look to outside forces to explain life's occurrences, Marxism does not only seek to understand the world but to change it. Based on this philosophy, capitalism is viewed as the exploitation of one social class by another, and this treatment results in the alienation of the worker from the overall purpose of the finished product. This alienation causes what Marxists term *reification*. Reification takes place when the concerns of capitalism—profit and loss—become primary, and consequently the worker is seen only as part of the labor force. The worker becomes no more than a cog in the machine—and as a result loses some of his/her humanity—people become things.

9. Frederick Engels, *The Origin of the Family, Private Property, and the State* (New York: International Publishers, 1975), 220.

10. Marx defines slavery, as opposed to capitalist production, as, among other things, those "relations under which the *laborers themselves, the living units* of labour power are still direct parts of the objective conditions of production and are appropriated as such. . . ." *Pre-Capitalist Economic Formations* (New York: New World Paperbacks, International Publishers, 1965), 98.

11. Karl Marx, *The German Ideology*, part 1 (1845; New York: International Publishers, 1970); "Pre-Capitalist Economic Formations" in Engels, *The Origin of the Family, Private Property, and the State,* 127, emphasis added.

12. Marx, *The German Ideology*, 103, emphasis added.

13. Karl Marx and Frederick Engels, *The Communist Manifesto* (1948; New York: Pathfinder Press, 1978), 62.

14. Marx and Engels, *The Communist Manifesto*, 46. The question might arise as to whether the expropriation of the bourgeoisie means the end of all private property and not the substitution of a new set of exploiters for the old ones. After all, the abolition of slave property did not mean the end of classes in general, but only of the slave owners and slaves as slaves, similarly with feudal property. The answer lay in

the unique character of modern society as opposed previous ones. Formerly, it was a question of one small class of exploiters overthrowing another, for example, the nascent bourgeoisie overthrowing the feudal class. Marx states:

> All the preceding classes that got the upper hand, sought to *fortify* their *already acquired status* by subjecting society at large to their conditions of appropriation. The proletarians cannot become masters of the productive forces of society, except by *abolishing* their own previous mode of appropriation, and thereby also every other previous mode of appropriation. They have nothing of their own to secure and to fortify; their mission is to destroy all previous securities for, and insurances of, individual property.

As further stated in the *Manifesto*:

> "All previous historical movements were movements of minorities, or in the interest of minorities. The proletarian movement is the self-conscious independent movement of the immense majority, in the interest of the immense majority. The proletariat, the lowest stratum of our present society, cannot stir, cannot raise itself up, without the whole superincumbent strata of official society being sprung into the air. " (p. 43)

In short the bourgeoisie does away with all forms of private property but its own. There is no longer slave, feudal, or "proletarian" private property to fortify. Thus the abolition of bourgeois property means the abolition of *all* private property. In a famous passage from the end of volume 1 of *Capital*, Marx sums up this process:

> The capitalist mode of appropriation, the result of the capitalist mode of production, produces capitalist private property. This is the first negation of individual private property, of individual private property as founded on the labour of the proprietor. But capitalist production begets, with the inexorability of a law of Nature, its own negation. It is the negation of the negation. This does not re-establish private property for the producer, but gives him individual property based on the acquisitions of the capitalist era: i.e., on co-operation and the possession in common of the land and of the means of production" (p. 763).

15. Marx and Engels, *The Communist Manifesto*, 32–33.
16. Marx and Engels, *The Communist Manifesto*, 35.
17. An extreme example is Russia after the October Revolution, where Lenin enumerated operating simultaneously *five* different modes of production (patriarchal economy, feudalism, capitalism, state capitalism, and socialism), the first four having been in existence before the Revolution. (See Vladimir Lenin, "Economics and Politics in the Era of the Dictatorship of the Proletariat," in *Collected Works*, vol. 30 [Moscow: Progress Publishers, 1973.])
18. Marx and Engels, *The Communist Manifesto*, 128–129.
19. Suffice it to say, the bourgeoisie did not evolve out of feudal production relations (e.g., manufacture by guilds, peasant or serf relations with landowners, etc.), but as *merchants* who in the beginning had no direct role in feudal or any other production or ownership of the means of production at all. It was only after they had achieved a certain wealth and power that they began attaching *themselves* to the old

forms of production and, with the power of money and the market, transforming them. In short, capital developed *first* as money and only later as productive capital (factories, large-scale machinery, capitalist farms, etc.). Aside from being of historical interest, this fact of capital's genesis is important because it is reflected in the way the bourgeoisie's intellectual "hegemony" was attained—largely by their attaching *themselves* to rather than destroying, wherever possible, the old ideas, particularly those that sanctioned material inequality. While the best bourgeoisie thinkers were truly revolutionary in their day, the bourgeoisie as a class could never be thoroughly so. That is left to the modern proletariat.

20. Marx and Engels, *The Communist Manifesto*, 35.

21. Marx and Engels, *The Communist Manifesto*, 34.

22. Marx and Engels, *The Communist Manifesto*, 39–40.

23. Karl Marx, *Capital*, vol. 1, 715.

24. Karl Marx, *Capital*, vol. 1, 760.

25. Capitalism, when it attacks a new region of the world or section of society, will leave the old forms of production in place for a greater or lesser period depending on their profitability. Capital, in other words, does not transform older forms of production as a matter of principle, but in order to make a profit, and thus does not do so fully or in every case. Thus, until recently, certain areas of the colonial world have remained backward, with either patriarchal or feudal modes of production continuing in certain areas alongside capitalist ones. These are the exceptions that prove the rule. And even they are rapidly changing in those colonial areas that remain under bourgeois domination—for example, the Brazilian Amazon, Sub-Sahara Africa, etc.

26. Karl Marx, *Capital*, vol. 1, 36.

27. Marx and Engels, *Selected Correspondence*, 103.

28. Etymologically, the remnants of the unity of the employers and wage laborers lie in the word "bourgeoisie" itself which means "town-dweller" ("burgher" in German), and has no class connotation. Through the time of the French Revolution, moreover, the term "third estate"—in opposition to the feudal aristocracy and the clergy—also was an umbrella term for both capitalists and proletarians, and the former fought long and hard to maintain the illusion of unity signified by it.

29. Marx and Engels, *The Communist Manifesto*, 41–42.

30. Lenin, *Collected Works*, vol. 5 (Moscow: Progress Publishers, 1973), 349–529.

31. Marx and Engels, *The Communist Manifesto*, 63–64.

32. Nineteenth- and twentieth-century European and U.S. history are full of attempts to establish "socialism" within capitalism, from the utopian colonies of the 1800s to the food and other co-ops of recent years. But such "droplets" of socialism inevitably become, within the environment of advanced capitalism, themselves capitalist enterprises or else they quickly go bankrupt.

33. This does not mean, of course, that workers cannot participate in the development of socialist theory, only that they do not do so as *workers*, but as intellectuals. Joseph Dietzgen is an example of such a worker who through his own intellectual activity approximated, independently of Marx and Engels, their theory of dialectical materialism.

34. Marx and Engels, *The Communist Manifesto* (London: Verso, 1998, with an Introduction by Eric Hobsbawn), 85.

35. Marx and Engels, *The Communist Manifesto*, 51.

36. Marx and Engels, *The Communist Manifesto*, 76.

37. Marx and Engels, *The Communist Manifesto*, 60.

38. Marx and Engels, *The Communist Manifesto*, 38.

39. Marx and Engels, *Selected Correspondence*, 371.

40. Marx and Engels, *Selected Correspondence*, 426–27.

41. "If we now talk of plantation-owners in America as capitalists, if they *are* capitalists, this is due to the fact that they exist as anomalies within a world market based upon free labour" (Karl Marx, *Pre-Capitalist Economic Formations*, 119).

Chapter Four

The State in Capitalist Society

THE PROBLEM OF RATIONALISM

The failure of rationalism from a Marxist perspective can be understood in terms of its Enlightenment construct of the state, which reinforced principles of class privilege. In a letter addressed to Joseph Weydemeyer, Marx argues in the following manner:

> And now as to myself, no credit is due to me for discovering the existence of classes in modern society or the struggle between them. Long before me bourgeois historians had described the historical development of this class struggle and bourgeois economists, the economic anatomy of the classes. What I did that was new was to prove: (1) that the *existence* of classes is only bound up with *particular*, *historical* phases of the development of production, (2) that the class struggle necessarily leads to the dictatorship of the proletariat, (3) that this dictatorship itself only constitutes the transition to the *abolition of all classes* and to *a classless society*.[1]

Any number of concepts can be identified in this passage, but what remains explicit is this: social classes and class conflict are *historical*, not ethereal, dimensions, "bound up with *particular*, *historical* phases of *production*" that only exist in a contingent manner.[2] Implied, although not stated specifically, is the correlation of the existence of classes and the existence of the state: "The abolition of all classes," socialism (or communism, of which socialism is the first of the lower stage) is both the result of the proletarian dictatorship and the cause of its "transition" to another political form in which the state as such does not exist. The existence of classes and class struggle gives rise to the state; the final form of the state is the dictatorship of the proletariat which, by abolishing classes, does away with its own raison d'être.[3]

The Marxist historical analysis of the state came into being both as a result of, and in struggle against, European rationalism. The culmination of this emerged in Hegelianism, rationalism, and liberalism (social contract), in which the Age of Reason provided the philosophical weaponry of the revolutionary bourgeoisie in its battle against the feudal estates system. Engels characterizes the rationalists (such as the French encyclopedists—François-Marie Voltaire, Denis Diderot, and so on) as follows:

> They recognize no external authority of any kind whatever. Religion, natural science, society, political institutions, everything was subjected to the most unsparing criticism: everything must justify its existence before the judgment seat of reason, or give up existence. Reason became the sole measure of everything. It was the time when, as Hegel says, the world stood upon its head; first in the sense that the human head, and the principles arrived at by its thought, claimed to be the basis of all human action and association but by and by, also, in the wider sense that the reality which was in contradiction to these principles had, in fact, to be turned upside down. Every form of society and government then existing, every old traditional notion was flung into the lumber room as irrational; the world had hitherto allowed itself to be led solely by prejudices; everything in the past deserved only pity and contempt. Now, for the first time, appeared the light of day, the kingdom of reason; henceforth superstition, injustice, privilege, oppression were to be superseded by eternal truth, eternal right, equality based on nature and the inalienable rights of man.[4]

The principles of rationalism transformed into shibboleths: "All men are created equal"; "Liberty, equality, fraternity"; "Life, liberty, and the pursuit of happiness," etc., transformed into political theory, that is, into a theory of society, both civil (economic and social) and political. In this context, nationalism became the philosophy of the modern democratic republic based economically on "free enterprise" and politically on the "social contract." Based on this transformation, "irrational" and outmoded privileges and customs of feudalism (the divine right of kings, the system of religious hierarchy, hereditary estates, serfdom, etc.) are now viewed as anachronistic. The transformed society based on rational self-interest now asserts that the human person is free to develop and live his or her life based upon individual conscience and rational choices with no preordained outcome established by previous customs and traditions. Rational actors within this construct are free individuals who enter into relationships with other free individuals for their mutual benefit. In economic relationships this notion of freedom takes the form of trade commodities among producers based on the principle of "enlightened self-interest" (self-interest based, that is, on the human person's understanding of his or her inalienable rights and others'), the only external constraint in activity being "the invisible hand" establishing market equilibrium.

Politically this freedom takes the form of a state based on a rational constitution that recognizes the freedom and equality of all its members is based
on representative democracy, and is designed to facilitate the free exercise of
the rights of all its members, "free enterprise," and minimal interference in
the lives of people. The rationalist state, in short, is a contract between each
member of society and all the others, entered into freely for the purpose of
guaranteeing the freedom (life, liberty, and pursuit of happiness) of all. The
rational basis of the state, with its laws and constitution, manifested itself in
juridical policies and administration.[5]

Does Marxism accept the rationalist model at face value? No! Engels states
in 1873:

> We know today that this kingdom of reason was nothing more than the idealized
> kingdom of the bourgeoisie; that this eternal fight found its realization in bour-
> geois justice; that this equality reduced itself to bourgeois equality before the
> law; that bourgeois property was proclaimed as one of the essential rights of
> man; and that the government of reason, the *Contract Social* of Rousseau, came
> into being, and only could come into being, as a democratic bourgeois republic.
> The great thinkers of the enlightenment century could, no more than their pred-
> ecessors, not go beyond the limits imposed upon them by their epoch.[6]

Rationalism, for Engels, was a philosophy that touted the "rights of man,"
which promoted a theory of the state where an idealized self-image of the antifeudal bourgeoisie is projected. Its iconoclastic assertion that there is "nothing sacred" in society was directed at its nemesis, the entrenched but moribund feudal aristocracy, not its own interests, which were understood to be
universal. Nevertheless, Engels' statement is based on a maturing notion of
Marxism, of a more precise notion of what is now known commonly as *historical materialism*. Even during the nascent stages of their work in the early
1840s, as radical democrats Marx and Engels were aware of, and enthusiastically exposed, the contradictions within eighteenth-century rationalism. This
was the case in rationalism's apotheosis within the Hegelian system, especially Marx's polemic against Hegel's political theory, *A Contribution to the
Critique of Hegel's Philosophy of Law (or Right)*.[7]

Hegel begins by recognizing empirically the separation of "civil society"
(essentially, economic life, the family, etc.) and the state body politic. This
"shows Hegel's profundity,"[8] because it signifies that he recognizes a fundamental fact about modern society, the separation of man himself (and by extension social groupings) into contradictory (private and public) aspects at
least potentially in conflict with each other. He envisions the state as an external, coercive force opposed to the family and individual (civil society). The
problem lies precisely in what Hegel does with this form of knowledge.

Rather than take it at face value, he attempts to rationalize it in the interest, on one level, of his unitary philosophical system, in which being is predicated on "the Idea," and, on another level, of his political aim, namely, justification of the Prussian constitutional monarchist state of his day as the ultimate political manifestation of the Idea. Thus he must find "Reason" at work in the most mundane and questionable behavior of the human person, terminating in the absolutizing of the ruling class and Prussian monarchy.[9]

Essentially, Hegel's political theory attempts to reconcile two contradictory propositions: the first a construct for rational freedom, and the second a justification for an authoritarian state. Marx and Engels argue, "Hegel here sets up an unresolved *antinomy. On the one hand* external necessity, *on the other hand* imminent end."[10] Thus the state (political society) is both an external force vis-à-vis civil society (authoritarian) *and* an internal force vis-à-vis its constitutive nature (freedom). Marx and Engels also accuse Hegel of uniting two irreconcilable propositions by asserting that (with recourse to their common origin in the Idea) rational freedom and choice are somehow related to authoritarian rule. Here, as elsewhere, "Hegel's chief error is to conceive the *contradiction of appearances* as *unity in essence, in the Idea*, while in fact it has nothing more profound for its essence, namely, an essential contradiction. . . ."[11]

This contradiction is elaborated further:

> The general law here appears in the individual. Civil society and the state are separated. Hence the citizen of the state is also separated from the citizen as the member of civil society. He must therefore effect a fundamental division with himself. As an actual citizen he finds himself in a two fold organization: the bureaucratic organization, which is an external, formal feature of the distant state, the executive, which does not touch him or his independent reality, and the social organization, the organization of civil society. But in the latter he stands as a private person outside the state; this social organization does not touch the political state as such. The former is a state organization for which he always provides the material. The second is a civil organization the material of which is not the state. In the former the state stands as formal antithesis to him, in the second he stands as material antithesis to the state. Hence, in order to behave as an actual citizen of the state, and to attain political significance and effectiveness, he must step out of his civil reality, disregard it, and withdraw from the whole organization into his individuality; for the sole existence which he finds himself for his citizenship of the state as executive is complete without him and his existence in civil society is complete without the state. He can be a citizen of the state only in contradiction to these available communities, only as an individual. His existence as a citizen of the state is an existence outside his communal existences and is therefore purely individual.[12]

The most visible evidence of the separation of civil man from the state is the coming into being in modern society of the nation-state (as opposed to small, feudal units), and with a large state bureaucracy, increasingly foreign to the citizen, complete with its own functionaries and dynamics. On a more fundamental level, modern (i.e., capitalist) society creates a gap between the civil (or economic) and the political person by abstracting the latter under the aegis of formal equality. Under this formal equality, society, previously assigned to social estates (social groupings), is atomized legally into myriad politically equal individuals, each of them "human" in general terms. This formal equality, absolutized in the constitution, is the ideal expression of the actual relations of production in capitalist society, in which many private and "equal" producers of commodities (equal in terms of the market with its common denominator, abstract human labor) buy and sell their wares freely; legally speaking, the capitalist, who owns property (means of production) and accumulates wealth, is equal to the propertyless proletarian, who *also* is free to trade his "property"—labor power, or ability to work.

However, lying beneath, and in contradiction to this formal equality, is actual inequality, particularly the *social* inequality between those who own property and those who do not—in modern times, the bourgeoisie and the proletariat. In political society, the realm of the wage laborer and the capitalist are equal; in civil society they are unequal not only quantitatively but *qualitatively*, forming opposite poles that become increasingly distant from each other as society advances. Marx states:

> It is an historical advance which has transformed the *political estates* into *social estates*, so that, just as the Christians are equal in heaven, but unequal on earth, so the individual members of the nation are *equal* in the heaven of their political world, but unequal in the earthly existence of society. The French Revolution completed the transformation of the *political* into *social* differences, into differences of civil life which are without significance in political life. With that, the separation of political life from civil society was completed.[13]

For the bourgeoisie, the establishment of complete legal equality through the abolition of the social privileges of the feudal aristocracy that had stifled their development is the *final* act, the *nec plus ultra* of their revolution. For Marx it is not. The social inequality that not only still remains but is, to a degree, actually aggravated by legal equality (free enterprise leads inevitably to monopoly, "The rich get richer and the poor get poorer") is not some unfortunate and temporary aberration from modern bourgeois progress and the democratic republic, but their inevitable result. Polarization of wealth and poverty not only continues to develop, but intensifies and becomes the principal social reality. In particular, the Industrial Revolution created on the one hand

phenomenal wealth and power, and on the other hand emiseration, brutaliza-
tion, starvation, disease, and degradation unheard of in the "irrational" Dark
Ages in the time before the dawning of the Age of Reason. The product of the
Hegelian state, "the actuality of the ethical idea—the ethical spirit as the
Manifest, substantial will, clear to itself," the product of and basis for this
"Actuality" are the eighteen-hour day, the sweatshop, the "Dark Satanic
Mills" of industrial England, and the Dickensian poorhouse. For Marx, the ultimate failure of the Hegelian synthesis lies in the social polarization that took
place in the nineteenth century. No amount of conceptual notion of "unity"
between civil life and the state can mask the material polarization of classes
and the fact that the state (and associated laws and policies), far from being
the reconciler of these contradictory social forces, stands on the side of one
against the other, serving "the religion of private property"[14] and its high
priest, the modern bourgeoisie.[15]

Even in 1844, while himself still working to a great extent within the
Hegelian framework, Marx draws revolutionary conclusions from his expo-
sure of the essentially antagonistic nature of bourgeois society and its political
expression, the modern state. Despite the idealistic Hegelian terms of this concept, a materialist reality undergirds this very system, surfacing as systematic,
historically determined analysis of not only the modern state, but historically
previous states and civilizations as well. Nonetheless, answering the question
about where the possibility of the emancipation of Germany lies, Marx states:

> In the formation of a class with radical chains, a class of civil society which is
> not a class of civil society, an estate which is the dissolution of all estates, a
> sphere which has a universal character by its universal suffering and claims no
> particular right because no particular wrong but wrong generally is perpetuated
> against it; which can no longer invoke a historical but only human title; which
> does not stand in any one-sided antithesis to the consequences but in an all-
> round antithesis to the premises of the German state; a sphere, finally which can-
> not emancipate itself without emancipating itself from all other spheres of soci-
> ety, which, in a word, is the complete loss of man and hence can win itself only
> through the complete rewinning of man. This dissolution of society as a partic-
> ular estate is the proletariat.[16]

In the letter to Weydemeyer previously quoted,[17] Marx clearly delineates the
cutting edge, the sine qua non of his thought—the theory of the dictatorship
of the proletariat. It is not the concept of the class struggle that makes his theory new and different. Such a concept can be acceptable even to traditional
thinkers, as long as the "classes" can be seen to be reconcilable and their
"struggle" resolvable by peaceful means. The dictatorship of the proletariat,
on the contrary, is not so malleable; it cannot be fit into a liberal critique of

capitalist society. Thus it is, as Lenin identifies,[18] that the reformist trend within the Marxist movement attempts to *amputate* the theory of the dictatorship of the proletariat from the rest of the Marxist *corpus*, thus reducing Marxism to "the theory of the class struggle," which has existed even prior to Marx among the bourgeois ideologists themselves. The revolutionary trend within the Marxist movement—on the contrary, following Marx himself—takes its stand *precisely* on the question of the dictatorship of the proletariat. Once the distinction between these two interpretations of Marxism is recognized, it becomes clear that in the over 150 years of Marxism's existence as a political credo (since approximately the date of the publication of the *Communist Manifesto,* written in 1848) the revolutionary trend within Marxism has, while continuing to develop based on analysis of actual historical practice, remained remarkably stable and consistent in its basic theoretical premises. The political thought of Marx and Engels, lifelong colleagues and collaborators after 1843, is a consistent, integrated body of thought, at least regarding the revolutionary role of the proletariat; Lenin's development of the thought, particularly in his writings on the state (namely, *State and Revolution*), does not "revise" it in any fundamental way, but merely sums it up and applies it in more advanced historical circumstances—that is, monopoly capitalism and the dawning of postcapitalist society. Joseph Stalin and Antonio Gramsci, although practically and theoretically maneuvering in divergent academic environments, both base their political analysis of their respective societies and state forms on the work of Lenin. Despite stylistic differences and emphases, there are no fundamental variations in the ideas of any of these Marxists. All agree on several basic points:

(1) The state did not always exist, but developed as a result of the breaking of society into antagonistic economic classes; (2) The state, far from being "the middle term," the "reconciler" of class antagonisms, is inevitably the tool of *one* class over another or others by which it maintains domination; (3) The essential content of the state, despite occasional (or frequent) appearances to the contrary, is based on *violence*; (4) The inevitable resolution of the basic antagonisms within the present order, capitalism, will be the seizure of political power by the proletariat, the destruction of the state, the dictatorship of the proletariat; (5) The proletariat will use its dictatorship to introduce socialist relations of production, characterized by the abolition of private property and with it the abolition of classes, which are based, historically, on one or another form of private property; and (6) This abolition of private property and, with it, classes will do away with class antagonisms, the historical basis of the existence of all states. Thus, the dictatorship of the proletariat, far from setting about, as all other states have, to perpetuate itself *ad infinitum*, in fact sets about to render itself superfluous, thus, in the long run, withering away.[19]

THE ORIGIN AND FUNCTION
OF THE CAPITALIST STATE

Both Marx and Engels based their theory on the most complete analysis of history possible during their time. In *Origin of the Family, Private Property, and the State*, Engels, using the most advanced anthropological work then available (in particular Lewis Henry Morgan's *Ancient Society*), traces the history of the development of classes, and with them, the state throughout history. Toward the end of his study Engels argues:

The state is therefore by no means a power imposed on society from without; just as little is it "the reality of the moral idea," the image and the reality of reason, as Hegel maintains. Rather, it is a product of society at a particular stage of development; it is the admission that this society involved itself in insoluble self-contradiction and is cleft into irreconcilable antagonisms which it is powerless to exorcise. But in order that these antagonisms, classes with conflicting economic interests, shall not consume themselves and society in fruitless struggle, a power, apparently standing above society, has become necessary to moderate the conflict and keep it within the bounds of "order"; and this power, arisen out of society, but placing itself above it and increasingly alienating itself from it, is the state.

In contrast to the old gentile organization, the state is distinguished by the grouping of its members on a *territorial* basis. . . .

The second distinguishing characteristic is the institution of a public force which is no longer immediately identical with the people's own organization of themselves as an armed power. This special force is needed because a self-acting armed organization of the people has become impossible since their cleavage into classes. . . . This public force exists in every state; it consists not merely of armed men, but also of material appendages, prisons and coercive institutions of all kinds, of which gentile society knew nothing. It may be very insignificant, practically negligible, in societies with still undeveloped class antagonisms and living in remote areas, as at times and in places in the United States of America. But it becomes stronger in proportion as the class antagonisms within the state become sharper and as adjoining states grow larger and more populous. . . . In order to maintain this public power, contributions from the state citizens are necessary—taxes. These were completely unknown to gentile society. We know more than enough about them today. . . . In possession of the public power and the right of taxation, the officials now present themselves as organs of society standing *above* society. The free, willing respect accorded to the organs of the gentile constitution is not enough for them, even if they could have it. Representatives of a power which estranged them from society, they have to be given prestige by means of special decrees, which invest them with a particular sanctity and inviolability. The lowest police officer of the civilized state has more "authority" than all the organs of gentile society put together; but the mightiest prince and the greatest statesman or general of civilization might envy the humblest of the gentile chiefs the unforced and unquestioned respect accorded to him. For the one stands in the midst of society; the other is forced to pose as something outside the above.[20]

The state is essentially an organ of force, consisting of "armed men," prisons, and other *coercive* elements. It is important here to recognize that the state is not coterminous with government or administration. Every society, no matter how small or primitive, has had some form of administration, some body of persons to lead and provide certain services. This is *not* in itself the state, that is, not simply a leadership but a coercive body. In modern society, for example, the state is a part of the government or general administrative apparatus; they are not identical. The latter includes many things—public transportation, sanitary systems, education, hospitals, for example—which are part of the government but not part of the state. Every society, as it grows in size and complexity, requires administration and special organs of leadership; these are not *in themselves* part of the state. This point is important because one trend in Marxist theory has tended to equate the entire *superstructure*   in Marxist terminology the legal and political system, education, philosophy, art, culture, etc.—with the state. In fact, the state is a part, albeit the decisive part, of the superstructure, but only a part. To this point Engels continues from the previous passage:

As the state arose from the need to keep class antagonisms in check, but also arose in the thick of the fight between the classes, it is normally the state of the most powerful, economically ruling class, which by its means becomes also the politically ruling class, and so acquires new means of holding down and exploiting the oppressed classes. The ancient state was, above all, the state of the slave-owners for holding down the slaves, just as the feudal state was the organ *of* the nobility for holding down the peasant serfs and bondsmen, and the modern representative state is the instrument for exploiting wage-labor by capital. . . . Further, in most historical states the rights conceded to citizens are graded on a property basis, whereby it is directly admitted that the state is an organization for the protection of the possessing class against the non-possessing class. . . . The highest form of the state, the democratic republic, which in our modern social conditions becomes more and more an unavoidable necessity and is the form of state in which alone the last decisive battle proletariat and bourgeoisie can be fought out—the democratic republic no longer officially recognizes differences of property. Wealth here employs its power indirectly, but all the more surely. It does this in two ways: by plain corruption of officials, of which America is the classic example, and by an alliance between the government and the stock exchange, which is effected all the more easily the higher the state debt mounts and the more the joint-stock companies concentrate in their hands not only transport but also production itself. . . .[21]

Thus the state is not a neutral, disinterested, reconciling force according to the Marxist vision. Martin Carnoy argues that the state and all its ideological underpinnings are merely "part of the class struggle."[22] In capitalist society, virtually the entire body of law is concerned with the definition and protection of property. Even laws that are theoretically neutral generally favor property by the sheer fact of maintaining the status quo, not to mention the fact that the rich are much better able than the poor to take advantage of the legal system, influence legislation, run for political office, etc. This is not to say that the class struggle is not manifested within the state itself. On the contrary, since according to Marxist theory, *force* is the final arbiter of social conflict, the state itself is susceptible to pressure from both inside and outside. The struggle of the working class against the employers is felt within the state in questions of legislation (e.g., protection of workers' health and safety in factories, right to organize unions, enfranchisement of propertyless persons, women's suffrage, etc.), just as diverse groups of capitalists fight among themselves. Large parts of volume 1 of Marx's *Capital* concern the class struggle in labor legislation, particularly the question of the length of the working day. Finally, a battle goes on within the state on the part of the capitalist class as a whole against individual capitalists. Most "government regulation," although much maligned by industrialists and financiers, falls into this category. Based on the anarchistic nature of capital accumulation, individual employers, left to their own devices, would quickly either "kill off" each other in cutthroat competition (which interstate commerce laws, laws regulating competition, antitrust laws, and so on, are meant to mitigate) or else "kill off" everyone, including themselves, by poisoning the air, water, and the earth by industrial pollution. Most government regulation is the result of capitalists collective (or "committee for managing the common affairs of the whole bourgeoisie," as Marx and Engels term the executive of the modern state[23]) trying to protect the capitalist class as a whole against its individual members from its own inherent monopolistic tendencies.

However, the recognition by Marxism that the class struggle takes place *within* the state does not mean that the class nature of a given state, at least in capitalist society, can be changed from within, or by formal changes in laws, personalities, and so forth. In themselves, reforms brought about by pressure from the working class tend to strengthen rather than weaken bourgeois rule by forcing it to rationalize itself and, in many cases, adding to its legitimacy. No reform, even one that helps the working class (such as the winning of the eight-hour day), challenges the basis of capitalist society and its state: private property, class antagonism, and the resulting polarization of wealth and power, which is present in the democratic republic, but, being so, "all the more sure."[24] Even pro-labor reforms may, in themselves, serve indirectly to aid capital. Eight-hour legislation and the passage of the National Labor Relations Act (or Wagner Act, 1935) are examples, because, among other things, they brought the working-class movement more under the control of the bourgeois superstructure.[25] The modern bourgeois state, in short, protects capitalism and the capitalist class not only from the proletariat, but from the individual capitalists or groups of capitalists as well. Even nationalization, which appears to violate the "sacred law" of private property, in fact is its final realization—first, because it takes from the bourgeoisie the burden of managing unprofitable enterprises and puts it on the (mainly proletarian) taxpayers; and second, because the bourgeoisie continues through the national debt to "own" the government, which now "owns" the nationalized industry.[26]

VIOLENCE AS THE ESSENCE OF THE STATE

Based on what has been established to this point, the position of classical Marxism on the question of the essential coercive character of the state should be clear. What needs to be touched on is the question of the relation of violence to "hegemony"—that is, in Gramsci's writing, the question of the bourgeoisie's ability in certain periods to rule more by moral authority and ideological domination than by open force. Thus, the bourgeoisie, by so thoroughly imbuing the workers with bourgeois ideology (again, either good or bad: individualism, acquisitiveness, consumerism, religious ideology, mysticism, etc.), has made force either totally unnecessary or else of minor importance next to hegemony—nonviolent persuasion. Gramsci, in particular, is credited by many European Marxist intellectuals with having given hegemony, as opposed to force, more its due than did Marx, Engels, and Lenin.[27] This view of Gramsci's thought is based on two misconceptions. The first is that classical Marxism did not adequately address hegemony. The second is that capitalism fundamentally changed between the period Marx wrote and the period Gramsci wrote, and that the latter set about, either consciously or unconsciously, to "correct" Marxism in light of new conditions.[28]

A basic tenet of Marxism is that "the ideas of a society are the ideas of its ruling class." In his *Introduction to a Contribution to a Critique of Political Economy*, Marx states how, in a given society, its "superstructure" and way of thinking are based on the relations of production or property relations. The ruling class does not control only the means of production and the state apparatus, but also the schools, cultural and religious institutions, scientific establishments, etc., either directly by ownership, or indirectly through influence, patronage, bribery, etc., all of which leads to its hegemony over the masses, who, generally speaking, have neither the education, the leisure, the money, nor (in ordinary times) the desire to put up a struggle against ruling class hegemony. Far from existing in contradiction to violence, hegemony is its complement, a dialectic that Lenin terms as rules "by the gendarme and the priest." In volume 1 of *Capital*, Marx describes in detail how the process of creating a proletariat (a process that he calls "primitive accumulation"[29]) has two stages. The first is the forcible eviction of the peasantry from the soil; they are burned, starved, chased off the land, reduced to pauperism, and driven into the cities, where laws against vagabondage force them to work for the industrialists. He says, "thus were the agricultural people first forcibly expropriated from the soil, driven from their homes, turned into vagabonds, and then whipped, branded, tortured by laws grotesquely terrible, into the discipline necessary for the wage system."[30] Here the direct and unadorned role of the state stands out—it is a direct tool of nascent capital in need of workers. The second stage is more gradual, and takes place after the violent expropriation. Marx continues:

> It is not enough that the conditions of labour are concentrated in a mass, in the shape of capital, at one pole of society, while at the other are grouped masses of men, who have nothing to sell but their labour-power. Neither is it enough that they are compelled to sell it voluntarily. The advance of capitalist production develops a working-class, which by *education, tradition, habit, looks upon the conditions of that mode of production as self-evident laws of nature. The organization of the capitalist process of production, once fully developed, breaks down all resistance.* The constant generation of a relative surplus-population keeps the law of supply and demand of labour, and therefore keeps wages, in a rut that corresponds with the wants of capital. The dull compulsion of economic relations completes the subjection of the labourer to the capitalist. Direct force, outside economic conditions, is of course still used, but only exceptionally. In the ordinary run of things, the labourer can be left to the "natural laws of production," i.e., to his dependence on capital, a dependence springing from, and guaranteed in perpetuity by, the conditions of production themselves. It is otherwise during the historic genesis of capitalist production. The bourgeoisie, at its rise, wants and uses the power of the state to "regulate" wages, etc.[31]

This clear exposition of the relationship of state force and coercion is the basis of hegemony. Gramsci himself seems quite satisfied with the Marxist theory of the state and ideology. Speaking about the role of the intelligentsia, Gramsci states:

> What we can do, for the moment, is to fix two major superstructural levels: the one that can be called "civil society," that is the ensemble of organisms commonly called "private," and that of "political society" or "the state." These two levels correspond on the one hand to the function of "hegemony" which the

dominant group exercises throughout society and on the other hand to that of "direct domination" or command exercises through the state and "juridical" government.[32]

Two "subaltern" and complementary functions, "social hegemony and political government" exist, according to Gramsci, through

[t]he "spontaneous" consent given by the great masses of the population to the general direction imposed on social life by the dominant fundamental group; this consent is "historically" caused by the prestige (and consequent confidence) which the dominant group enjoys because of its position and function in the world of production. . . . The apparatus of state coercive power . . . "legally" enforces discipline on those groups who do not "consent" either actively or passively. This apparatus is, however, constituted for the whole of society in anticipation of moments of crisis or command and direction when spontaneous consent has failed.[33]

There is no substantive difference between Gramsci's statement and Marx's previous one. Gramsci's view is based on nothing more (or less) than that of solid Marxist analysis. It is true that in his writings Gramsci dwelt a great deal on the question of revolution and the revolutionary movement as an *intellectual* process, and that his views at times are susceptible to reformist misconceptions. (Thus, for example, his discussion of the necessity of the Revolutionary Party's fighting for hegemony in the working-class movement has been distorted, particularly by Italian "Eurocommunists," to mean that the Communist Party must gain hegemony within or control over society as a whole—economically and politically.) Thus the "historic compromise" of Enrico Berlinguer, who boasts to the bourgeoisie that he can run capitalist society better than they. But this is not Gramsci's position. This was a difference of *emphasis*, not *kind*, on Gramsci's part, and differed little if at all from Lenin's emphasis on the role of the *conscious* element, the Party, in the Revolutionary process. To understand why this emphasis was different from that of Marx, it is important to focus on the period and conditions in which they wrote, one of upsurge in which the transition from capitalism to socialism was an immediate and practical question, not simply a more or less distant inevitability. Gramsci, in particular, was grappling with a situation in which all the objective conditions for revolution were present (the period after World War I until the establishment of Fascism) but in which the subjective factor (both the Socialist movement, hamstrung by reformism and sectarianism, and a large section of the masses themselves) was lagging behind, owing to historical and cultural weaknesses in the Italian working class movement.[34]

BEYOND BOURGEOIS DEMOCRACY

The inevitability of the dictatorship of the proletariat stems from the inevitability of a final decisive clash between the two great classes of modern society, the bourgeoisie and the proletariat.[35] This clash, although it develops first in the economic realm (exploitation, strikes, etc.) and is retarded politically by the common struggle of both workers and employers against feudalism, must finally take a political form in that "every class struggle is a political struggle."[36] That is, it can take place only in the realm of state power. In the words of the *Manifesto*, "the first step in the revolution by the working class is to raise the proletariat to the position of ruling class, to win the battle of democracy."[37] Marx and Engels further state:

> The proletariat will use its political supremacy to wrest, by degrees, all capital from the bourgeoisie, to centralize all instruments of production in the hands of the State, i.e., of the proletariat organized as the ruling class. . . .
>
> When, in the course of development, class distinctions have disappeared, and all production has been concentrated in the hands of a vast association of the whole nation, the public power will lose its political character. Political power, properly so called, is merely the organized power of one class for oppression of another. If the proletariat during its contest with the bourgeoisie is compelled, by the force of circumstances, to organize itself as a class, if, by means of a revolution, it makes itself the ruling class, and, as such, sweeps away by force the old conditions of production, then it will, along with these conditions, have swept away conditions for the existence of class antagonisms and of classes generally, and will thereby have abolished its own supremacy as a class.[38]

In summation the salient points are as follows:

1. "The State" is "the proletariat organized as the ruling class" after the overthrow of the bourgeois rule.
2. The proletarian state is an instrument of the proletariat by which it establishes socialism, i.e., "wrest(s), by degrees, all capital from the bourgeoisie."
3. By doing so, by sweeping "away by force the old conditions of production," the proletarian and its state sweep away "conditions for the existence of class antagonisms," different property relations of different social classes. By abolishing the bourgeoisie the proletariat abolishes itself as a proletariat, that is, a propertyless mass of wage laborers.
4. This abolition of classes and the disappearance of class distinctions do not happen all at once, but "by degrees" and "in the course of development." The proletariat's political victory, in other words, is the precondition for its final victory, but not identical to it. Its "despotic inroads on the rights of property, and on the conditions of bourgeois production"[39] imply a long-term, bitter struggle carried on by the dictatorship of the proletariat.

As Lenin remarks in *State and Revolution*, Marx and Engels' theory of the state develops and matures from the time of the writing of the *Manifesto* (1848) through Marx's *The Eighteenth Brumaire of Louis Bonaparte* (1851) through *The Civil War in France* (1871), the latter being the summing up of the first real proletarian revolution, the Paris Commune.[40] This is because their theory is based on actual historical experience, not abstractions, and, once established in its broad outlines, can only advance based on new experience. The principal development of the Marxist theory of the state from 1848–1871 lies in its further concretization of what the proletariat state is. The state is *not* simply the substitution of the proletariat for the bourgeoisie within the same political apparatus, but the *destruction* of the old state machinery and the construction of a brand new one. Lenin quotes Marx and Engels saying, in their preface to the new German edition of the *Manifesto*, 1872, "one thing especially was proved by the Commune, viz., that 'the working class cannot simply lay hold of the ready-made state machinery and wield it for its own purposes. . .'";[41] Lenin further remarks, "thus, Marx and Engels regarded one principal and fundamental lesson of the Paris Commune as being of such enormous importance that they introduced it as an important correction into the *Communist Manifesto*."[42] And, "Marx's idea is that the working class must break up, smash the 'ready-made state machinery,'[43] and not confine itself merely to laying hold of it."[44]

The proletarian state is qualitatively different from its predecessor. Since it represents the power not of a small minority of exploiters, but of the vast majority of working people (the proletariat allied with other laboring classes, especially the landless peasantry, or for that matter high-tech and white-collar workers), it can no longer operate on the best of elite institutions whose raison d'être, under the old conditions, was the keeping of the majority out of political life and their actual suppression. Instead of a special, highly paid caste of civil servants or bureaucrats whose main purpose, aside from defending bourgeois property is its self-perpetuation, a government in the proletarian state is constructed by the workers themselves, consisting of persons who work for "workmen's wages" and who are subject to immediate recall by their constituency, the working class. Rather than a balance of powers, in which those making laws lack power to put them into effect, and where the judiciary enjoys a "sham independence," there is a unitary government based on the principle that those who legislate have the responsibility for executing the law.[45] Parliamentarianism—the system of bourgeois democracy in which the public legislators put on a show in a "talk shop" (parliament or congress), while the real decisions are made in committees of unrelated officials (cabinets, armed forces, FBI, etc.)—is replaced by a new form. Lenin sums up Marx's analysis of the Commune thusly:

The Commune . . . appears to have replaced the smashed state machine "only" by fuller democracy: abolition of the standing army; all officials to be elected and subject to recall. But as a matter of fact this "only" signifies a gigantic replacement of certain institutions by other institutions of a fundamentally different type. This is exactly a case of "quantity being transformed into quality": democracy, introduced as fully and consistently as is at all conceivable, is transformed from bourgeois into proletarian democracy; from the state (a special force for the suppression of a particular class) into something which is no longer the state proper.[46]

The Commune form of state organization came to fruition in the revolution of 1905 in Russia and, finally, in the October Revolution of 1917. In these revolutions, more definitively than in the French, the proletariat *in practice* realized that it had to form its own organs of power separate from those of the bourgeoisie. These were the Soviets. Lenin himself further develops Marx's theory of the state and the dictatorship of the proletariat during and after the Russian Revolution in a number of his writings—namely, *Left-Wing Communism*, "Economics and Politics in the Era of the Dictatorship of the Proletariat," and many others. The conditions under which his theoretical development takes place are different from those anticipated by classical Marxism, namely, the conditions of a proletariat state in a predominantly peasant country and in a situation in which the revolution is surrounded by powerful, hostile, bourgeois states. Lenin makes it clear that this extremely difficult internal and external environment in which the dictatorship of the proletariat is operating creates difficulties and conditions that make "the era" of its existence one of sharp struggle, inevitable setbacks, compromise, the danger of the recrudescence of bureaucracy owing to the relative backwardness of the masses and the necessity of enlisting the help of former members of the previous state apparatus, etc.

According to Marxism, revolutionary theory is the summation of the *entire* experience of the working class movement, not in one country, but worldwide. This experience is a continuing thing, of course, and the development of theory never ends. Just as Marx and Engels continued throughout their lives to deepen their understanding of the state in general and the proletariat state in particular throughout their lives, Lenin, and after him Stalin and Gramsci, continued their work under new historical conditions. The final word has not been written either on the socialist state or even on the bourgeois state, since even the latter has taken on new forms during the period of fascism, state monopoly capitalism, and the revolutions in the colonial world that have given rise to new forms of the bourgeois state and the new theoretical problems (e.g., the existence of the "non-capitalist, non-socialist path" of development with its corresponding political forms or non-forms, the anti-imperialist but procapitalist state, the concept of more than one class sharing power, and so on). However, an important distinction needs to be made at this point between the legitimate (in Marxist terms) development of theory based on new historical experience and the altering of basic tenets of historical materialism under the guise of development, elaboration, etc. An example of the latter is the assertion that the "complexity" of the modern state and its democratization through universal suffrage and education render the traditional class nature of the state obsolete. True or false as this in fact might be, such a concept is contrary to Marxism as a method of historical analysis.

NOTES

1. Karl Marx and Frederick Engels, *Selected Correspondence* (Moscow: Progress Publishers, 1965), 64, emphasis added.

2. The *historical* foundation of Marx's analysis of various structures of social production is a constitutive part of his entire doctrine, not exclusively one related to his theory of the state. It is, arguably, the *core* principle for his theorizing. For example, it is his ability to separate conceptually what is eternal about human society (the production of means of subsistence, "Use Values") from what is *transient* (the production of commodities, or "Exchange Values") that enables him to "defetishize" commodities and thus break through the cul-de-sac into which classical bourgeois political economy has gotten itself. See, e.g., *Capital*, vol. 1 (Moscow: Foreign Language Publishing House Edition, 1959), 81. Classical economists, believing capitalist production to be "eternally fixed by nature for every state of society," were unable to differentiate between the utility of an object (the relation between it and the user) and its value form, that is, money.

3. Frederick Engels, *Anti-Dühring* (New York: International Publishers, 1965), 307.

4. Frederick Engels, *Socialism: Utopian and Scientific* (New York: International Publishers, 1975), 32.

5. Hegel (on the French Revolution) "thought the concept of law, all at once makes itself felt, and against this the old scaffolding of wrong could make no stand. In this conception of law, therefore, a constitution has now been established, and henceforth everything must be based upon this" ("Philosophy of History," 1840, 535, quoted in Engels, *Socialism: Utopian and Scientific*, 31).

6. Engels, *Socialism: Utopian and Scientific*, 32.

7. Karl Marx and Frederick Engels, *Collected Works*, vol. 3 (New York: International Publishers, 1975).

8. Marx and Engels, *Collected Works*, 75.

9. Marx and Engels, *Collected Works*, 127 and passim.

10. Marx and Engels, *Collected Works*, 6, emphasis added.

11. Marx and Engels, *Collected Works*, 91, emphasis added.

12. Marx and Engels, *Collected Works*, 77.

13. Marx and Engels, *Collected Works*, 80.

14. Marx and Engels, *Collected Works,* 138.

15. See Marx and Engels, *Collected Works*, 84, for Marx's criticism of the Hegelian synthesis, in particular Hegel's use of "The Legislative" to reconcile the monarch and civil society, which Marx terms "Mystical Dualism."

16. Marx and Engels, "Introduction to the Contribution to the Critique of Hegel's Philosophy of Law," in *Collected Works*, vol. 3, 186.

17. Marx and Engels, *Collected Works*, 64.

18. Vladimir I. Lenin, "State and Revolution," in *Collected Works*, vol. 25 (Moscow: Progress Publishers, 1964), 386.

19. This last thesis, on the withering away of the state, has been a point of great controversy in the Marxist movement, serving as a key point of attack on Marxist theory by its critics, who point particularly to the example of the former USSR where the state had certainly not withered away in the aftermath of the establishment of socialism. This subject deserves a full treatment in its own right to investigate whether Marx was wrong on this point or not. Suffice it to say, here both Marx and Engels were assuming, in discussing the withering away of the state, the victory of socialism in at least all the main industrial nations and thus did not take into consideration the possibility of socialism's being built in a hostile environment of "cordon sanitaire." (See Joseph V. Stalin, "Report to the Eighteenth Congress of the C.P.S.U. (B)," in *Problems of Leninism* (Peking: Foreign Languages Press, 1976), 927–942, emphasis added.

20. Frederick Engels, *The Origin of Family, Private Property and the State* (New York: International Publications, 1975), 230.

21. Engels, *The Origin of Family, Private Property and the State,* 231–232. The power of the energy companies or banks over the government in the United States might be examples of this last point. The banks' takeover of New York City in 1975 by strictly financial means is an indication of the power of financial institutions in this country. See also, Roger E. Alcaly and David Mermelstein, eds., *The Fiscal Crisis of American Cities* (New York: Vintage Books, 1976).

22. Martin Carnoy, *The State and Political Theory* (Princeton, N.J.: Princeton University Press, 1984), 101.

23. Marx and Engels, *The Communist Manifesto* (Moscow: Progressive Publications, 1971), 34.

24. Engels, *The Origin of Family*, 231–232.

25. The point here is not that Marxism argues against the desirability of fighting for reforms, merely that it sees the struggle for reform in itself as dead ended. (See, e.g., the final section of Marx's *Value, Price and Profit* [New York: International Publishers, 1935] for a criticism of modern trade unionism). Also, Stalin, *Foundations of Leninism*, 97–100.

26. See Engels, *Socialism: Utopian and Scientific*, 66.

27. This idea is particularly popular among Althusser and his followers, with their notions of "ideological state apparatuses," etc., which they deduce from Gramsci. Thus Marx and Lenin are criticized for having had an oversimplified or "perceptual" view of the state, as opposed to Gramsci's (and Althusser's) more "dialectical" and developed view.

28. A variation on this second view is that Marx had understood hegemony but has been perverted or oversimplified "undialectically" by Engels, Lenin, and Stalin, and that Gramsci was returning to the fount.

29. See Marx's *Capital*, chapters 26–33, passim.

30. Marx, *Capital*, 737.

31. See Marx's *Capital* (emphasis added).

32. Antonio Gramsci, "Problems of History and Culture," in *Selections from the Prison Notebooks* (New York: International Publishers, 1971), 12.

33. Gramsci, *Selections*, 12.

34. It should be noted that here, as elsewhere, the attempt to review Marxism is based on an either conscious or unconscious misunderstanding of Marx's actual thinking, particularly on the question of the relation of economics to politics or, more generally, the "basis" to the "superstructure." Thus the "economic" Marx is counterpoised by the more "political" or "ideological" Lenin or Gramsci or whomever. Those who do this forget, among other things, that one of the reasons for Lenin's, Gramsci's, et al.'s ability to dwell less on the economic and more on the political or ideological side of their respective political situations—apart from the aforementioned necessity of doing so due to the political exigencies of their times—stemmed largely from the fact that they *didn't have to rediscover or reargue* the fact of the economic basis of politics, ideology, etc., including the state. Marx had already done so definitively, thus freeing them to study their concrete circumstances. But to find a contradiction here between the theoretical foundation that he had laid and the edifices they constructed on it is like finding a contradiction between the study of architecture and the construction of the buildings. (See, Engels's letter to Bloch, September 21–22, 1890: "Marx and I are ourselves partly to blame for the fact that the younger people sometimes lay more stress on the economic side than is due to it. We had to emphasize the main principle vis-à-vis our adversaries, who denied it, and we had not always the time, the place or the opportunity to give their due to the other elements involved in the interaction. But when it came to presenting a section of history, that is, to making a practical application, it was a different matter and there no error was permissible" (Marx and Engels, *Selected Correspondence*, 396).

35. See, e.g., Marx and Engels, *The Communist Manifesto*, 44.

36. See Marx and Engels, *The Communist Manifesto*, 41.

37. See Marx and Engels, *The Communist Manifesto*, 53.

38. See Marx and Engels, *The Communist Manifesto*, 54 (emphasis added).

39. See Marx and Engels, *The Communist Manifesto*, 54.

40. Lenin, "State and Revolution," in *Collected Works*, vol. 25, 381–492, passim.

41. Quoted in Lenin, "State and Revolution," in *Collected Works*, vol. 25, 414.

42. See Lenin, "State and Revolution," in *Collected Works*, vol. 25, 414.

43. See Lenin, "State and Revolution," in *Collected Works*, vol. 25, 414.

44. Martin Carnoy, *The State and Political Theory*.

45. See Carnoy, *The State and Political Theory*, 419.

46. See Lenin, "State and Revolution," in *Collected Works*, vol. 25, 414.

Chapter Five

Comparative Models of Welfare Policy

In liberal welfare regimes, such as the U.S. and, in the last decade, the U.K. and New Zealand, the dominant welfare threats to competitiveness are not those of disincentives, crowding-out, state redistribution, regulation and other leading issues in current debates. The dominant threat is of inequality and its effects.

—Ian Gough, *Global Capital, Human Needs and Social Policies*

Some theorists argue that society and government have a direct obligation to meet the needs of its members and to do so unconditionally. The topic of welfare rights is one that elicits numerous and complicated questions. Regarding welfare policy, Nicholas Rescher states:

In what respects and to what extent is society, working through the instrumentality of the state, responsible for the welfare of its members? What demands for the promotion of his welfare can an individual reasonably make upon his society? These are questions to which no answer can be given in terms of some a priori approach with reference to universal ultimates. Whatever answer can appropriately be given will depend, in the final analysis, on what the society decides it should be.[1]

Rescher's point regarding the a priori nature (metaphysical assumptions) of welfare rights may in fact prove to be a significant intellectual challenge to those interested in the debate on welfare. Nevertheless, his response to his own question is that from a policy perspective a society has only those responsibilities for its members that it *believes* it has through legislative and constitutional decree. Although this claim is nonetheless true regarding the legislative implementation of welfare policy, we argue that it is inadequate precisely because it violates the fundamental rights of individuals to secure economic sustenance and thus provides a threat to the general welfare and common good. Moreover, we argue that welfare rights must be understood in the same philosophical capacity that life and liberty are understood and interpreted in a similar constitutional manner. For example, if one imagines the case of an affluent society that leaves its blind, disabled, and needy to die of starvation, the incompleteness of Rescher's account becomes obvious. In this imagined case, one is naturally led to raise the question as to whether those in power ought to supply those in need with the necessities of life. Though the needy have no precise legal right to welfare benefits of any kind, at least based on constitutional decree at this point in time, one might very well argue persuasively that they ought to have such a right. Hugh Heclo argues that this issue is the most significant "social question" confronting American society.[2]

DOES SOCIETY HAVE AN OBLIGATION TO HELP THE POOR?

Trudy Govier examines three divergent views on welfare. The first position is what she describes as the individualist position: In an affluent society, one ought not have any legal right to state-supplied welfare benefits. The second is the permissive position: In a society with sufficient resources, one ought to have an unconditional legal right to receive state-supplied welfare benefits. (That is, one's right to receive such benefits ought not to depend on one's behavior; it should be guaranteed.) The third is the puritan position: In a society with sufficient resources one ought to have a legal right to state-supplied welfare benefits; this right ought to be conditional, however, on one's willingness to work.[3]

The individualist view maintains the position that a person in need has no legitimate moral claim on those around him or her, and a society that leaves its citizens to beg or starve cannot rightly be held accountable for doing so. This view, which has some significant support in contemporary social thinking, manifests itself in libertarian theory and the writings of Ayn Rand and her devotees.[4] The individualist position establishes a high value on uncoerced personal choice where each person is an "individual actor." The individualist view insists that with the freedom to make decisions goes the responsibility for the consequences of those decisions. For example, persons have every right to spend their time in whatever capacity chosen. But if, as a result of this choice, they are unemployable, they ought not to expect others to labor on their behalf. This is because no one has a proper claim on the labor of others, or on the income ensuing from that labor, unless he can repay the laborer in a way acceptable to that laborer. Thus, since government welfare schemes provide benefits from funds gained largely by taxing earned income, people are forced to work to provide a standard of living for others.

According to Govier, the individualist position argues that money appropriated by government for social programs—of which a significant proportion is public support—may not necessarily be endorsed by working individuals. The substance of this argument is that the beneficiaries of these programs—those who do not work—are as though they have people working for them gratis. Supported by government and legitimate authority, these people are able to live off the income of others. People financially supporting others through public assistance do not do so voluntarily on a charitable basis; they are coerced by government. Libertarian John Hospers states:

> Someone across the street is unemployed. Should you be taxed extra to pay for his expense? Not at all. You have not injured him, you are not responsible for the fact that he is unemployed (unless you are a senator or bureaucrat who agitated for further curtailing of business which legislation passed, with the result that your neighbor was laid off by the curtailed business). You may voluntarily wish to help him out, or better still, try to get him a job to put him on his feet again; but since you have initiated no aggressive act against him, and neither purposefully nor accidentally injured him in any way, you should not be legally penalized for the fact of his unemployment.[5]

Govier argues that this orientation need not lack empathy for the poor and destitute.[6] In fact, people who possess libertarian beliefs may, out of empathy for the poor, give generously to charitable organizations from their own income. Moreover, a libertarian may believe as a matter of "empirical fact" that existing government programs do not actually help the poor. Instead, government programs support a cumbersome bureaucracy that depletes financial resources which, if untaxed, might be used by those with initiative to pursue entrepreneurial enterprises that in turn create jobs. Reflecting this position, Neil Gilbert and Gordon Tullock acknowledge that the welfare system itself is overextended, and they argue that this is largely because much of the funding is diverted to pay the salaries of middle-class service providers and overpaid bureaucrats.[7] The major thrust of the individualist position, based on Enlightenment ideals, is that each person owns his or her own body and labor. Thus each person has virtually an unconditional right to the income of which that labor can earn in a free and competitive market. John Locke states:

> Though the earth and all inferior creatures be common to all men, yet every man has a property in his own person. This nobody has a right to but himself.

> The labor of his body and the work of his hands, we may say, are properly
> his. Whatsoever, then he removes out of the state that nature hath provided
> and left it in, he hath mixed his labor with it, and joined to it something that
> is his own, and thereby makes it his property. It being by him removed from
> the common state nature placed it in, it hath by this labor something annexed
> to it that excludes the common right of other men. For his labor being the un-
> questionable property of the laborer, no man but he can have a right to what
> that is once joined to, at least where there is enough, and as good left in
> common for others.[8]

Taking part of a worker's earnings without that worker's consent is morally
illicit according to Locke and classical liberal theory. The fact that the government is the intermediary through which this deed is committed does not at
all change its moral status. Those in need should be cared for by charities or
through other organizations to which contributions are voluntary. Consequently, there is no moral justification for government-sponsored welfare
programs financed by taxpayers since the notion of private property is in no
way conditioned by social circumstances or the priority of a risk-management
scheme.

The permissive view is in direct contrast to the individualist view of welfare according to Govier.[9] According to this position, every individual in a society who has sufficient resources and necessities ought to be given the legal
right to social security without this right being contingent on individual behavior. Prior to the Personal Responsibility and Work Opportunity Reconciliation Act of 1996 (PRWORA), the permissive approach had been the dominant form of welfare policy in the United States. Aid is given if, and only if,
one can demonstrate the need for public assistance through "means testing."
This position holds that society must provide sufficient goods to everyone—
for example, food, clothing, shelter, and other basic needs—if and only if individuals cannot provide these basic needs for themselves. In fact, an individual's life is threatened if he or she lacks these basic goods. Thus a society
that takes no steps to change this state of affairs implies by its inaction that
the life of such a person is without substantive value. Based on the permissive position, a society that can rectify these circumstances, and does not, can
be justly accused of imposing upon the needy either death or lifelong deprivation. Those characteristics that make a person needy—whether they be illness, old age, insanity, feeblemindedness, inability to find paid work, or even
poor moral character—are insufficient to make him deserve the fate to which
an inactive society would in effect condemn him.

The adoption of a permissive view of welfare has significant practical implications. If there were a legal right, unconditional upon behavior, to a spec-
ified level of state-supplied benefits, then state investigations of the prospec-

tive welfare recipient could be kept to a minimum, as Govier asserts.[10] Why a person is in need, and whether he or she can or is willing to work, and what this person does while receiving welfare benefits is quite irrelevant to a person's right to receive those benefits. Even though the permissive position has been predominant in American society, it still presents a difficult challenge with respect to the perception of dependence and social stigma.[11] Even liberals such as Kenneth Arrow argue, "if everyone is guaranteed an income, no one will work."[12] In fact, in the late 1960s the permissive view manifested itself not only in traditional Aid to Families with Dependent Children (AFDC) programs, but also in the Family Assistance Plan of 1969. It was proposed by conservative President Richard Nixon and liberal Senator Patrick Moynihan. Moynihan argued in the late sixties that a guaranteed income would cost less than social security payments administered through the present bureaucracies. It was thought that these savings would result from a drastic cut in administrative costs especially if it were administered through income tax returns.[13]

Another form of permissive welfare policy is formulated by democratic socialist Michael Harrington. Harrington contends that "the poor get less out of the welfare state than any other group in America."[14] In fact, while not seeking to abolish the welfare state, Harrington argues that full employment—and if need be subsidies from tax revenues—is a better course of direction for the poor and underclass by freeing them from relying on welfare measures. Harrington states: "[I]f one followed a vigorous full-employment program, it would partly finance itself. It would, in Lyndon Johnson's characteristic phrase, 'turn tax eaters into taxpayers.'"[15] This alternate "permissive" measure is justified, according to Harrington, not because the federal government subsidizes big business and should also subsidize the poor; rather, the federal government can also subsidize work programs or encourage market measures that strive for full employment given the economic reality of classic market failures and imperfect competition.

The permissive view also asserts that private property is not an absolute right, but rather a limited right relative to the common good. That is, superfluous wealth can be redistributed legitimately if this is to the benefit of the most needy in society. This argument has been asserted by ancient philosophers such as Aristotle, to John Keynes in the early twentieth century, to present day neo-Marxists and communitarians.[16] The problem, according to these perspectives, is one of a market economy in which a grossly inequitable distribution of wealth is manifested both within and between nations. Frances Moore Lappé and Joseph Collins argue that "the market left to its own devices will concentrate wealth and purchasing power and therefore undermine its usefulness in meeting human needs."[17] According to Harrington, it makes no difference in how well-intended the capitalist class is in creating jobs for the poor, since capitalists would never undermine themselves and their profitability by freely paying people living wages. In fact, Harrington and other left-leaning scholars such as Harry Magdoff, Paul Sweezy, and Paul Baran believe that capitalism may never cure poverty and resolve the welfare dilemma even with limited government intervention. Harrington states:

> [T]he assumption of Keynesian social democracy that, with some adjustments at the edges, corporate-based growth would generate the solution to most of society's problems has to be abandoned. John F. Kennedy made a classic statement of this attitude when he said, "a rising tide lifts all boats." We know from the experience of the last quarter century that this is not true (and Kennedy himself had begun to suspect that fact). Indeed, one can fairly say that a rapidly rising tide will now sink some boats.[18]

Although Harrington advances a structural solution to ending poverty and welfare through subsidized work, he nevertheless argues for the enduring nature of a permissive welfare state as a byproduct of a capitalist system.

Another perspective, the puritan view of welfare, is a compromise position between the individualist and the permissive views. According to Govier, a person who works also helps to produce the goods that all use in daily living and, when paid, contributes through taxation to government endeavors.[19] Conversely, the person who does not work, according to this position, is not entitled to a share of the goods produced by others if he or she chooses not to take part in the labor involved. Unless this person can demonstrate that there is some justification for his or her not making the sacrifice of time and energy that others make, he or she has no legitimate claim to welfare benefits. However, if a person is disabled or unable to obtain work, this person needs to be supported by the community either indefinitely, in the case of a disabled person, or for a contingent period of time, in the case of the unemployed person. Moreover, if persons choose not to work, they would have to justify their choice to let others sacrifice on behalf of them. This notion, a version of what John Rawls refers to as the "free-rider principle," is a difficult position to rationally defend.[20] According to Govier, "to deliberately avoid working and benefit from the labors of others raises serious questions of equity."[21]

Based on these principles, the right to welfare is conditioned upon one's satisfactory accounting for his or her failure to obtain the necessities of life by his or her own efforts. An individual who is severely disabled, mentally or physically, or who for some other reason cannot work, is entitled to receive welfare benefits. Someone who chooses not to work is not entitled. This is currently the case in the United States, albeit in a limited way, even with the implementation of the new federal welfare policy of 1996, which places time limits on assistance. Thus a welfare system based on this puritan view—that is, on the relationship between welfare and work—provides a rationale for three interconnected principles. These three principles are: (1) those on welfare should never receive a higher income than the working poor; (2) if the income is higher, then eligibility should be only for a limited amount of time; and (3) a welfare policy should, in some way or other, incorporate incentives to work. The categories mentioned, according to Govier, presuppose that it is better to work than not to work and emerge naturally from the contingency that is at the basis of the puritan view: the goods essential for social security are products of the labor of some members of the community.[22] The continued supply of these social goods, with certain stipulated conditions attached, is nevertheless essential for a decent society under this perspective.

Conservative Mickey Kaus argues that a "workfare" program is a practical alternative to welfare. Because welfare payments may equal or exceed unskilled job pay, many do not seek work. He argues in effect that these two principles are violated by the past welfare schemes. Kaus further argues that if workfare is implemented, unemployed adults will find jobs before their welfare payments are stopped.[23] Critics of this position, such as Richard Cloward and Francis Fox Piven, argue that these programs are unrealistic. They point out that many year-round, full-time workers receive wages that are below the poverty level. Moreover, former AFDC mothers under this rubric would be fortunate to get any employment, and it is likely to be part-time, poorly paid, and lacking health and pension benefits. Nevertheless, the operating assumption of the puritan view is that welfare should not be a way of life and that neither the nation nor the states can afford the escalating costs. Kaus believes that welfare time limits and putting poor people to work will make working for benefits more equitable, restore family and community cohesion, and reduce crime and poverty.

Donna Shalala, former secretary of health and human services in the Clinton administration, asserted in the 1990s, the welfare system in the United States was a major problem. Shalala argued that the 1988 Family Support Act was an important initial step in "ending welfare as we know it." This law was intended to develop state-run programs that would help individuals who received welfare assistance to break away from their dependency on benefits through work, training, and education. Fundamental change, according to Shalala, did not follow. In reinforcing the puritan view, she asserted that a welfare reform strategy must encompass three major principles: work, responsibility, and ending intergenerational dependence on welfare. She concluded that these reforms would make welfare a transitional system leading to work. These important elements were critical components of the new 1996 welfare reform law. She argued that to truly make welfare policy transitional, special attention needed to be given to funding education, job training, childcare, and job creation. As Shalala saw it, basic human needs still needed to be secured in some fashion. The rational use of government in this capacity could be a source of support for people in need.

ASSESSMENT OF MODELS

The individualist perspective would abolish all nonoptional government programs that have as their goal the improvement of anyone's personal welfare. This rejection extends to health schemes, pension plans, and education, as well as to welfare and unemployment insurance. Suffice it to say, implementation of the individualist position would lead to sweeping changes. Furthermore, it will be claimed that on the whole, this non-scheme will bring beneficial consequences. This is reminiscent of policy strategies urged by the Austrian school of economics in which Friedrich von Hayek has argued that government intervention in society and the economy ultimately hurts the poor more than it helps them, though Hayek admits, in *The Road to Serfdom*, that there are people who would suffer some form of deprivation if welfare and other social security programs were simply terminated. Yet it is very difficult to assume, as does Tullock, that spontaneously developing charities would comprehensively address the needs of the poor. Nevertheless, the individualist seeks to identify the benefits that would accrue to the business community and to working people and their families if funding for these programs were drastically cut. The argument is that consumption would rise, hence production would rise, job opportunities would be extended, and there would be an economic boom—if only people could spend all their earned income as they desired. This economic growth would benefit both rich and poor alike.[24]

There are significant conditions that are necessary in order to render the individualist's optimism plausible. Workers and businesspersons would have to fund insurance schemes of various kinds, either for themselves or their workers. If they did have insurance to cover health problems, old age, and possible job loss, then they would have to pay for it. Hence consumers would not be spending most of their earned income on consumer goods, but rather on exorbitant insurance rates, especially if individuals or firms had to fund their own unemployment insurance. Furthermore, the goal of increased consumption and increased productivity must be questioned from an ecological viewpoint: many necessary materials are available only in limited quantities.[25] Scarce resources would need to be allocated—the economic implication is that prices would fluctuate according to this allocation. Finally, once society and the economy are liberated from welfare programs, it cannot be rationally assumed that those who are at the mercy of charities will improve their state, either materially or psychologically. Choice in charities might be every bit as expensive as government-supported benefit schemes are now. There is no guarantee that charities are more efficient in the utilization of funds than is the federal government. Thus the consequences of extreme individualism, or personal choice, do not easily translate into new and improved public policy.[26]

Today welfare schemes operating in the United States are almost without exception based upon the principles of the puritan view. For example, PRWORA ended AFDC, the largest entitlement program in United States history, and allowed states to establish their own programs within federal guidelines. Welfare benefits are now time-limited and are closely tied to work requirements that are intended to move welfare recipients off welfare and into the labor force. Welfare reform in the state of Arizona, under the title of EM-POWER Redesign, is a program that emphasizes work and promotes personal responsibility for one's and his or her dependents' well-being. Features of this law include a provision in which participants must sign a personal responsibility agreement. This means that a mandatory work requirement is stipulated. Participants must engage in work activities. Temporary deferrals are allowed for heads-of-household with a child under one, parents under age eighteen caring for a child under twelve weeks of age, high school students, persons who are disabled or caring for a disabled person, and victims of domestic violence. Related to this is the JOBStart program, which allows for a three-year demonstration project to evaluate the effect of replacing AFDC and food stamp benefits with wages from guaranteed employment in the private sector. Transportation to and from work is also part of this program. Nevertheless, this cashes out assistance and food stamp benefits for use by employers.

Time limits are also part of this legislation. This curtails adult eligibility for cash assistance to twenty-four months per sixty-month period. Good cause exceptions may be approved and a limited percentage of the population can be eligible for extensions. Children are not subject to this limit; they are subject to the federal five-year lifetime limit. School attendance is also important in local welfare reform in Arizona. Dependent children between six and sixteen years of age must attend school. Immunization of dependent children is also mandatory for temporary aid. Childcare assistance is provided for cash assistance recipients to engage in work activities. Families who leave cash assistance due to employment may receive up to twenty-four months of transitional childcare assistance. Childcare is allowed for working families with incomes below 135 percent of the federal poverty level.

This welfare model can be commended for its intent to place people back in the work force and encourage them to be contributors and stakeholders in society. On the other hand, this model can be criticized for its demoralization of recipients, who often must deal with several levels of government and are vulnerable to arbitrary interference on the part of administering officials. EMPOWER Redesign possesses mechanisms that are even more intrusive into the lives of its clientele. Welfare officials have the power to check on welfare recipients and cut off or limit their benefits under a large number of circumstances. The potential dangers to welfare recipients in terms of anxiety, threats to privacy, and loss of dignity are real. According to Tom Joe and Cheryl Rogers, welfare recipients experience bureaucratic rigidities that often result in the degradation, humiliation, and alienation of recipients. Joe and Rogers and Leonard Goodwin argue that there are too many instances of humiliation, leaving the impression that these are too easily found to be incidental aberrations. They further argue that concern over a welfare recipient's ability to work can easily turn into concern about how he or she lives, how many children he or she has, etc. In short, an almost dehumanizing invasion into the life of a welfare recipient results from puritan models of welfare.[27]

At this point it must be noted that bureaucratic checks and controls are not exclusively a feature of the puritan welfare system; permissive systems would have to incorporate them as well. Within those systems, welfare benefits would be given only to those whose income was inadequate to meet basic needs. There would be, however, no checks on "willingness to work," and there would be no need for welfare workers to evaluate the merits of the daily activities of recipients. If a guaranteed income system or a subsidized funding for work were administered through tax returns, the special status of welfare recipients would not be required." Govier claims, "They would no longer be singled out as a special group within the population. It is to be expected that living solely on government-supplied benefits would be psychologically easier in that type of situation."[28] In this sense it can be argued that a permissive scheme has more advantages than a puritan one. But the concern that most theorists would have regarding the permissive scheme relates to its costs and its dangers to the "work ethic." Thus if a guaranteed income or subsidized work scheme were adopted by the government, then incentives to work would disappear. The fear is that a great many people—even some with relatively pleasant jobs—might simply cease to work if they could receive nonstigmatized government money on which to live. The economic efficiency of society would be damaged as a result.

The counterargument to this position is that welfare benefits are set to ensure that only those who do not work have a life based on subsistence, that is, with an income sufficient for basic needs, and that they have a tolerable existence with an income regardless of why they fail to work. Govier argues that permissive welfare benefits will not finance luxury living for a family of five. She states: "[I]f jobs are adequately paid so that workers receive more than the minimum welfare income in an earned salary, then there will still be a financial incentive to take jobs. What guaranteed income schemes will do is to raise the salary floor. This change will benefit the many nonunionized workers in service and clerical occupations."[29] Furthermore, people do not work simply for money and the things it can buy. People work for other reasons, such as personal satisfaction and other intrinsic values. They also tend to be happier when their time is structured in some way, when they are active outside their own homes, when they feel themselves part of a project whose purposes transcend their particular egoistic ones—at least according to Goodwin. With these and other factors operating, Govier and others argue that in no way will the adoption of a permissive welfare scheme "be followed by a level of slothfulness which would jeopardize human well-being."[30]

The merits of individualism, puritanism, and permissivism must be analyzed with respect to their impact on the distribution of the goods necessary for well-being. Robert Nozick describes, from an individualist perspective, distributive justice schemes as "manna from heaven" policies that are taken unjustly from people by government and redistributed to nondeserving persons. Nozick has argued against the entire concept of distributive justice on the grounds that it presupposes the free gift of collective goods by taking other people's property and redistributing it. Nozick states:

> Whether it is done through taxation on wages or on wages over a certain amount, or through seizure of profits, or through there being a big social pot so that it's not clear what's coming from where and what's going where, patterned principles of distributive justice involve appropriating the actions of other persons. Seizing the results of someone's labor is equivalent to seizing hours from him and directing him to carry on various activities. If people force you to do certain work, or un-rewarded work, for a certain period of time, they decide what you are to do and what purposes your work is to serve apart from your decisions.[31]

The individualist attempts to justify extreme variations in income—with some people below the level where they can fulfill their basic needs—with reference to the fact of people's actual accomplishments. This view of welfare can be derived from Locke's doctrine of property. If labor is what makes the possession of property legitimate, then without labor one would not deserve to possess anything. Within this sort of framework, welfare benefits would be regarded as gifts conferred on those who did not deserve to receive them. Interpreting Locke, Charles Frankel states:

[W]elfare is the child of charity—it is associated with the notion of unearned re-
lief from distress. It is something that cannot be brought within the sphere of the
controlling doctrine that work is the sole justification for receiving any benefit
from others. Welfare activities, accordingly, have been regarded as essentially
exceptional in character; they deal with boundary-line conditions. The recipients
of welfare, if they are not always beyond the pale, are not quite within the pale
either." [32]

Consequently, the individualist stresses the unfairness of a system that would
do this, as it makes no attempt to distinguish between those who choose not
to work and those who cannot work. No one should be able to take advantage
of another under the auspices of a government program and institution. The
puritan scheme seeks to eliminate this possibility, and for that reason, the puritan strategy would argue, it is a more just scheme than the individualist or
permissive models.

Permissivists can best reply to this contention by acknowledging that any
instance of free-riding would be an instance where those working were done
an injustice, but by showing that any justice that the puritan preserves by
eliminating free-riding is outweighed by *injustice* perpetrated elsewhere. For
example, consider the children of the puritan's free riders. They will suffer,
more or less, for the negligence of their parents. Within the institution of the
family, the puritan cannot suitably deter the culpable without cruelly depriv-
ing the innocent. There is a sense, too, in which the puritan position does an
injustice to the many people on welfare who are free riders. It perpetuates the
notion that they are noncontributors to society and this doctrine, which is
oversimplified if not false, has a harmful effect upon welfare recipients. Suffice it to say, the puritan scheme addresses the need for human work and self-
fulfillment that comes from maintaining one's independence and dignity
while providing an opportunity to participate and contribute to society.

The permissivist position on social justice is not simply a matter of the distribution of goods, or the income with which goods are to be purchased. It is
also the matter of the protection of rights. Western societies claim to give their
citizens equal rights in political and legal contexts; they also claim to endorse
the larger conception of a right to life. Now it is possible to interpret these
rights in a limited and formalistic way, so that the duties correlative to them
are minimal. On the limited or negative interpretation, to assert that one has
a right to life is simply to say that others have a duty not to interfere with another's attempt to keep himself or herself alive. This interpretation of the right
to life is compatible with individualism as well as puritanism, at least insofar
as all three positions can find some common ground. But it is an inadequate
interpretation of the right to life and to other rights. Thus the right to life is
meaningless unless basic needs are made accessible to all persons, even those

parents of small children who are unable or refuse to work for basic needs. The obligation to support the right to life of these children emerges as a priority of justice in a democratic society. Similarly, the right to vote is virtually meaningless if one is starving and unable to get to the polls; a right to equality before the law is meaningless if one cannot afford a lawyer.[33]

Even a permissive welfare scheme will go only a small way toward protecting people's rights. It will amount to a meaningful acknowledgment of a right to life by ensuring income adequate to purchase food, clothing, and shelter—at a minimal level. These minimum necessities are presupposed by all other rights a society may endorse in that their possession is a precondition of being able to exercise these other rights. Such diverse philosophers as Aristotle and Marx have argued this position consistently in their works. The permissivist contends that all should receive at least the floor income, or as Bertrand Russell argued for, a "vagabond's wage," and that the individualists are tendentious and disingenuous to insist that taxation to support welfare schemes amounts to "legalized robbery."[34] Nevertheless, because it protects the rights of *all* within society, the permissive view can rightly claim a more precise notion of justice since it tends to promote greater equality—the right to life and access to basic needs and well-being—and secures human needs more comprehensively than the puritan and individualist positions. Yet all three approaches—permissive, puritan, and individualist—are suspect from a postmodern Marxist welfare perspective. It is exactly this discussion about equality in the United States that literally invites intense partisan politics, but simultaneously broaches the issues of class analysis and postmodern welfare policy.

NOTES

1. Nicholas Rescher, *Welfare: The Social Issues in Philosophical Perspective* (Pittsburgh, Pa.: University of Pittsburgh Press, 1972), 114.

2. Hugh Heclo, "The Social Question," in *Poverty, Inequality, and the Future of Social Policy*, eds. Katherine McFate, Roger Lawson, and William Wilson (New York: Russell Sage Foundation, 1995), 669.

3. Trudy Govier, "The Right to Eat and the Duty to Work," *Philosophy of the Social Sciences* 5 (June 1975): 123–143.

4. See any of Rand's works, such as *Atlas Shrugged* (New York: Random House, 1957); *Anthem* (Caldwell, Idaho: Caxton Printers, 1960); *The Virtue of Selfishness* (New York: New American Library, 1965); and *Capitalism: The Unknown Ideal* (New York: New American Library, 1966).

5. John Hospers, *Libertarianism: A Political Philosophy for Tomorrow* (Los Angeles: Nash Publications, 1971): 67.

6. Trudy Govier, "The Right to Eat and the Duty to Work."

7. Neil Gilbert, *Capitalism and the Welfare State* (New Haven, Conn.: Yale University Press, 1983); Gordon Tullock, "Private Charity, Public Aid," *Society* 23, no. 2 (January/February 1986); Gordon Tullock, *Wealth, Poverty, and Politics* (New York: Blackwell, 1988).

8. John Locke, *The Second Treatise on Government: An Essay Concerning the True Original, Extent and End of Civil Government* (New York: Oxford University Press, 1947), 17–18.

9. Govier, "The Right to Eat and the Duty to Work."

10. Govier, "The Right to Eat and the Duty to Work."

11. Leonard Goodwin, *Causes and Cures of Welfare: New Evidence on the Social Psychology of the Poor* (Lexington, Mass.: Lexington Books, 1983).

12. Kenneth Arrow, "Redistribution to the Poor: A Collective Expression of Individual Altruism," in *Poverty and Social Justice: Critical Perspectives*, ed. Francisco Jimenez (Tempe, Ariz.: Bilingual Press), 46.

13. Daniel Patrick Moynihan, *The Politics of a Guaranteed Income: The Nixon Administration and the Family Assistance Plan* (New York: Random House, 1973).

14. Michael Harrington, *The Other America* (New York: Macmillan, 1964), 161.

15. Michael Harrington, *The New American Poverty* (New York: Holt, Rinehart, and Winston, 1984), 244.

16. Renford Bambrough, *The Philosophy of Aristotle* (New York: A Mentor Book, 1963); Rodney G. Peffer, *Marxism, Morality, and Social Justice* (Princeton, N.J.: Princeton University Press, 1990); Tom Rochmore, *Marx after Marxism: The Philosophy of Karl Marx* (Malden, Mass.: Blackwell, 2002); Charles Taylor, "On Social Justice," *Canadian Journal of Political and Social Theory* 1 (Fall 1977).

17. Frances Moore Lappé and Joseph Collins, *World Hunger: Twelve Myths* (New York: Grove Press, 1986), 82.

18. Michael Harrington, *Socialism: Past and Future* (New York: A Mentor Book, 1992), 230.

19. Trudy Govier, "The Right to Eat and the Duty to Work."

20. John Rawls, *A Theory of Justice* (Cambridge, Mass.: Harvard University Press, 1971) 124, 136.

21. Govier, "The Right to Eat and the Duty to Work," 133.

22. Govier, "The Right to Eat and the Duty to Work."

23. Mickey Kaus, *The End of Equality* (New York: Basic Books, 1992).

24. Frederick von Hayek, *The Mirage of Social Justice*, vol. 2, in *Law, Legislation, and Liberty* (London: Routledge and Kegan Paul, 1982).

25. Robert Lekachman, *Greed Is Not Enough* (New York: Pantheon Books, 1982).

26. Lekachman, *Greed Is Not Enough.*

27. Tom Joe and Cheryl Rogers, *By the Few for the Few: The Reagan Welfare Legacy* (Lexington, Mass.: Lexington Books, 1981). Also see Leonard Goodwin, *Causes and Cures of Welfare.*

28. Govier, "The Right to Eat and the Duty to Work," 138–39.

29. Govier, "The Right to Eat and the Duty to Work," 139.

30. Govier, "The Right to Eat and the Duty to Work," 140.

31. Robert Nozick, "Distributive Justice," *Philosophy and Public Affairs* (Fall 1973), 68.

32. Charles Frankel, "The Moral Framework of Welfare," in *Welfare and Wisdom* (Toronto: The University of Toronto Press, 1966), 168.

33. James Sterba, *Morality and Social Justice* (Lanham, Md.: Rowman & Littlefield, 1996).

34. Bertrand Russell, "Proposed Roads to Freedom," in *Selected Papers of Bertrand Russell* (New York: Random House, 1955).

Chapter Six

The Decline of the Capitalist Welfare State

In short, the crisis of the welfare state was the consequence of its triumph, not the result of some original sin of an economic policy flawed from the outset.

—Michael Harrington, *Socialism: Past and Future*

Along with liberty and individualism, equality long has been understood to be a fundamental component of the American political culture. The French political philosopher Alexis de Tocqueville begins *Democracy in America* by writing:

No novelty in the United States struck me more vividly during my stay there than the equality of conditions. It was easy to see the immense influence of this basic fact on the whole course of society. . . . The more I studied American society, the more clearly I saw equality of conditions, the creative element from which each particular fact derived, and all my observations constantly returned to this nodal.[1]

From Tocqueville's perspective the egalitarian ethos of the democratic revolution was able to bloom more rapidly in the United States than elsewhere because the United States had been "born free" of feudalism. Careers were more open to individual talents and skills in the United States (except in the South, because of slavery) than in most other countries. He also believed that equality in America was both a source of dynamism (promoting mobility and prosperity) and a chronic source of discontent. In Tocqueville's words, "the more equal men are, the more insatiable will be their longing for equality."[2] Thus Tocqueville came to the melancholy conclusion that equality generates needs that never can be satisfied.

The fact that the United States is committed to equality has not meant that disputes over it have been avoided. Egalitarian questions have been deeply involved in most of the great dramas in American history: the American Revolution, the Jacksonian era, the Civil War and Reconstruction, the Populist–Progressive period, the New Deal, the Great Society, and the civil rights struggles of the 1960s and 1970s. According to Sidney Verba:

> In each period, challenging groups sought both political and economic equality, for themselves and on behalf of others. Inevitably, each battle led to some progress toward egalitarianism on both fronts. In the end, however, each upheaval did relatively little to redress inequalities in the distribution of income and wealth. The enduring and significant result of these historical battles was rather the achievement of greater political equality through the expansion of political rights or the dispersion of political influence. In other words, the principal legacy of the drives for equality in the United States has been a steadily increasing democratization.[3]

However, this "democratization" has not prevented the steadily increasing distribution of inequality taking place in the United States today.

America's seeming tendency to support egalitarianism has almost always been tempered by its support of liberty, individualism, self-reliance, limited government, and federalism. Such values are at times in conflict with public policies designed to promote equality, such as affirmative action or even in the case of California's CalWORKs program or Arizona's EMPOWER Redesign. There also has been a split among Americans concerning competing visions of equality—that is, equality of opportunity versus equality of outcome. These two views appeared to be similar at the time of the American Revolution because, as Gordon Wood writes, "it is widely believed that equality of opportunity would necessarily result in a rough equality of station, that as long as the channels of ascent and descent were kept open, it would be impossible for artificial aristocrats or overgrown rich men to maintain themselves for long."[4] Individuals pursuing their economic interests in unregulated markets would produce prosperity and equality. In the twentieth century, most egalitarians no longer believe that equal opportunity is a sufficient condition for achieving equal results. As Richard Ellis contends, "today, it is widely believed that the opportunity to compete creates unconscionable inequalities, and that the call for equal treatment is often little more than an excuse to perpetuate existing inequalities."[5] As a result, these two visions of equality, which were mutually supportive in our earlier history, have become more contentious in the latter half of the twentieth century.

Egalitarian notions also are associated with what can be defined as "the American Dream." Economists operationalize the American Dream when they point out that in much of the United States history the standard of living has doubled roughly every thirty years. Each generation expects to live considerably better than the previous one. When egalitarianism merges with American optimism, it becomes a society of "haves and will haves." This particular history and myth suggests that all can hope to share in United States' prosperity. For the Left, the American Dream has had a stifling effect on their efforts to mobilize the poor in support of redistributive programs because so many of the poor do not want to eliminate the rich—they tend to see their well-being as dependent upon the rich or, perhaps more to the point, they too desire to become like the rich. The poor and lower classes then become a threat to the wealthy and elite. As a result, Richard Cloward and Frances Fox Piven argue that the "natural" relationship between politics and economics, or politics and its insulation from public policy, is neither neutral nor coincidental. Large governments evolve through history in order to protect great accumulations of property and wealth. In societies where wealth and property are controlled by a select class of persons, a state develops to protect the interests of the "haves" from the "have-nots." As John Locke states, "the great and chief end . . . of Men's uniting into Commonwealths, and putting themselves under Government, is the Preservation of their Property."[6] Furthermore, Adam Smith, the founding father of capitalism, asserted that "the necessity of civil government grows up with the acquisition of valuable property. . . . Till there be property there can be no government, the very end of which is to secure wealth, and to defend the rich from the poor."[7]

Some theorists, such as John Maynard Keynes and John Kenneth Galbraith, argue that welfare state programs exist because their economic support systems are functional for capitalism.[8] The welfare state was constructed to pacify and depoliticize insurgent or potentially insurgent groups. Consequently, social welfare programs are thus seen as part of the strategy by which the ruling class governs, a strategy through which working people are enticed to cash in their political capacities and political intelligence for a pittance in material benefits. With the expansion of these programs, the body politic presumably grows more compliant to the demands of the capitalist class.[9] Others such as James O'Connor have argued that social welfare programs presumably contribute to profitability by lowering the costs incurred by employers in order to maintain a healthy and skilled labor force. Without these programs, employers would have to pay for health and education services directly, or raise wages to permit workers to purchase them.[10] While not rejecting these views necessarily, Cloward and Piven argue that to some large degree the welfare state has not turned out to be beneficial for a capitalist economy at all. Because of the income maintenance programs, "the reserve army is no longer quite so ready and willing to be called up in defense of profits . . .; it has always been recognized that the most effective way to 'regulate the poor' in the labor market is to close off access to alternative means of subsistence."[11]

A significant turning point for liberals in their orientation toward equality was reflected in President Lyndon Johnson's announcement, in June 1965, that equal opportunity was not enough to overcome the inequalities caused by racism. President Johnson proclaimed, "we seek . . . not just equality as a right and a theory but equality as a fact and equality as a result."[12] To this point Ellis concludes, "in the contemporary period, it has been the attempt to help blacks and other minorities that has perhaps contributed most to the collapse of the belief that securing equal process is sufficient to achieve more equal results."[13] Arguably, this shift has been costly from an electoral perspective for liberal Democrats because the idea of equality of opportunity has more public support and appears to be more compatible with the American political tradition than equality of results. To bring about an equality of results would seem to require a more intrusive government than most Americans want or are willing to finance.

Reacting to growing income disparities, many liberals such as John Kenneth Galbraith and Lester Thurow still advocate progressive income taxes and welfare policies to redistribute income from the rich to the poor.[14] Although he mentions a ceiling on income for the rich, Michael Parenti and more progressive thinkers argue for raising the living standards of the poor through more government sponsored work programs.[15] Conservative Mickey Kaus argues that liberals have created a whole repertoire of "fudge phrases" to avoid specifying that "they want 'to tilt the balance in favor of ordinary people'; they want 'a good deal more equality than we now have'; they believe 'the strong owe a duty to the weak'; they favor—in F.D.R.'s earlier version—the 'underprivileged' over the 'overpriviledged . . .'"[16] When liberals refuse to define the kind of equality they want, however, it arouses conservative suspicions that liberals have a secret agenda.

Galbraith and Thurow concede that competitive markets are efficient, but claim that government interference may be necessary to assure social justice. Without social justice modern political systems cannot sustain their legitimacy. If a capitalist system continues to create increased inequalities and increased personal insecurities, liberals fear that the democratic political system will be undermined.[17] Thurow cautions: "[S]ince accurate data have been kept, beginning in 1929, America has never experienced falling real wages for a majority of its work force while its per capita GDP was rising. In effect, we are conducting an enormous social and political experiment—something like putting a pressure cooker on the stove over a full flame and waiting to see how long it takes to explode."[18] As Robert Reich, President Bill Clinton's first secretary of labor, suggests: "unlike the citizens of most other nations, Americans have always been united less by a shared past than by shared dreams of a better future. If we lose the common future, we lose the glue that holds our nation together."[19]

In general, American conservatives tend to emphasize individual freedom far more than equality according to theorists such as Lawrence Mead and George Gilder. They argue, as did ancients such as Aristotle, that while all share an equal human nature, it would be an injustice to treat unequals as equals.[20] Whereas liberals believe that equality and liberty can be reconciled to some significant degree, conservatives do not. While liberals tend to think of equality as promoting social justice, conservatives believe that equality brings about stifling uniformity, leveling, and bureaucratic oppression. For conservatives, according to Conrad Waligorski, "[A]ny attempt to apply [equality] to groups or to consider the conditions for equality, beyond identical treatment by the law and equal right to attempt to compete in free markets, is illegitimate and must destroy freedom. Beyond these narrow limits, freedom and equality are mutually exclusive."[21] In essence, the modern conservative is arguing that America's yearning for equality should be pacified by the condition of equality of opportunity.

John Rawls, Sar Levitan, and other liberals are concerned that the unequal access to resources in markets prevents participants from being able to compete effectively, while conservatives, such as Robert Nozick and Robert Rector, argue that market rationality will produce the best results in the long run. Liberals, nevertheless, are skeptical at the conservative notion of equality of opportunity, stated best by R. H. Tawney: "the equal right to be unequal."[22] Responding to this, conservative social critic R. Emmett Tyrrell reacts, "our only safeguard . . . from all the baseness that issues from equalitarians is reverence for personal liberty as the ultimate political value. . . . The intelligent quest is for the free society with equality of opportunity. The quest for equality of result is the path to the widest inequality of all: despotism."[23] Likewise, conservative economist Milton Friedman warns: "a society that puts equality—in the sense of equality of outcome—ahead of freedom will end up with neither equality nor freedom."[24]

These differing perspectives toward equality suggest increasing hostility between liberals and conservatives. While for liberals equality is a moral incentive leading to a more socially just society, for conservatives it is economically counterproductive, politically dangerous, and a demagogic appeal to envy. Liberals (Galbraith, Thurow, Piven, and Cloward) tend to believe that freedom can be threatened by growing inequalities; conservatives (Hayek, Friedman, Mead, and Nozick) are confident that personal freedom will be sacrificed if government attempts to reduce disparities. This final conservative scenario seems to carry the day philosophically and explains why the permissive model of welfare has been rejected. Thus the welfare state appears to have currently reaffirmed the puritan model with some individualist dimensions, as far as time limits are concerned.

RAWLS, LIBERAL DEMOCRATIC THEORY, AND THE WELFARE STATE

Liberal democratic theory has traditionally justified the existence of the welfare state as a buffer to a free market system. One of the chief spokespersons today for this version of the welfare state is John Rawls, whose monumental work, *A Theory of Justice*, has influenced most of the second half of the twentieth century. Being faithful to liberal tradition, Rawls sets out to justify the philosophical basis of liberal society that defines human rights in terms of the maximum amount of freedom and autonomy for all persons. Yet for Rawls, it is problematic for a society to posit some universal objective concept of justice. Recognizing this, Rawls establishes as a starting point, a hypothetical situation from behind a "veil of ignorance." Behind this veil, parties know neither their individual natural abilities, nor their position in society. By implication, then, they would not know what their position would be once the agreed-upon concept of justice were implemented, though according to theorists such as Derek Phillips, this may be virtually impossible to accomplish.[25]

Though Phillips's critique of Rawls's original position may be on the mark, Rawls's reconstruction of the liberal tradition, nevertheless, is built on what Rawls describes as a "general conception" of justice. This conception is a normative standard for determining which inequalities in society are justified and which are not. Rawls thus formulates this standard by asserting that, "all social values—liberty and opportunity, income and wealth, and the bases of self-respect—are to be distributed equally unless an unequal distribution of any, or all, of these values is to everyone's advantage."[26] Here Rawls's special conception of justice, and ultimately his rationale for welfare, consists of essentially describing, at least theoretically, the way justice should be promoted in U. S. culture and constitutional decree. The heart of this theory is based on a procedural "fairness" that contains two basic principles. The first claims a principle of basic equal liberties for all, in that "each person is to have an equal right to the most extensive total system of basic liberties compatible with a similar system of liberty for all."[27] The second asserts an equality that negotiates or conditions fairness, in that "social and economic inequalities are to be arranged so that they are both: (a) to the greatest benefit of the least advantaged . . . and (b) attached to offices and positions open to all under conditions of fair equality of opportunity."[28] Thus the "difference principle," which reprioritizes social relationships "to the greatest benefit of the least advantaged," provides the rationale that "everyone benefit[s] from economic and social inequalities,"[29] which according to Rawls, "would make everyone better off."[30]

In Rawls's theory the two principles of justice are not of equal weight. They are ordered "lexically." This order of priority is one "which requires us to satisfy the first principle in the ordering before we move on to the second. . . . A principle does not come into play until those previous to it are either fully met or do not apply."[31] Thus the first principle, the principle of equal liberty, has an "absolute weight" and takes priority over the second principle, which calls for basic societal structures designed to benefit the least advantaged. "[L]iberty," according to Rawls, "can be restricted only for the sake of liberty."[32] The basic liberties that the first principle defends are the fundamental rights of liberal democracy. Here, it is important to keep in mind how Rawls's notion of liberty is restricted to the equal right to vote, eligibility for public office, freedom of speech and assembly, freedom of conscience and thought, the right to own property, and freedom from arbitrary arrest and seizure. "These liberties," according to Rawls, "are all required to be equal by the first principle, since citizens of a just society are to have the same basic rights."[33] Rawls surmises that this ordering should not be objectionable to the poor or those who are otherwise disadvantaged because they are guaranteed the same liberty as the well off, by the first principle. At the same time, the second principle assures the poor that whatever inequalities exist in the economic sphere—as the result of increased productivity, efficiency, and economic growth—will be to their benefit. In other terms, in Rawls's version of liberalism the question of satisfying social and economic needs arises only after the basic liberal rights have been secured. There can be no trade-offs between the right of liberty and such rights as the right to food or housing or work. In fact, Rawls does not consider economic claims rights. Additionally, he does not theoretically defend welfare rights, but sees them simply as political arrangements that can be negotiated in a democratic society. Consequently for Rawls, "social justice is the principle of rational prudence applied to an aggregate conception of the welfare of the group,"[34] and "injustice, then, is simply inequalities that are not to the benefit of all."[35]

Can Rawls coherently maintain the priority of liberty and still defend the view that the goods of liberty, opportunity, income, wealth, and self-respect are to be equally distributed unless inequalities are to the benefit of the poor in society? Unfortunately he does not address this question directly, whereas for example, Marxists and socialists would argue directly for a redistribution of wealth and limitation on liberties.[36] Karl Marx asserts that "right can never be higher than the economic structure of society and the cultural development conditioned by it."[37] Yet Rawls contends that there are cogent arguments which, if factual and true, would lead to the conclusion that liberalism, manifested in capitalism, is incompatible with basic notions of justice.[38] Notwithstanding, what Rawls tries to do with his fundamental principles of justice is to prevent others from suffering as a result of others' liberality. For Rawls, the most humane social institutions will be those in which the many beliefs and values are pursued in such a way that the institution continues to protect liberty and its "lexical" priority.

Many significant questions are pursuant to Rawls's position. For example, why is it that Rawls posits liberty as the prior good for society and not equality? In other words, equality could be a major supposition upon which to base social, political, and economic relationships just as easily as liberty. On this point Rawls is ambivalent. Rawls believes that people are not unconcerned about other values such as equality. His general conception of justice calls for an equal distribution of "primary social goods" unless inequality will benefit those who are worse off. Primary goods, according to Rawls's definition, are "things which it is supposed a rational man wants whatever else he wants."[39] They include liberty, opportunity, income, wealth, and self-respect. These goods are desirable to those in very different types of societies—for example, both to those living in advanced industrial societies and those in societies near or below the level of subsistence. However, liberals themselves, such as H. L. A. Hart, are prepared to admit in their critique of Rawls that it may be naive or pretentious for Rawls to point out to a starving person that he or she is politically "free" to eat whatever food can be earned.[40] So too, this may be simplistic to argue that a single mother with three children is politically free to pursue whatever rational ends she chooses without public support, time-limited or otherwise.

In response to this criticism, Rawls is willing to acknowledge that the provisions of a system of equal civil liberties will be of no less value to the poor, and that these liberties can be negotiated to advance the cause of those most in need. Thus Rawls's general conception of justice appears to call for distributing these primary goods within societies and between societies in such a way that the least advantaged will benefit. A trade-off between individual liberty and other social goods seems permissible by his general conception of justice in at least some social situations. Rawls himself admits this, for he acknowledges that the priority of liberty can be limited "if it is necessary to raise the level of civilization"[41] to the point where basic needs have been generally met and where individual liberty can reasonably be called the primary value. Later Rawls also moves beyond basic needs to declaring that liberty can be placed in check, "if it is necessary to *enhance* the quality of civilization so that in due course the equal freedoms can be enjoyed by all."[42]

This tension within Rawls's theory reveals a fundamental problem facing the liberal theory of rights, especially as it manifests itself in current welfare policy. The defense of liberty in current culture has become an urgent and central concern. Generally, the resistance offered, primarily by libertarians and conservatives, to restrictions of civil and political rights provides strong evidence for the reality of this concern. At the same time, inequalities in levels of economic development make inescapable the question of the legitimacy of restricting the economic liberty of the rich in the interests of those in extreme deprivation. Rawls's theory, and the liberal tradition it represents, provides some substantive support for the poor and marginalized in society, but ultimately this same theory lacks an adequate strategic answer to guarantee subsistence for the poor, since welfare policies can and have been negotiated away in current welfare policy. Rawls states:

> To be sure, it is not the case that when the priority of liberty holds, all material wants are satisfied. Rather these desires are not so compelling as to make it rational for the persons in the original position to agree to satisfy them by accepting a less than equal freedom. The account of the good enables the parties to work out a hierarchy among their several interests and to note which kinds of ends should be regulative in their rational plans of life. Until the basic wants of individuals can be fulfilled, the relative urgency of their interest in liberty cannot be firmly decided in advance. It will depend on the claims of the least favored as seen from the constitutional and legislative stages.[43]

Given the market's precarious and independent nature, current welfare policy assumes too much in that the market itself will provide a living wage inclusive of decent housing, food, transportation, health care, childcare, etc. A permissive form of welfare policy that subsidizes private sector work programs might best support this position and thus promote greater social justice and cohesion within communities. Public administrators and policy analysts are arguing for a "guaranteed adequate income," which would in no way delegitimize the emphasis on work, contribution, participation, and self-esteem with regard to receiving public support. It would provide choices for people to utilize in relation to their unemployed status. This would include anywhere from receiving a flat sum of money for subsistence to government work programs that pay a living wage.[44]

Nevertheless, if Rawls's theory of justice states that liberty can be restricted through legislative means, and if the claims (welfare rights) of the least favored in society are subject to constitutional and legislative interpretations, then "power" ultimately becomes the criterion for social relationships. David Easton defines power as a "relationship in which one person or group is able to determine the actions of another in the direction of the formers' own ends."[45] Thus power relationships result from the interests of the participants in a social relationship. In turn, these interests are defined in part by wider economic and cultural forces. For Easton, the point is that power is used not only to pursue interests, but also to predefine the field of choice within which one must then define one's interests. Following this same line of thought, Richard Merelman states, "what makes one person or group so much more powerful than others are those very others who give him or her their empowering responses."[46] Thus Marxists and neo-Marxists argue that the institutional and cultural structure of a society will reflect whomever possesses or lacks power. Likewise, Michael Zweig argues that power is primarily a matter of social class, not outcome.[47] Still others, such as Michel Foucault, argue that both conflict and power need to be understood in terms of their unique social logic and history. Foucault concludes that universal notions of conflict, such as those espoused by Marxists, must be abandoned since power can be and is located in dimensions other than the state. Power, for Foucault, is a tool that can be used for legitimization or domination, and which needs to be understood in terms of "local, flexible, and provisional discourses whose value is proven by their political engagement, specifically one focused on resistance."[48] Consequently, Foucault argues for a postmodern approach where power is understood as a tool for resistance on behalf of marginalized communities. He states, "the role for theory seems to me to be just this: not to formulate the global systematic theory which holds everything in place, but to analyze the specificity of mechanisms of power, to locate the connections and extensions, to build little by little a strategic knowledge."[49]

WELFARE AND "POSTMODERN" CAPITALISM

In the contemporary political discourse taking place among those who assume a critical, oppositional stance to the demise of welfare, a significant question is being posed as to whether the emancipatory potential of modernity (e.g., Rawls), which expressed its resistance to domination in the universal terms of liberal justice, reason, and progress, is now at an end.[50] Theorists such as Peter Leonard tend to answer this question in the affirmative, precisely because of the new 1996 welfare policy. According to Leonard, postmodern deconstruction challenges modernism's attempt to uncover a universal rational principle or scientific system aimed at the betterment of humanity.[51] Rooted in Enlightenment philosophy, modernism has manifested itself today in rational and universal strategies from politics to economics. Steven Seidman argues that modernism leads to the domination of others.[52] This is because, according to Seidman, the sweeping universal natures of grand theories such as socialism or capitalism are themselves rigid and dogmatic.

Modernity as a historical period in Western culture may be seen as having its origins in the Age of Enlightenment, which began toward the end of the eighteenth century. Intellectually, this school of thought asserts that reason and the scientific method are the foundations upon which society can progress and humanity can be emancipated from ignorance.[53] Capitalism and socialism as rival versions of modernity have both promised emancipation; socialism as a political and economic system has for all intents and purposes collapsed, and the other, capitalism, now transformed into a global reality, has yet to demonstrate that it can solve the issue of poverty on both a domestic and international level. Nevertheless, the intellectual architects of modernism (e.g., Kant, Smith, Rousseau, Hegel, Marx, Mills, Rawls, Nozick, Friedman) are convinced—from diverse perspectives—that modernity and autonomous reason are the vehicles for emancipation.[54] Postmodernists, on the other hand, argue that modernity has represented, in practice, a Eurocentric, patriarchal, and destructive triumphalism over populations and over nature itself. Modernity, it is maintained, represents the "triumph of the West" reflected in colonialism and postcolonial domination, according to both Seidman and Leonard.[55] It is claimed that the interests of Western capitalism lead to the attempted homogenization of a world with diverse cultures, beliefs, and histories; nevertheless, postmodern neo-Marxists such as Habermas attempt to salvage some elements of modernity by arguing that modernity, though imperfect, can still emphasize a concept of reason based on egalitarian communication and the development of consensus amongst pluralities.[56]

Zygmut Bauman argues that, as grand theories of modernism, capitalism and socialism are simply a family quarrel inside modernity—it is a quarrel about how best to implement modernity.[57] Furthermore, Bauman argues that the value of modernity's world-view is now in question. Postmodernity's iconoclastic position, for Bauman, has helped dismiss the assumptions of an old, now-discredited order such as modernity. Bauman argues, nonetheless, that the erosion of modernity's vision of the world leaves the individual and society without the authority to identify what is true, good, and just. Whether or not postmodernity will provide a structure for promoting justice for the poor via a welfare state, Bauman remains skeptical. Bauman believes that modernity is self-destructive, and postmodernity follows down the same path. Bauman states:

> The main feature ascribed to "postmodernity" is thus the permanent and irreducible pluralism of cultures, communal tradition, ideologies. . . . Things which are plural in the postmodern world cannot be arranged in a revolutionary sequence, or seen as each other's inferior or superior stages; neither can they be classified as "right" or "wrong" solutions to common problems. No knowledge can be assessed outside the context of the culture, tradition, language game, etc., which makes it possible and endows it with meaning. Hence no criteria of validation are

available which could be themselves justified "out of context." Without universal standards, the problem of the postmodern world is not how to globalize superior culture, but how to secure communication and mutual understanding between cultures.[58]

The key to making some sense of postmodernism, for Bauman, is to embrace postmodernism as a form of social criticism.[59] Others, like Ben Agger, influenced by the thinking of Habermas argue that postmodernism only strengthens Marxism as an ongoing critique of the excesses of capitalism.[60] Bauman's response to this position is that social critique, from Marx to Habermas, has claimed legitimacy by typically appealing to universal abstractions and social laws. A postmodern social critique, however, would preserve the emancipatory hopes of the modern but without the anchor of any theoretical certitude. In this way, postmodernism dispels any myth of a messianic system of belief or social theory that is, according to Bauman, "the faith in a historical agent waiting in the wings to take over and to complete the promise of modernity using the levers of the political state. . . ."[61] Thus postmodern critics imagine change as less millennial; they look less to the state as an agency of change or support. Local, private organizations thus act in a democratic capacity to provide for the legitimate needs of communities. Moreover, postmodern critics such as Bauman, Habermas, Foucault, Jameson, and Baudrillard gesture more toward a postmodern criticism whose aim is to enlighten citizens to their unique role as historical agents in resisting postmodern capitalism (international capital and market consumerism) which they believe ultimately threatens to diminish freedom and political democracy.[62] For these theories, capitalism on a local and international scale cannot solve its crisis tendencies and will not be able to provide adequately for the basic human needs of all people. Therefore postmodern capitalism must be resisted in an enlightened manner.

Critics of capitalism argue that under the old imperialist system capitalism did not have to organize all the various forms of production; it simply had to control them.[63] In many colonies there were enclaves of subsistence agriculture that were older and more traditional. The colonizers simply made workers toil longer in the fields, in their traditional methods, and then extracted tribute from them. However, with each new stage of capitalist development, certain enclaves were destroyed, assimilated, and adapted into capitalism itself.[64] For example, capitalist agricultural adaptations have included the green revolution, innovations in informational technologies, atomic energy, cybernetics, chemical products, and hybrids. This has resulted in older, more traditional methods of farming being replaced by agribusiness, while robots have replaced craftsmen. Yet the penetration of capital is not limited to areas of agribusiness and technologies; it is also assimilated into the unconscious, according to Fredric Jameson, by means of culture and the media.[65] This can be discovered from media stereotypes and symbols that are supplanted within the minds of people. These images are filtered through television, movies, radio, newspapers, billboards, Internet, etc., on a twenty-four-hour basis. With this tremendous explosion of information and simultaneous infusion of values—in this case capitalist because of its methods of controlling wealth, and bourgeois because of prevailing concern for the acquisition of material interests and emphasis on subsequent respectability—people's desires are often formed and patterned on these stereotypes. The absolute criterion for this is financial profit. Thus the capitalist-media system imprints this into the minds of people and perpetuates its own existence. This is the foundation of what Jameson defines as postmodern capitalism.[66]

An entire way of life, not only in the United States but internationally as well, is organized around this form of capital.[67] Since the lives of individuals are so thoroughly integrated into the workings of a postmodern capitalist system, critical distance from this phenomenon may be difficult to achieve. This is because postmodern capital is simply an accepted part of people's lives in which there is really no substantial critique of the system. In fact, the resistance to any other consideration or variation of capital is generally met with skepticism.[68] The reason for this unconditional acceptance—and simultaneous resistance—is that the entire postmodern capitalist system itself has developed more subtle yet ubiquitous dimensions within its dynamic nature. It is precisely through the conduit of the media that postmodern capitalism has been embedded universally in the psyches of people to constantly and habitually consume. This form of "consumer capitalism," according to Jameson,

> constitutes the purest form of capitalism to have yet emerged, a prodigious expansion of capital into hitherto uncommodified areas. This purer capitalism of our time thus eliminates the enclaves of pre-capitalist organizations it had hitherto tolerated and exploited in a tributary way. One is tempted to speak in this connection of a new and historically original penetration and colonization of Nature and the Unconscious: that is, the destruction of pre-capitalist Third World agriculture by the Green Revolution, and the rise of the media and the advertising industry.[69]

The power of social critique is uncommodified and thus subsumed by capitalist culture through what Jameson describes as the "colonization of the Unconscious."[70] As Edward Herman and Noam Chomsky observe, the media has played a large role in nurturing uncritical reflection—especially television, capitalism's most ubiquitous tool—that has, in essence, formatted the human consciousness so that the very possibility of thinking in ways that are self-critical appear to be circumspect.[71] Herbert Marcuse and the New Left have argued that originality as a concept has been defined by capitalist culture's images disguised as a new form of control. What has emerged is a new type of fetishism, manifested at times in crass and even vulgar talk shows that operate under the pretense of a forum or exchange of ideas.

Jameson asserts that the "subversive contents" of history (censored perspectives critical of postmodern capitalism) have been forgotten or simply dismissed by what he describes as the process of "schizophrenic disjunction."[72] This disjunction, he argues, is the result of postmodern capitalism's global captivity of people's minds, hearts, and values. Thus any attempt to change the world, or move people away from a self-centered, consumeristic worldview, becomes increasingly problematic. To counter this disjunction, Jameson argues for a commitment to postmodern resistance, which he believes contains the seeds to check this uncritical and unconscious perspective. For Jameson, in this sense, a community and lifestyle of "resistance" provides the self-critical distance needed to check the excesses of postmodern capitalism while simultaneously promoting justice within concrete settings.[73]

Still for Jameson, it is easy to miss the critical point of contemporary postmodern capitalist ethos: the trivial productions of the culture (television shows, movies, fashionable clothing, stylish automobiles, Britney Spears and Pepsi, Lebron James and Nike, etc.) are its very driving force and conduit for profits and simultaneous exploitation.[74] The consumption of commodities driven by media lore has become, for Jameson, a powerful symbolic force that gives expression to both a contemporary moral code and social hierarchy. For social critics such as Jean Baudrillard, this form of capital consumerism is now the axis of culture.[75] Conformity to this unwritten but powerful code, for Baudrillard, is the force that drives consumer culture in which people no longer buy products based upon the values of need and utility, but rather on the conformity to the code of consumption. This form of "conspicuous consumption," as Thorstein Veblen describes it in *The Theory of the Leisure Class*, is according to Baudrillard a form of play for the rich, whereas for the middle class and poor, commodity consumption gives expression to a Nietzschean "slave morality."[76] It is precisely the design of the capitalist class to keep certain sectors and social classes within society captive to the consumeristic trends of postmodern capitalism. The rationale for this strategy is the expansion of markets and increased profits. Consequently, Baudrillard argues that "certain poorer classes are consigned to finding their salvation in objects, consecrated to a social destiny of consumption."[77]

In effect, the subtext of advanced postmodern capitalist culture can be understood as a radical dislocation from oneself, others, and community, as Jameson and Baudrillard believe. This new cultural subtext creates a "hyperreality" or "simulation" in which consumers are immersed in a media-created world that is passed off as reality itself. In this sense the capitalist culture and its habituated consumers prefer the hyper-real to the real which, according to

Baudrillard, "is no longer a question of false representation of reality (ideology), but of concealing the fact that the real is no longer real."[78] The recent success of reality TV programs, such as *The Osbournes*, *Survivor*, and *Scare Tactics* (a post-modern version of the 1960's *Candid Camera*) offer insights into this new subtext of capitalist culture. For Baudrillard, this is how a media-driven, postmodern capitalist society can divert attention from the substantive issues at hand (i.e., the causes of hunger, oppression, and environmental exploitation) with no analysis of the media-capitalist system that operates automatically to the benefit of increasing consumption and profitability.[79] Nevertheless, what is at issue here is an unspoken code of conformity, "commodity consumption," which is deeply embedded in the culture and psyches of a postmodern capitalist society, perpetuating itself through marketing extravaganzas to maximize profits.[80] Here the very nature of postmodern capitalism, based on habitual consumption, threatens to undermine the well-being of the planet by endless consumption of natural resources and commodities. Thus Jurgen Habermas, Max Horkheimer, and other postmodern neo-Marxists argue that the result of postmodern bourgeois society is in social crisis.[81]

Based on this analysis of postmodern capitalism, the rationale for a welfare state has become increasingly obscure, that is, if consumeristic capital is a significant factor in the economic interactions of a society.[82] As the acquisition for greater wealth and material consumption increases, the rational justification for economic support for the poor (through welfare policy) takes on less significance, for Leonard. Thus the domination of the state through postmodern capitalism, for Bauman, epitomizes the contradiction between domination and emancipation that has historically been an issue unique to modernity.[83]

Postmodernists argue that the old, liberal, and social democratic welfare state is under attack not only by the radical Right, but as part of the overall challenge to modernity and its knowledge claims. These views assert that welfare, even with the 1996 welfare law in the United States, is still rooted in modern domination. This is because modernity focuses on the organization of welfare as a manifestation of modernity within a state system of surveillance, monitoring, and control.[84] While postmodernists would agree that it is possible to envisage a form of welfare that reflects the emancipatory side of modernity, they would nevertheless argue that a reconstructed project of emancipation is central to the future of human welfare. According to Leonard, this must be built upon "the liberator potential of the whole idea of emancipation still expressed, sometimes in muted form, within socialist, feminist, anti-racist and other struggles against domination."[85]

Here the question is what to do about welfare as well as how to theorize about it.[86] The postmodern emphasis on difference and its accompanying

disillusionment with "big government" solutions to social problems leads to
a focus on the liberatory potential for local, small-scale forms of welfare,
community-based advocacy, and consumer-controlled projects and agencies.
These organizations of welfare, close to the people they serve, are able, it is
argued, to relate to the diverse and unique needs of specific populations with
their particular configurations of gender, class, culture, ethnicity, and other
social characteristics.[87] (Examples could be the Urban League, Chicanos Por
La Causa, Habitat for Humanity, etc.). In fact, Saul Alinsky and the "people
power" movement of the 1960s may very well have been responsible for the
beginnings of this postmodern trend, especially by influencing those who
started to see that local government initiatives made more political sense
than federal solutions. But such postmodern political solutions—micropolit-
ical resistance rather than the modern mass politics of confronting and attempting to win state power—pose serious problems. As Leonard asserts, in
relinquishing the universalistic ideas of welfare, more credence is given to
the neoconservative political discourse of less government and continued
"devolution." Parties traditionally of the Left or center-Left who have always embraced this same political agenda are not given serious credit for
their critiques of mammoth government and their advocacy to consequently
bypass government.[88] What is different is that this new conservative discourse on the nature of government and welfare aims to drastically reduce
state social expenditures, establish residual lower-cost forms of welfare,
fragment opposition, and divide sites of resistance, all in the name of local
diversity and control. The "greater good" espoused by this right-wing discourse is that leaner models of welfare using minimal state resources (or its
entire elimination) serve ultimately to improve a country's competitiveness
in the global market through reducing corporate taxation, increasing the rate
of return on capital, reducing labor costs, and returning to the traditional
virtues of family cohesiveness and hard work.[89]

In attempting to ameliorate government "responsiveness," conservatives
and libertarians have focused on theories of bureaucratization.[90] An argument put forth by David Ellwood is that government bureaucracy tends to
accumulate increasing power to itself, thus undermining the political con-
stituencies it is intended to serve.[91] Thus the de-bureaucratization of government is in order through what has been coined a "public choice." This
means that the managerial hierarchies of government are to be replaced by
more flexible market exchanges. In this case, the underlying premise is that
market structures such as those found in the private sector work best and
that this model will naturally improve the public sector.[92] This also translates into the shrinking of the welfare state and the emergence of a post-
welfare political agenda. As a result, one salient feature of postmodernity is

the strengthening of market forces at the expense of the historically strong role of the nation state.[93] Recommodification through the twin processes of the privatization of the public sector and the deregulation of the private sector has occurred in the Western capitalist societies as well. As Michael Rustin states:

> [T]he underlying purpose of this [strategy] was to remove collectivist threats to capital accumulation and authority, and to give private capital access to potential markets (in health, insurance, pensions, education and training, transportation, energy, prison building and management) from which it had been previously excluded. Capital as a whole sought to gain by recommodifying sectors recently excluded from the market, and by the disorganization of resistance to capital which followed from the restoration of market disciplines.[94]

The modernization of Western capitalism in the twentieth century saw the emergence of a "mixed economy" as a result of the rationalization of the relationship between individual interests represented by the market and the public interest represented by the state. In this symbiotic relationship the market economy provided the state with resources, mainly through the mechanism of taxation, and the state provided the market with planning (or "steering") as well as subsidies for social and technological risks. Richard Green and Lawrence Hubbell argue that this arrangement is now breaking down.[95] Consequently, due to the accumulation of fiscal deficits, failures of bureaucratic planning, negative effects of bureaucratic regulations, and intensified global competition, support for state intervention has fallen and the role of markets has grown. David Cheal, however, argues that "a predictable consequence of the shrinking of the welfare state and the expanded market competition is an increase in economic inequality. The pluralization of lifestyles in postmodern societies is therefore accompanied by the polarization of incomes."[96]

Addressing this welfare problem, Seidman argues that despite postmodernism's reluctance to envisage a mass struggle for justice other than at the grassroots level, postmodernism has something to offer in terms of an ethics that might underpin a new collective politics of human and social welfare.[97] Commentary on the political potential and limitations of the new social movements and politics of identity, and their relationship to struggles over welfare, leads to a preliminary discussion of possibilities of an organized solidarity emerging from a politics of difference. Seidman argues that, on its own, postmodernism is unable to provide an intellectual or practical basis for the kind of mass politics necessary to support a new welfare project. Yet, Leonard argues that as a movement based on the possibility of constructing a party as a confederation of diversities—through strategies of collective resistance and welfare support—postmodernism can provide a vision for organized alliances among a range of social movements. Leonard argues that this in turn will create political momentum for an increased demand by society for social capital.[98] It can do this by providing a structure in which each social movement pursues its own vision and interests, but with the potential for solidarity rooted in a commitment to the struggle to meet the concrete human needs of the poor.[99] In this sense postmodernism can be understood as a cultural and political critique of the present state of affairs, and a useful tool in attempting the support of welfare rights. For both Leonard and Seidman contemporary postmodern culture has thus turned to the method of embracing resistance as a strategy for attempting to maintain some dimension of justice on behalf of the poor. Albeit, postmodern welfare has barely served as a stopgap in addressing the welfare rights of people during the enactment of PRWORA. Whether postmodern "communities of resistance" can help the poor, or help the poor help themselves and fill the void left by government welfare programs, remains doubtful at this point in time. And while TANF programs appear to provide some incentive for recipients to exit welfare programs, the element of social power and control remains preeminent. Similarly, whether the market can provide sustainable work for former welfare recipients, as conservatives and libertarians argue it will, bears little recent historical evidence based on early findings on people transitioning from welfare to work. This is further bolstered by the formidable Marxist insight that downward pressure on wages is an optimal profit-maximizing strategy that may in turn lead to fragmented policy efforts to provide subsidies to minimum- and low-wage earners in order to make TANF programs more effective.

NOTES

1. Alexis de Tocqueville, *Democracy in America* (New York: Harper and Row, 1988), 9.

2. Tocqueville, *Democracy*, 538.

3. Sidney Verba, *Elites and the Idea of Equality: A Comparison of Japan, Sweden and the United States* (Cambridge, Mass.: Harvard University Press, 1987), 44.

4. Cited in Richard J. Ellis, "Rival Visions of Equality in American Political Culture," *The Review of Politics* 54 (1992): 258.

5. Ellis, "Rival Visions of Equality," 256.

6. John Locke, *Treatise on Civil Government* (New York: Appleton-Century-Croft, 1937), 32.

7. Adam Smith, *An Inquiry into the Nature and Causes of the Wealth of Nations* ([1776] Chicago: Encyclopedia Britannica, 1952), 309, 311.

8. John Maynard Keynes, *The General Theory of Employment, Interest, and Money* (New York: Harcourt, Brace & Ward, 1964); John Kenneth Galbraith, *The Good Society: The Humane Agenda* (Boston: Houghton-Mifflin, 1996).

9. Sheldon Wolin, "Why Democracy?" *Democracy* (January 1981).

10. James O'Connor, *The Fiscal Crisis of the State* (New York: St. Martin's Press, 1973).

11. Frances Fox Piven and Richard A. Cloward, *The New Class War: Reagan's Attack on the Welfare State and Its Consequences* (New York: Pantheon Books, 1982), 32.

12. John Kenneth White, *The New Politics of Old Values*, 2nd ed. (Hanover, N.H.: University Press of New England, 1990), 65.

13. Ellis, "Rival Visions of Equality," 265.

14. John Kenneth Galbraith, *The Good Society* (Boston: Houghton Mifflin, 1996); Lester Thurow, *The Future of Capitalism* (New York: William Morrow, 1996).

15. Michael Parenti, *Democracy for the Few*, 6th ed. (New York: St. Martin's Press, 1995).

16. Mickey Kaus, *The End of Equality* (New York: Basic Books, 1992), 12.

17. Ted Robert Gurr, *Why Men Rebel* (Princeton, N.J.: Princeton University Press, 1970).

18. Lester Thurow, "The Rich: Why Their World Might Crumble," *The New York Times Magazine*, November 19, 1995, 78.

19. Robert Reich, "The Fracturing of the Middle Class," *New York Times*, August 31, 1994, 13.

20. Renford Bambrough, *The Philosophy of Aristotle* (New York: A Mentor Book, 1963).

21. Conrad Waligorski, *The Political Theory of Conservative Economists* (Lawrence, Kans.: University Press of Kansas, 1990), 29.

22. Cited in Kaus, *The End of Equality*, 192.

23. R. Emmett Tyrrell, *The Liberal Crack-Up* (New York: Simon and Schuster, 1984), 219.

24. Milton Friedman, *Capitalism and Freedom* (Chicago: University of Chicago Press, 1962), 195.

25. According to Derek Phillips there is a flaw in Rawls's argument. In his attempt to place everyone in what he calls the "original position" behind the veil of ignorance, Rawls strips away from them not only their social status, but also all characteristics that distinguish them from each other. Phillips points out that this makes it impossible for them to have different viewpoints about the choice of principles to guide the just society. Phillips states, "[I]f . . . agents are deprived of all knowledge of their own specific identity, what is the nature of the 'beings' who are supposed to think about social justice?" See Derek L. Phillips, *Toward a Just Social Order* (Princeton, N.J.: Princeton University Press, 1986), 63.

26. John Rawls, *A Theory of Justice* (Cambridge, Mass.: Harvard University Press, 1971), 63.

27. Rawls, *A Theory of Justice*, 302.

28. Rawls, *A Theory of Justice*, 302.

29. Rawls, *A Theory of Justice*, 65.

30. Rawls, *A Theory of Justice*, 62.

31. Rawls, *A Theory of Justice*, 43.

32. Rawls, *A Theory of Justice*, 302.

33. Rawls, *A Theory of Justice*, 61.

34. Rawls, *A Theory of Justice*, 24.

35. Rawls, *A Theory of Justice*, 63.

36. Robert Amdur, "Rawls and His Radical Critics: The Problem of Equality," *Dissent* 27, no. 3 (Summer 1980): 333.

37. Karl Marx, "Critique of the Gotha Program," in *Karl Marx: Selected Writings*, ed. Thomas B. Bottomore (New York: McGraw-Hill, 1964), 119.

38. John Rawls, "Fairness to Goodness," *Philosophical Review* 84 (October 1975): 564.

39. Rawls, "Fairness to Goodness," 92.

40. Herbert Lionel Adolphus Hart, "Rawls on Liberty and Equality," in *Reading Rawls: Critical Studies on Rawls' A Theory of Justice*, ed. Norman Daniels (New York: Basic Books, 1975).

41. Hart, "Rawls on Liberty," 152.

42. Hart, "Rawls on Liberty," 542.

43. Hart, "Rawls on Liberty," 543.

44. The French theorist Philippe Van Parijs has called for a *universal basic income*: an income that is unconditionally granted to every person, without any means test or work reqirement. For a discussion of what kind of democratic possibilities exist in a capitalist market economy, see *Politics and Society*, vol. 32 no. 1 March 2004.

45. David Easton, *The Political System* (New York: Knopf, 1953), 143.

46. Richard Merelman, "On the Neo-Elitist Critique of Community Power," *American Political Science Review* 62 (June 1968): 455.

47. Michael Zweig, *The Working Class Majority: America's Best Kept Secret* (Ithaca, N.Y.: Cornell University Press, 2000).

48. Michel Foucault, "Two Lectures," *Power/Knowledge: Selected Writings and Other Interviews* (New York: Pantheon, 1980), 83.

49. Foucault, "Two Lectures," 83.

50. Peter Leonard, *Postmodern Welfare: Reconstructing an Emancipatory Project* (Thousand Oaks, Calif.: Sage Publications, 1997).

51. Leonard, *Postmodern Welfare*.

52. Steven Seidman, *Contested Knowledge: Social Theory in the Postmodern Era*, 2nd ed. (Malden, Mass: Blackwell Publishers, 1998).

53. Seidman, *Contested Knowledge*.

54. Seidman, *Contested Knowledge*.

55. Seidman, *Contested Knowledge*. See also Leonard, *Postmodern Welfare*.

56. Jürgen Habermas, *The Philosophical Discourse of Modernity* (Cambridge, Mass: MIT Press, 1987).

57. Seidman, *Contested Knowledge*.

58. Zygmut Bauman, *Intimations of Postmodernity* (New York: Routledge, 1992), 102.

59. Bauman, *Intimations of Postmodernity,* 102.

60. Ben Agger, *A Critical Theory of Public Life: Knowledge, Discourse and Politics in an Age of Decline* (New York: Falmer Press, 1991).

61. Agger, *A Critical Theory*, 109.

62. Leonard, *Postmodern Welfare*.

63. Seidman, *Contested Knowledge*.

64. Seidman, *Contested Knowledge*.

65. Fredric Jameson, *Postmodernism, or the Cultural Logic of Late Capitalism* (Durham, N.C.: Duke University Press, 1992).

66. Jameson, *Postmodernism*.

67. Jameson, *Postmodernism*.

68. Jameson, *Postmodernism*.

69. Jameson, *Postmodernism*, 36.

70. Jameson, *Postmodernism*, 36.

71. Edward Herman and Noam Chomsky, *Manufacturing Consent: The Political Economy of the Mass Media* (New York: Pantheon Books, 1988).

72. Jameson, *Postmodernism*.

73. Jameson, *Postmodernism*.

74. Jameson, *Postmodernism*.

75. Jean Baudrillard, *The Consumer Society: Myths and Structures* (Thousand Oaks, Calif.: Sage Publications, 1997). Also see Alan Aldridge, *Consumption* (Cambridge: Polity Press, 2003).

76. Baudrillard, *The Consumer Society.*

77. Jean Baudrillard, *For a Critique of the Political Economy of the Sign*, trans. Charles Levin (Saint Louis, Mo.: Telos Press, 1981), 37.

78. Jean Baudrillard, *Simulations,* trans. Paul Foss, Paul Patton, and Philip Beiteman (New York: Semiotext, 1983), 25.

79. Baudrillard, *Simulations*, 25.

80. Baudrillard, *Simulations*, 25.

81. Jürgen Habermas, *Theory and Practice* (Boston. Beacon Press, 1973); Max Horkheimer, *Eclipse of Reason* (New York: Seabury Press, 1974).

82. Leonard, *Postmodern Welfare*.

83. Zygmut Bauman, *Postmodernity and its Discontents* (Cambridge, Mass.: Blackwell Publishers, 1997).

84. Seidman, *Contested Knowledge*.

85. Leonard, *Postmodern Welfare*, xiii.

86. Leonard, *Postmodern Welfare*.

87. Leonard, *Postmodern Welfare*.

88. Leonard, *Postmodern Welfare*.

89. Leonard, *Postmodern Welfare*.

90. David Ellwood, "Political Science," in *The State of Public Management*, eds. Donald Kettl and H. Brinton Milward (Baltimore, Md.: Johns Hopkins University Press, 1996).

91. Ellwood, "Political Science."

92. Ellwood, "Political Science."

93. Richard Green and Lawrence Hubbell, "On Governance and Reinventing Government," in *Refounding Democratic Public Administration: Modern Paradoxes, Postmodern Challenges,* eds. Gary Wamsley and James Wolf (Thousand Oaks, Calif.: Sage Publications, 1996).

94. Michael Rustin, "The Politics of Post-Fordism: Or, the Trouble with 'New Times,'" *New Left Review* (1989): 175.

95. Green and Hubbell, "On Governance and Reinventing Government."

96. David Cheal, *New Poverty: Families in Postmodern Society* (Westport, Conn.: Greenwood Press, 1996), 185.

97. Seidman, *Contested Knowledge.*

98. Leonard, *Postmodern Welfare.*

99. Leonard, *Postmodern Welfare.*

Conclusion: The Welfare State and Alternative Futures

SOCIAL SOLIDARITY

> If participatory democracy is potentially a basis for effective forms of democratic bargaining power over both state apparatuses and the concentration of private economic power, local efforts at popular control must be able to percolate upwards through the political system, if only to transform it and break up its hierarchies in the process.
>
> —Hilary Wainwright, *Reclaim the State*

For the most part, the Marxist tradition rejects liberalism's attempt to justify the division of the general conception of justice into two principles, one governing the sphere of civil and political freedoms and the other governing the distribution of wealth, economic opportunity, and social participation. Where the liberal democratic rights theory grants primacy to the individual's negative immunity from interference or political coercion, Marxist discussion of human rights stresses positive entitlements to participate fully in the public life of society and decries the exploitation of the human person. What has thus developed in Marxist thought is a definition of human solidarity quite distinct from liberal theory. The individual ethos that springs from liberal thought, according to Marx, is "an individual separated from community, withdrawn into himself, wholly preoccupied with his private interest and acting in accordance with his private caprice. . . . The only bond between men is natural necessity, need and private interest, the preservation of their property and their egoistic persons."[1]

Marx argued the inseparability of personal freedom and social solidarity that is the cornerstone of Marxist social philosophy. Individual and social freedoms can only be realized if they are connected in a meaningful way by

making political and economic rights correlative. The outcome of this combination is the creation of a society that has the form of, as Marx states, "an
association in which the free development of each is the condition for the
free development of all."[2] Yet in their attempt to implement this vision, totalitarian command economies of Eastern Europe and China were brutal and
repressive. Nevertheless, Marx based his principle of human dignity and social solidarity on the "Declaration of the Rights of Man and the Citizen,
1791." Marx argued that the prevention of exploitation and oppression is of
urgent importance and that "Communism deprives no man of the power to
appropriate the products of society; all it does is to deprive him of the power
to subjugate the labor of others by means of such appropriation."[3]

Notions of Marxist solidarity are based on the perspective that the human
person is to be understood within the context of the common good. In his
early writings Marx argues that human nature is not radically individual, but
essentially social, a part of a community, a "species-being." Marx states:

> [I]t is above all necessary to avoid postulating "society" once again as an ab-
> straction confronting the individual. The individual is the social being. The man-
> ifestation of his life—even when it does not appear directly in the form of a
> communal manifestation, accomplished in association with other men—is,
> therefore, a manifestation, and affirmation of social life. Individual human life
> and species-life are not different things, even though the mode of existence of
> individual life is necessarily either a more specific or a more general mode of
> species-life, or that of species life a specific or more general mode of individual
> life.[4]

For Marx, not only is the person fundamentally social in his relationships, but
also fundamentally social in action and reflection. Thus, in order to promote
greater social solidarity a deeper social and cultural commitment is needed
beyond the one provided by liberalism.

The centrality of socioeconomic rights for Marxism is based on the conviction within which authentic individual freedom is manifested in a given
social milieu. Individual freedom cannot be achieved by a person acting in
isolation, but rather in community with others. Marx states:

> In his species-consciousness man confirms his real social life, and reproduces
> his real existence in thought; while conversely, species-life confirms itself in
> species-consciousness and exists for itself in its university as a thinking being.
> Though man is a unique individual—and it is just his particularity which makes
> him an individual, a really individual communal being—he is equally the whole,
> the ideal whole, the subjective existence of society as thought and experienced.
> He exists in reality as the representation and the real mind of social existence,
> and as the sum of human manifestations of life.[5]

In fact, for Marx, a person can only be fulfilled as an individual within the context of community. He states, "activity and mind are social in their content as well as in their origin; they are social activity and social mind."[6] For this reason Marx regarded liberal individualism as "egoistic" and "bourgeois," values that were counterproductive to the human family and which invariably lead "every man to see in other men, not the realization, but rather the limitation of his own liberty."[7]

Marx regarded human rights in liberal theory as spurious because these rights ignore the fuller context of "species-being," or the social nature of the human person. The "bourgeois" rights of the individual over and against society are reflections of the failure of society to understand the communal context in which individual rights can flourish in the first place. Moreover, equality in liberal theory holds that while all persons share the same fundamental human nature, not all are necessarily deserving of satisfaction for basic human needs and aspirations. Such notions of equality, for Marxist theory, are abstract and one-dimensional, precisely because they do not abolish the unequal distribution of power in economic and social life. If human rights, dignity, and social solidarity are to have real significance, then political liberties must coexist with social and economic equality. Inequalities, especially inordinate distributions of wealth, continue to be reinforced by the dominant class. For Marxist theorists, liberalism, even in its Keynesian manifestation, continues to perpetuate class antagonisms. Thus, for Marx, "rights" must be rooted in fundamental economic equality and only secondarily can political rights be prioritized, since the fundamental right to secure basic human needs is prior to notions of political rights. For Marx, therefore, "right can never be higher than the economic structure of society and the cultural development conditioned by it."[8] However, the primary goal of Marxist liberation is not simply the abolition of economic injustice and class division, but rather a "communist" society in which full and concrete freedom and equality are brought into being in order to promote greater social justice, human dignity, and social solidarity.[9]

Since the proletarian class in Marxist thought is generally viewed as the agent of this new revolutionary movement of justice and solidarity, the interests of the proletariat are to be the determining interests in shaping the political and economic life of society so long as classes exist. When the goal of the revolution has been attained, the priority of social participation over strict political liberty will be prioritized. Marxist thought denies that genuine social solidarity and mutual interdependence are possible if society and the economy function in accordance with class divisions in maximizing political freedom and rights while failing to guarantee economic freedom and rights. But if social and economic rights were genuinely guaranteed by law, then the Marxist objection to liberalism would lose much of its force. On the other hand, liberal democracy is built largely on the conviction that a pluralistic society cannot easily be brought to agreement on social and economic policies without resorting to totalitarian measures. Thus if the protection of social and economic rights were pursued in such a way that continued to guarantee basic civil and political liberties, the liberal objections to socialism would be less persuasive. This option, suffice it to say, would be ideal precisely because it presents the best of both models. Yet it is difficult to move beyond this ideal option since "justice" is interpreted in numerous ways.

Liberal democratic theory holds that not all individuals are willing to have society guarantee social and economic rights and concludes that these rights are not really rights at all. Rights are identified with claims to political liberty. Marxism, on the other hand, notes that unrestricted liberty in a society stratified according to classes leads to a denial of social and economic rights. If this tension is to be mitigated, then political liberty, according to Marxist thought, must be restricted if social and economic claims are to be guaranteed. Hence, both liberal and radical traditions assert that the effective recognition of rights depends on a choice regarding how political power will be used: in one case for the protection of claims to individual liberty, in the other for the protection of claims to social participation and solidarity.[10]

Postmodernism is in need of a greater notion of solidarity if it is to make a significant impact on current welfare reform. Arguably, the Marxist tradition can be of benefit here. Solidarity in the Marxist tradition prioritizes relationships with others as an integral dimension of human experience. On the other hand, organic solidarity, according to Emile Durkheim, attempts to describe the underlying causes of societal cohesiveness. While this approach to solidarity is beneficial, it nevertheless fails to provide a holistic understanding of solidarity that the Marxist tradition does present. This is because the coherence and interconnectedness of human relationships for Marx is critical in the promotion of "just" relationships in society. The Marxist approach moves beyond an empirical description to a normative understanding of solidarity. Solidarity in the Marxist tradition maintains the preeminence of mutual interdependence, which promotes the good of the individual and community. This is abundantly clear since individuals in isolation from others may jeopardize their well-being and the fulfillment of others in community.[11]

Western thinking has been historically dominated by an artificial dualism which, for the most part, has failed to recognize the holistic and integrated nature of human experience. This intellectual polarity has maintained the separation of body from soul, secular from sacred, spirit from matter, reason from emotion, and intuition from knowledge. It is this dualism that has tended to lay the foundation for minimizing the temporal order precisely because the nonmaterial elements were seen as superior to the material order. Postmodern feminists argue that this dichotomy has provided an intellectual disservice to humanity since it undermines notions of social solidarity and mutual interdependence.[12] There are other ontological assumptions, such as those based on solidarity, that can provide a foundation for restructuring a new worldview that is appropriate for securing greater justice and equality. On the other hand, an absence of mutual interdependence, which is at the heart of solidarity, can provide a framework for exploitative relationships. Potential injustices can manifest themselves in benign paternalism, elitism, sexism, ethnocentrism, racism, and violent forms of domination. In this capacity, solidarity is more than simply a political theory that empathizes with those marginalized in society. Solidarity serves as a foundation for resistance to oppressive schemes based on modernist traditions.

What postmodern strategy based on Marxist social solidarity might rejuvenate a commitment to the welfare state? David Stroesz and Howard Karger argue for a "reconstructed" welfare policy that is relevant to the nation's needs in a postmodern era.[13] Such a policy, described as "radical pragmatism," would focus on five principles: productivity, family, social cohesion, community, and social choice. Productivity here refers to reestablishing the "legitimacy" of the welfare state. Establishing legitimacy is essential in order to demonstrate how social programs contribute to the nation's productivity rather than drag it down. Social welfare must also assist the family in a constructive manner in order to mitigate tensions that surface when families are financially vulnerable. Support of the American family during times of serious financial crisis must be a priority in order to maintain the integrity of the family itself. Welfare policy must also reinforce social cohesion. A collective social entity in which groups or classes understand their interdependence is critical, since this self-understanding is what fundamentally legitimizes the welfare state in the first place. No one group or subculture must be considered "expendable," especially if social cohesion and solidarity are considered important values within a democratic society. Related to this is the importance of fostering community. Attempting to nurture relationships among people of diverse histories and backgrounds—especially for those who have been, for one reason or another, traditionally left out of policy discussions—can only help policy to be less fragmented and more focused on achieving solidarity goals. Finally, social choice, according to Stroesz and Karger, provides a battery of options for welfare recipients as incentives to be proactive in sustaining themselves and eventually exiting assistance. Social choice presupposes that these work incentives pay sustainable or living wages and be calibrated accordingly based on family and other basic human needs.

Stroesz and Karger argue that the American welfare state can be made more congruent with domestic demands for "work first" by restructuring social programs around "radical pragmatic" principles. Creatively developed, these strategies for promoting productivity, family, social cohesion, community, and social choice can serve as the principles through which the American welfare state may be reorganized and improved. The challenge to American welfare advocates, then, is to integrate these values into public policy so that the public itself can appreciate how social programs contribute to the "general welfare" of the United States in a postmodern era. Specific policies, or a "politics of care" argued by Cheryl King and Camilla Stivers et al.,[14] would advocate that welfare recipients take on vital roles in constructing the very welfare policies that affect their lives.

CLASS, SOLIDARITY, AND WELFARE POLICY

One means for empowering marginalized persons to maximize opportunities for people to empower themselves to become self-determining moral agents is through "collective resistance." This construct is basically made up of grassroots groups, organizations, and networks who operate on an informal agenda that is proactive on behalf of marginalized persons. These collective resistance associations can be private or nonprofit, made up of educators, counseling and therapy groups, social workers, housing support groups, churches, charities, environmentalists, even families—in short, activist special interest groups. This can be contrasted to elite special interest groups who co-opt the bureaucratic, hierarchical monolith of the state. Collective resistance would incorporate collective decision making with its goal of challenging dominant forces in culture who control a vast majority of assets and resources to the detriment of marginalized persons. The goal of collective resistance in order to promote postmodern welfare, we argue, must focus primarily on the destructive nature of late or postmodern capitalism, the cultivated dependence on the consumer market, and the power of a commodified culture. Peter Leonard argues that this phenomena has reached destructively into the family:

> [C]hildren become as vulnerable as adults to the manufacture of desire . . .
> and homogenizing messages about the moral superiority of individualism . . .
> over all concern for solidarity, collectivity, wider communities and the well-being of others. The fact that a mass culture serves predominantly to reproduce the ethics of capitalist exploitation, to induce submission through the internalization of dominant discourses in the constitution of subjectivities, is the central thrust of that counter-discourse upon which collective resistance rests.[15]

Coupled with the globalization phenomena—capital mobility, increased profits, decreased labor expenses, and downsizing of personnel—postmodern capital presents itself as an impersonal and rationalistic force within the domestic and international market, and therefore free from considerations of equity and justice.

With the continued search for higher profits in order to maintain global competitiveness and accountability to shareholders, capitalist strategies focused on vulnerable social policies directed at providing human services as opposed to military spending and subsidies to corporations.[16] Cutting social spending on fundamental human needs was an effort to cut taxes (personal and corporate), the funds from which would then be reinvested in capital investment, which in turn would increase the overall wealth of the country. The point of collective resistance to this devastation should focus on the ideological critique of the late or postmodern capitalist strategy that legitimizes, in rational terms, an economic system that is argued to be as normal and impartial as nature itself. The fact is that such a system is far from impartiality, and intentionally leverages economic relationships to its own advantage while proclaiming that this form of self-interest indeed promotes the common good. Resistance movements argue that this does not promote the common good, but instead creates deeper fissures in society and further alienates communities. What resistance movements should mobilize around is a strategy of mutual interdependence and the implications of coalitions that may arise from this vision. To this strategy Leonard argues that "ultimately, the aim of organizing such resistance and dissent amongst those most negatively affected by continuous economic restructuring in the interests of profitability is to generate a legitimation crisis with which to confront governments and corporations faced with having to manage the crisis tendencies of the economic system as a whole."[17]

In order to reconstruct postmodern welfare, we argue that this process must be based on the principle of mutual interdependence, or what is otherwise known as social solidarity. We believe that the notion of class solidarity best complements postmodern attempts to reestablish some form of economic provision for the marginalized of society. A reconstructed postmodern welfare, based on the principles of social solidarity and mutual interdependence, will attempt to direct its concerns primarily to fundamental human needs, that is, if people are to develop as moral agents. This can be contrasted with current state systems, whether the former AFDC or current TANF program. The modern nation-state, which was conceived in modernity itself, is profoundly flawed. It was the modern nation-state that was created as the manifestation of universal reason while simultaneously laying the groundwork for domination by the state itself. Yet it is in reconstructing a postmodern welfare system that the power and resources of the state must be tapped in order to be a conduit for diversity and interdependence.

We argue that the proponents of solidarity must push its agenda as a "special interest" that would seek support for those marginalized persons within a given population. This can also become the agenda of a political party—in that it seeks public policies to promote greater solidarity in a community—which would be most beneficial to those living in economically deprived situations. The future of welfare policy rests on the recognition that social solidarity is at the core of mutual interdependence and greater equality and liberty for all people. Currently, welfare policy in the United States, as manifested in PRWORA, fails in this capacity. Moreover, that market structures are leading to further "crises" with respect to corporate greed, boom–bust cycles, unemployment trends, and negative effects of globalization indeed presages the importance of rethinking social welfare policy from a postmodern perspective. Dialogue in this venue may prove to be the policy strategy to implement greater social security and cohesion in Western democracies. As it stands, liberal Western democracies continue to mirror class stratification, to the detriment of democratic institutions and principles.

Without some form of subsistence, it would be risky for any society, especially a democracy, to permit hundreds of thousands of people to be cast adrift without a stake in that very society and its political system.[18] Yet federal interventions in the complex realm of social policy have brought their share of frustrations and excesses. The more important issues are the extent to which social welfare policies and programs have been revised to reflect the lessons of the past and the standards by which progress in the welfare system is measured. A balanced and reasonable assessment suggests that there have been mistakes made—some inevitable, others the result of overly ambitious efforts—during two decades of frequently bold innovation. The past gains have been generally encouraging in light of competing goals set out for the liberal welfare state.[19] This is because the designers of the welfare system, from the New Deal to the founding of the Great Society, tended to underestimate the deep-seated problems associated with poverty. Christopher Jencks argues that the designers of the Social Security Act of 1935 assumed that a needs-tested public assistance would wither away as young workers became fully covered by social insurance—an expectation that was shattered by changing demographics and steadily expanding welfare rolls and benefits during the postwar period.[20] Similarly, a central premise of President Johnson's War on Poverty was that investments in education and training, health care, civil rights protections, and community organizations representing the poor could dramatically lift this generation's poor out of deprivation and ensure their children a decent life.[21] Cycles of poverty and dependency have proved considerably more intractable. It became increasingly clear that there are no easy answers or immediate solutions to discrimination, economic deprivation, and other social ills.[22] As some of the experiments turned out to be counterproductive as well as politically divisive (i.e., accounts of welfare abuse and fraud), the ensuing disillusionment sorely taxed the nation's will to sustain the welfare system in pursuit of steady but incremental gains.

Because many social problems have proved more pervasive and persistent than originally believed, the welfare system has been forced to rely upon more varied and costly strategies for long-term amelioration.[23] Such comprehensive, long-term approaches frequently involved offering preferential treatment to targeted groups at the cost of legitimate aspirations of the more fortunate, such as the middle class. It has proven extremely difficult politically to defend these actions. Social programs requiring high initial investments have often been abandoned, becoming victims of public resentment. Even when government interventions have achieved their intended results, the process of change in some instances has generated unwanted side effects and posted new problems for policy makers. One clear lesson provided by the experience of the past two decades is that the search for remedies to complex social problems is inherently difficult, particularly when the process involves helping the "have-nots" to compete effectively with those who have "made it." In a democratic society, those who have gained privileged status generally have the clout to abort such changes. Observing this phenomena, Frances Fox Piven and Richard Cloward state, "this tact is taken in an analysis descended from the Marxist tradition, which explains the construction of the welfare state primarily as a process of ideological domination . . . with the consequence that democratic political capacities were suppressed."[24]

The experience of recent decades suggests that the federal government must proceed on several fronts simultaneously if it is to be successful in efforts to alleviate poverty. For example, unless suitable employment and economic development programs are also initiated, the training of low-income workers is unlikely to have a significant impact on overall poverty levels or welfare caseloads when provided amid high unemployment or in declining economic regions. In contrast, although income transfers address the immediate needs of the poor, they do not result in lasting improvements in earning capacity and self-sufficiency unless complemented by public efforts to enhance the skills of recipients and to alter the institutions that trap them in poverty. The interdependence of these antipoverty strategies can create the appearance of failure when individual initiatives are viewed in isolation, particularly when concomitant interventions necessary for their success are not undertaken. At the same time, the benefits of comprehensive approaches are cumulative and can far exceed the potential of isolated efforts. Failure to pursue this strategy, according to Peter Edelman, "would engage in further punishment of the millions who lack skills or, having skills, lack the possibility of obtaining employment because there are not enough jobs to go around."[25]

America's experience with the modern welfare system is that poverty cannot be eliminated solely through reliance upon income transfers. In fact, this was never the purpose of welfare, according to Edelman.[26] Nevertheless, income maintenance is an essential component of any antipoverty effort, but a strategy relying upon transfers alone can neither enhance self-sufficiency nor avoid conflicts in labor markets. In a society in which wages for millions of workers are too low to lift them out of poverty, the provision of adequate cash assistance to the nonworking poor—if unaccompanied by incentives to supplement assistance with earnings—inevitably raises serious questions of equity and generates strong political opposition among taxpayers. Income transfers large enough to lift low-income households above the poverty threshold, if not tied to work efforts, would trigger large drops in labor force participation or force massive public expenditures to the nonpoor in order to preserve acceptable work incentives. According to Edelman, the political and economic realities have contributed to the demise of successive guaranteed income schemes during the past two decades and further demonstrate the need for federal strategies that assist both the working and dependent poor.

The rhetoric of the Great Society and subsequent initiatives often placed heavy emphasis on the expansion of economic opportunity for the less fortunate. This promise, according to Edelman, has never been fulfilled through a sustained and adequate commitment of societal resources.[27] Many of the dilemmas posed by the modern welfare system—perverse incentives discouraging work by welfare recipients, neglect of the needs of the working poor, high levels of youth and minority unemployment, and burgeoning costs for universal entitlements—arise from an inadequate emphasis on the extension of economic opportunity in current policies. Beyond fundamental guarantees of equal access and civil rights, the welfare system's attempts to broaden opportunity have relied upon relatively small and frequently sporadic investments in job training, public employment, compensatory education, and meaningful work incentives. These initiatives, despite yielding promising results, have fallen far short of their necessary role as equal partners with income maintenance in advancing the goals of the welfare system. To help the millions of unskilled and undereducated, Edelman asserts that it is necessary to recognize that work and welfare go together as an appropriate public policy.[28] Edelman warns, however, that the reality of minimum-wage jobs tends to perpetuate the problem of poverty and the need for welfare assistance.

The difficulties associated with the expansion of economic opportunity through the welfare system are substantial, ranging from the technical and economic to the cultural and political. Heavy reliance upon transfer programs in recent years, that is, prior to the 1996 Welfare Reform Act, tended to reflect the fact that assurances of income security were thought to be less threatening to established interests. They were easier to adopt than broader efforts to open avenues to self-support and advancement, given the ambiguities of the market and its cycles. Nevertheless, there appears to be no alternative to reviving the promise of opportunity in America than simply assuming that free markets, personal liberty, and the absolute right to private property alone will solve the employment–poverty problem as conservatives and libertarians such as Robert Nozick argue. James Sterba argues that liberty makes no sense if some form of capital, either social and/or material, is not available for individuals and communities to fulfill their most basic rights in the first place.[29] In fact, left-leaning scholars such as Allen Buchanan argue that work and self-advancement are themselves libertarian rights that must necessarily translate into welfare rights. This is fundamental for any society, according to Buchanan, since one has the right to participate in political processes, the right to freedom of expression, and the right to the benefits of the legal system. Moreover, for Buchanan, this is the case since "there is no defensible notion of a property right that is strong enough to block the derivation of welfare rights from libertarian rights. This is not to say, however, that considerations concerning the proper scope of a right to property will not play an important role in determining what measures are appropriate for minimizing inequalities in the effectiveness of the exercise of equal rights."[30]

Rather than viewing welfare as a "failure," Buchanan argues that it plays a vital role in supporting people in the event that their fundamental needs are not met within society. In this sense it may be critical to view libertarian rights in terms of welfare rights and the profound impact liberty and welfare can have in the development of a community of resistance that acts as an advocate for those who, for whatever reason, are not participating in the economic structure of society.

Racialized inequality remains a vexing problem in the United States. Prior to the Great Society programs, racialized ethnic minorities were systematically excluded from welfare programs. With the implementation of civil rights and progressive federal legislation, people of color began to access entitlement programs. The expansion of welfare policy, during the 1960s, was a direct result of aggressive civil rights advocacy. During the late 1970s and early 1980s, progressive social policies like welfare policy had come under increased attack by neoconservative ideologues and policy wonks. The context of this right-wing agenda was articulated during the Reagan era, which embodied downward pressure on labor and wages, regressive taxation, loosening environmental regulations, expansion of criminal justice and military spending, and an attack on welfare programs and affirmative action guidelines. However, as a result of the recent changes in welfare policy (PRWORA) initiated by the Clinton administration, African Americans and Chicano/Latino

welfare recipients now outnumber Anglos by two to one.[31] The Bush initiatives
have promised to further undermine welfare policy even more than the Reagan conservatives and Clinton pragmatists. Indeed, the Bush administration
has proposed legislation that would take "compassionate conservatism" to another level. Under its 2003 proposal, the Bush administration would compel
welfare recipients to work up to forty hours a week, regardless of family com-
mitments and job training under TANF. Sixty percent of these recipients are in
low-paying minimum wage jobs. Sometimes the wages are even below the legal minimum wage requirement, justified under the rationale of job training.
With the growing budget deficits around the country, states may need to real-
locate their resources to programs other than human services and TANF programs. The consolidation of the neoliberal model for welfare reform has indeed jeopardized the American safety net. The impact on the poor and
racialized groups may prove to be devastating. As we have argued in these
pages the "savage state"—in its structure and role—is a functional imperative
of the capitalist political economy. Thus a democratic alternative to welfare
capitalism will depend on the levels and forms of a renewed class struggle.
This movement for a more just and humane future will require a new kind of
class-based coalition of working- and middle-class families across the "racial
divide." Political initiatives that are outlined here will come at considerable
cost, but the benefits could be enormous—a democratic economy and society.

NOTES

1. Karl Marx, "On The Jewish Question," in *Karl Marx, Early Writings*, ed.
Thomas B. Bottomore (New York: McGraw-Hill, 1964), 26.

2. Karl Marx and Frederick Engels, *The Communist Manifesto* (New York:
Pathfinder Press, 1978), 34.

3. Marx and Engels, *The Community Manifesto*, 30.

4. Marx and Engels, *The Community Manifesto*, 158.

5. Marx and Engels, *The Community Manifesto*, 158.

6. Marx and Engels, *The Community Manifesto*, 157.

7. Marx, "On The Jewish Question," 25.

8. Karl Marx, "Critique of the Gotha Program," in *Karl Marx, Selected Writings*, ed.
Lawrence H. Simon (Indianapolis, Ind.: Hackett Publishing Company, 1994), 119.

9. Jon Elster, *Making Sense of Marx* (Cambridge: Cambridge University Press,
1985); Hilliard Aronovitch, "Marxian Morality," *Canadian Journal of Philosophy* 10,
no. 3 (September 1980); Isaiah Berlin, *Karl Marx*, 4th ed. (Oxford: Oxford University Press, 1978); Richard W. Miller, "Marx and Morality," in *Canadian Journal of
Philosophy*, supplement, vol. 3, eds. Nielsen and Patten (1977).

10. Richard Rorty, "Solidarity or Objectivity," in *Consequences of Pragmatism: Essays 1972–1980* (Minneapolis: University of Minnesota Press, 1982).

11. Karl Marx, "Private Property and Communism" and "Alienated Labor" in *Karl Marx, Early Writings*, trans. by Thomas B. Bottomore (New York: McGraw-Hill, 1964).

12. Beverly Harrison, *Making the Connections: Essays in Feminist Social Ethics*, ed. Carol Robb (Boston: Beacon Press, 1985); Carol Gilligan, *In A Different Voice* (Cambridge, Mass.: Harvard University Press, 1982).

13. David Stroesz and Howard Karger, *Reconstructing the American Welfare State* (Lanham, Md.: Rowman & Littlefield Publishers, 1992).

14. Cheryl King and Camilla Stivers, et al., *Government Is Us: Public Administration in an Anti-Government Era* (Thousand Oaks, Calif.: Sage Publications, 1998).

15. Peter Leonard, *Postmodern Welfare: Reconstructing an Emancipatory Project* (Thousand Oakes, Calif.: Sage Publications, 1997), 171–72.

16. Martin Shaw, "The State of Globalization: Towards a Theory of State Transformation," in *State/Space: A Reader*, eds. Neil Brenner, Bob Jessop, Martin Jones, and Gordon MacLeod (Oxford: Blackwell, 2003).

17. Leonard, *Postmodern Welfare*, 173.

18. Frances Fox Piven and Richard Cloward, *The New Class War* (New York: Random House, 1982).

19. Peter Rossi, *Down and Out in America: The Origins of Homelessness* (Chicago: University of Chicago Press, 1989).

20. Christopher Jencks, "How Poor Are the Poor?" *The New York Review of Books*, May 9, 1985.

21. Michael Harrington, *The New American Poverty* (N.Y.: Holt, Rinehart and Winston, 1984).

22. Ted Lowi, "Why Is There No Socialism in the United States?" *Society 22*, (January/February 1985): 34 42.

23. Robert Clark, *The War on Poverty: History, Selected Programs, and Ongoing Impact* (Lanham, Md.: University Press of America, 2002).

24. Piven and Cloward, *Regulating the Poor*, 416.

25. Peter Edelman, "Work and Workfare: An Alternative Perspective on Entitlements," *Budget and Policy Choices* (1983): 54.

26. Edelman, "Work and Workfare," 54.

27. Edelman, "Work and Workfare," 54.

28. Edelman, "Work and Workfare," 54.

29. James Sterba, "The Welfare Rights of Distant Peoples and Future Generations: Moral Side-Constraints on Social Policy," *Social Theory and Practice* 7 (Spring 1981); James Sterba, *The Demands of Justice* (South Bend, Ind.: University of Notre Dame Press, 1980).

30. Allen Buchanan, "Deriving Welfare Rights from Libertarian Rights," in *Income Support: Conceptual and Policy Issues*, 245.

31. Tony Platt, "The State of Welfare: United States 2003," *Monthly Review* (October 2003): 13–27.

Appendix

PRESIDENT LYNDON B. JOHNSON'S ANNUAL MESSAGE
TO THE CONGRESS ON THE STATE OF THE UNION

January 8, 1964
[As delivered in person before a joint session]

Mr. Speaker, Mr. President, Members of the House and Senate, my fellow Americans:

I will be brief, for our time is necessarily short and our agenda is already long.

Last year's congressional session was the longest in peacetime history. With that foundation, let us work together to make this year's session the best in the nation's history.

Let this session of Congress be known as the session which did more for civil rights than the last hundred sessions combined; as the session which enacted the most far-reaching tax cut of our time; as the session which declared all-out war on human poverty and unemployment in these United States; as the session which finally recognized the health needs of all our older citizens; as the session which reformed our tangled transportation and transit policies; as the session which achieved the most effective, efficient foreign aid program ever; and as the session which helped to build more homes, more schools, more libraries, and more hospitals than any single session of Congress in the history of our Republic.

All this and more can and must be done. It can be done by this summer, and it can be done without any increase in spending. In fact, under the budget that I shall shortly submit, it can be done with an actual reduction in federal expenditures and federal employment.

We have in 1964 a unique opportunity and obligation—to prove the success of our system; to disprove those cynics and critics at home and abroad who question our purpose and our competence.

If we fail, if we fritter and fumble away our opportunity in needless, senseless quarrels between Democrats and Republicans, or between the House and the Senate, or between the South and North, or between the Congress and the administration, then history will rightfully judge us harshly. But if we succeed, if we can achieve these goals by forging in this country a greater sense of union, then, and only then, can we take full satisfaction in the state of the union.

II.

Here in the Congress you can demonstrate effective legislative leadership by discharging the public business with clarity and dispatch, voting each important proposal up, or voting it down, but at least bringing it to a fair and a final vote.

Let us carry forward the plans and programs of John Fitzgerald Kennedy—not because of our sorrow or sympathy, but because they are right.

In his memory today, I especially ask all members of my own political faith, in this election year, to put your country ahead of your party, and to always debate principles; never debate personalities.

For my part, I pledge a progressive administration which is efficient, and honest, and frugal. The budget to be submitted to the Congress shortly is in full accord with this pledge.

It will cut our deficit in half—from $10 billion to $4,900 million. It will be, in proportion to our national output, the smallest budget since 1951.

It will call for a substantial reduction in federal employment, a feat accomplished only once before in the last ten years. While maintaining the full strength of our combat defenses, it will call for the lowest number of civilian personnel in the Department of Defense since 1950.

It will call for total expenditures of $97,900 million—compared to $98,400 million for the current year, a reduction of more than $500 million. It will call for new obligational authority of $103,800 million—a reduction of more than $4 billion below last year's request of $107,900 million.

But it is not a standstill budget, for America cannot afford to stand still. Our population is growing. Our economy is more complex. Our people's needs are expanding.

But by closing down obsolete installations, by curtailing less urgent programs, by cutting back where cutting back seems to be wise, by insisting on a dollar's worth for a dollar spent, I am able to recommend in this reduced budget the most federal support in history for education, for health, for retraining the unemployed, and for helping the economically and the physically handicapped.

This budget, and this year's legislative program, are designed to help each and every American citizen fulfill his basic hopes—his hopes for a fair chance to make good; his hopes for fair play from the law; his hopes for a full-time job on full-time pay; his hopes for a decent home for his family in a decent community; his hopes for a good school for his children with good teachers; and his hopes for security when faced with sickness or unemployment or old age.

III.

Unfortunately, many Americans live on the outskirts of hope—some because of their poverty, and some because of their color, and all too many because of both. Our task is to help replace their despair with opportunity.

This administration today, here and now, declares unconditional war on poverty in America. I urge this Congress and all Americans to join with me in that effort.

It will not be a short or easy struggle, no single weapon or strategy will suffice, but we shall not rest until that war is won. The richest nation on earth can afford to win it. We cannot afford to lose it. One thousand dollars invested in salvaging an unemployable youth today can return $40,000 or more in his lifetime.

Poverty is a national problem, requiring improved national organization and support. But this attack, to be effective, must also be organized at the state and the local level and must be supported and directed by state and local efforts.

For the war against poverty will not be won here in Washington. It must be won in the field, in every private home, in every public office, from the courthouse to the White House.

The program I shall propose will emphasize this cooperative approach to help that one-fifth of all American families with incomes too small to even meet their basic needs.

Our chief weapons in a more pinpointed attack will be better schools, and better health, and better homes, and better training, and better job opportunities to help more Americans, especially young Americans, escape from squalor and misery and unemployment rolls where other citizens help to carry them.

Very often a lack of jobs and money is not the cause of poverty, but the symptom. The cause may lie deeper in our failure to give our fellow citizens a fair chance to develop their own capacities, in a lack of education and training, in a lack of medical care and housing, in a lack of decent communities in which to live and bring up their children.

But whatever the cause, our joint federal–local effort must pursue poverty, pursue it wherever it exists—in city slums and small towns, in sharecropper shacks or in migrant worker camps, on Indian reservations, among whites as well as Negroes, among the young as well as the aged, in the boomtowns and in the depressed areas.

Our aim is not only to relieve the symptom of poverty, but to cure it and, above all, to prevent it. No single piece of legislation, however, is going to suffice.

We will launch a special effort in the chronically distressed areas of Appalachia.

We must expand our small but our successful area redevelopment program.

We must enact youth employment legislation to put jobless, aimless, hopeless youngsters to work on useful projects.

We must distribute more food to the needy through a broader food stamp program.

We must create a National Service Corps to help the economically handicapped of our own country as the Peace Corps now helps those abroad.

We must modernize our unemployment insurance and establish a high-level commission on automation. If we have the brainpower to invent these machines, we have the brainpower to make certain that they are a boon and not a bane to humanity.

We must extend the coverage of our minimum wage laws to more than two million workers now lacking this basic protection of purchasing power.

We must, by including special school aid funds as part of our education program, improve the quality of teaching, training, and counseling in our hardest hit areas.

We must build more libraries in every area and more hospitals and nursing homes under the Hill-Burton Act, and train more nurses to staff them.

We must provide hospital insurance for our older citizens financed by every worker and his employer under Social Security, contributing no more than one dollar a month during the employee's working career to protect him in his old age in a dignified manner without cost to the Treasury, against the devastating hardship of prolonged or repeated illness.

We must, as a part of a revised housing and urban renewal program, give more help to those displaced by slum clearance, provide more housing for our poor and our elderly, and seek as our ultimate goal in our free enterprise system a decent home for every American family.

We must help obtain more modern mass transit within our communities as well as low-cost transportation between them.

Above all, we must release $11 billion of tax reduction into the private spending stream to create new jobs and new markets in every area of this land.

IV.

These programs are obviously not for the poor or the underprivileged alone. Every American will benefit by the extension of social security to cover the hospital costs of their aged parents. Every American community will benefit from the construction or modernization of schools, libraries, hospitals, and nursing homes, from the training of more nurses and from the improvement of urban renewal in public transit. And every individual American taxpayer and every corporate taxpayer will benefit from the earliest possible passage of the pending tax bill from both the new investment it will bring and the new jobs that it will create.

That tax bill has been thoroughly discussed for a year. Now we need action. The new budget clearly allows it. Our taxpayers surely deserve it. Our economy strongly demands it. And every month of delay dilutes its benefits in 1964 for consumption, for investment, and for employment.

For until the bill is signed, its investment incentives cannot be deemed certain, and the withholding rate cannot be reduced—and the most damaging and devastating thing you can do to any businessman in America is to keep him in doubt and to keep him guessing on what our tax policy is. And I say that we should now reduce to 14 percent instead of 15 percent our withholding rate.

I therefore urge the Congress to take final action on this bill by the first of February, if at all possible. For however proud we may be of the unprecedented progress of our free enterprise economy over the last three years, we should not and we cannot permit it to pause.

In 1963, for the first time in history, we crossed the seventy-million-job mark, but we will soon need more than seventy-five million jobs. In 1963 our gross national product reached the $600 billion level—$100 billion higher than when we took office. But it easily could and it should be still $30 billion higher today than it is.

Wages and profits and family income are also at their highest levels in history—but I would remind you that four million workers and 13 percent of our industrial capacity are still idle today.

We need a tax cut now to keep this country moving.

V.

For our goal is not merely to spread the work. Our goal is to create more jobs. I believe the enactment of a thirty-five-hour week would sharply increase costs, would invite inflation, would impair our ability to compete, and merely share instead of creating employment. But I am equally opposed to the forty-five- or fifty-hour week in those industries where consistently excessive use of overtime causes increased unemployment.

So, therefore, I recommend legislation authorizing the creation of a tripartite industry committee to determine on an industry-by-industry basis as to where a higher penalty rate for overtime would increase job openings without unduly increasing costs, and authorizing the establishment of such higher rates.

VI.

Let me make one principle of this administration abundantly clear: All of these increased opportunities—in employment, in education, in housing, and in every field—must be open to Americans of every color. As far as the writ of federal law will run, we must abolish not some, but all racial discrimination. For this is not merely an economic issue, or a social, political, or international issue. It is a moral issue, and it must be met by the passage this session of the bill now pending in the House.

All members of the public should have equal access to facilities open to the public. All members of the public should be equally eligible for federal benefits that are financed by the public. All members of the public should have an equal chance to vote for public officials and to send their children to good public schools and to contribute their talents to the public good.

Today, Americans of all races stand side by side in Berlin and in Viet Nam. They died side by side in Korea. Surely they can work and eat and travel side by side in their own country.

VII.

We must also lift by legislation the bars of discrimination against those who seek entry into our country, particularly those who have much needed skills and those joining their families.

In establishing preferences, a nation that was built by the immigrants of all lands can ask those who now seek admission: "What can you do for our country?" But we should not be asking: "In what country were you born?"

VIII.

For our ultimate goal is a world without war, a world made safe for diversity, in which all men, goods, and ideas can freely move across every border and every boundary.

We must advance toward this goal in 1964 in at least ten different ways, not as partisans, but as patriots.

First, we must maintain—and our reduced defense budget will maintain—that margin of military safety and superiority obtained through three years of steadily increasing both the quality and the quantity of our strategic, our conventional, and our antiguerilla forces. In 1964 we will be better prepared than ever before to defend the cause of freedom, whether it is threatened by outright aggression or by the infiltration practiced by those in Hanoi and Havana, who ship arms and men across international borders to foment insurrection. And we must continue to use that strength as John Kennedy used it in the Cuban crisis and for the test ban treaty—to demonstrate both the futility of nuclear war and the possibilities of lasting peace.

Second, we must take new steps—and we shall make new proposals at Geneva—toward the control and the eventual abolition of arms. Even in the absence of agreement, we must not stockpile arms beyond our needs or seek an excess of military power that could be provocative as well as wasteful.

It is in this spirit that in this fiscal year we are cutting back our production of enriched uranium by 25 percent. We are shutting down four plutonium piles. We are closing many nonessential military installations. And it is in this spirit that we today call on our adversaries to do the same.

Third, we must make increased use of our food as an instrument of peace—making it available by sale or trade or loan or donation to hungry people in all nations which tell us of their needs and accept proper conditions of distribution.

Fourth, we must assure our preeminence in the peaceful exploration of outer space, focusing on an expedition to the moon in this decade—in cooperation with other powers if possible, alone if necessary.

Fifth, we must expand world trade. Having recognized in the Act of 1962 that we must buy as well as sell, we now expect our trading partners to recognize that we must sell as well as buy. We are willing to give them competitive access to our market, asking only that they do the same for us.

Sixth, we must continue, through such measures as the interest equalization tax, as well as the cooperation of other nations, our recent progress toward balancing our international accounts.

This administration must and will preserve the present gold value of the dollar.

Seventh, we must become better neighbors with the free states of the Americas, working with the councils of the OAS, with a stronger Alliance for Progress, and with all the men and women of this hemisphere who really believe in liberty and justice for all.

Eighth, we must strengthen the ability of free nations everywhere to develop their independence and raise their standard of living, and thereby frustrate those who prey on poverty and chaos. To do this, the rich must help the poor—and we must do our part. We must achieve a more rigorous administration of our development assistance, with larger roles for private investors, for other industrialized nations, and for international agencies and for the recipient nations themselves.

Ninth, we must strengthen our Atlantic and Pacific partnerships, maintain our alliances and make the United Nations a more effective instrument for national independence and international order.

Tenth, and finally, we must develop with our allies new means of bridging the gap between the East and the West, facing danger boldly wherever danger exists, but being equally bold in our search for new agreements which can enlarge the hopes of all, while violating the interests of none.

In short, I would say to the Congress that we must be constantly prepared for the worst, and constantly acting for the best. We must be strong enough to win any war, and we must be wise enough to prevent one.

We shall neither act as aggressors nor tolerate acts of aggression. We intend to bury no one, and we do not intend to be buried.

We can fight, if we must, as we have fought before, but we pray that we will never have to fight again.

IX.

My good friends and my fellow Americans: In these last seven sorrowful weeks, we have learned anew that nothing is so enduring as faith, and nothing is so degrading as hate.

John Kennedy was a victim of hate, but he was also a great builder of faith—faith in our fellow Americans, whatever their creed or their color or their station in life; faith in the future of man, whatever his divisions and differences.

This faith was echoed in all parts of the world. On every continent and in every land to which Mrs. Johnson and I traveled, we found faith and hope and love toward this land of America and toward our people.

So I ask you now in the Congress and in the country to join with me in expressing and fulfilling that faith in working for a nation, a nation that is free from want and a world that is free from hate—a world of peace and justice, and freedom and abundance, for our time and for all time to come.

Source: *Public Papers of the Presidents of the United States: Lyndon B. Johnson, 1963–1964.* Volume I, entry 91, pp. 112–118. Washington, D. C.. Government Printing Office, 1965.

Bibliography

Adorasky, Victor. *Dialectical Materialism*. New York: International Publishers, 1932.

Agger, Ben. *A Critical Theory of Public Life: Knowledge, Discourse and Politics in an Age of Decline*. New York: Falmer, 1991.

Alcaly, Roger E., and David Mermelstein, eds. *The Fiscal Crisis of American Cities*. New York: Vintage Books, 1976.

Aldridge, Alan. *Consumption*. Cambridge: Polity Press, 2003.

Althusser, Louis. *Lenin and Philosophy and Other Essays*. New York: MR Press, 1971.

Amdur, Robert. "Rawls and His Radical Critics: The Problem of Equality." *Dissent* 27, no. 3 (Summer 1980): 333.

Arneson, Richard. "Liberalism, Distributive Subjectivism, and Equal Opportunity for Welfare." *Philosophy & Public Affairs* 19, no. 2 (Spring 1990): 158–194.

Aronovitch, Hilliard. "Marxian Morality." *Canadian Journal of Philosophy* 10, no. 3 (September 1980).

Arrow, Kenneth. "Redistribution to the Poor: A Collective Expression of Individual Altruism." In *Poverty and Social Justice: Critical Perspectives*, edited by Francisco Jimenez. Tempe, Ariz.: Bilingual Press, 1987.

Bambrough, Renford. *The Philosophy of Aristotle*. New York: A Mentor Book, 1963.

Bane, Mary Jo, and David Ellwood. *Welfare Realities: From Rhetoric to Reform*. Cambridge, Mass.: Harvard University Press, 1994.

Baudrillard, Jean. *The Consumer Society: Myths and Structures*. Thousand Oaks, Calif.: Sage Publications, 1997.

———. *For a Critique of the Political Economy of the Sign*. Translated by Charles Levin. Saint Louis, Mo.: Telos Press, 1981.

———. *Simulations*. Translated by Paul Foss, Paul Patton, and Philip Beiteman. New York: Semiotext, 1983.

Bauman, Zygmut. *Intimations of Postmodernity*. London: Routledge, 1992.

———. *The Left in Search of a Center*. Edited by Michael Crozier and Peter Murphy. Urbana: University of Illinois Press, 1996.

———. *Postmodernity and Its Discontents*. Cambridge, Mass.: Blackwell Publishers, 1997.

Bello, Walden. *Dark Victory: The United States, Structural Adjustment and Global Poverty*. Oakland, Calif.: Institute for Food and Development Policy, 1994.

Berlin, Isaiah. *Karl Marx*. 4th ed. Oxford: Oxford University Press, 1978.

Blank, Rebecca M., and Ron Haskins, eds. *The New World of Welfare*. Washington, D.C.: Brookings Institution Press, 2001.

Bottomore, Thomas B. *Classes in Modern Society*. New York: Vintage Books, 1966.

Bowles, Samuel, and Herbert Gintis. "Capitalism and Alienation." In *Capitalist System: A Radical Analysis of American Society*, edited by Richard Edwards et al. Englewood Cliffs, N.J.: Prentice-Hall, 1978.

———. "Power and Wealth in a Competitive Capitalist Economy." *Philosophy & Public Affairs* 21, no. 4 (Fall 1992): 324–353.

Boyte, Harry. "A Democratic Awakening." *Social Policy* (September/October 1979).

Brenner, Neil, Bob Jessop, Martin Jones, and Gordon MacLeod. *State/Space: A Reader*. Oxford: Blackwell, 2003.

Buchanan, Allen. *Ethics, Efficiency and the Market*. Totowa, N.J.: Rowman and Allenheld, 1985.

Carnoy, Martin. *The State and Political Theory*. Princeton, N.J.: Princeton University Press, 1984.

Cheal, David. *New Poverty: Families in Postmodern Society*. Westport, Conn.: Greenwood Press, 1996.

Clark, Robert. *The War on Poverty: History, Selected Programs, and Ongoing Impact*. Lanham, Md.: University Press of America, 2002.

Cloward, Richard, and Frances Fox Piven. "Punishing the Poor, Again: The Fraud of Workfare," *The Nation* (May 24, 1993).

Dahrendorf, Ralf. *Class and Class Conflict in Industrial Society*. Stanford, Calif.: Stanford University Press, 1959.

Denhardt, Robert. "Toward a Critical Theory of Public Organization." *Public Administration Review* 41 (November/December 1981).

Durkheim, Emile. *The Division of Labor in Society*. New York: Free Press, 1933.

Easton, David. *The Political System*. New York: Knopf, 1953.

Economic Justice for All: Pastoral Letter on Catholic Social Teaching and the U.S. Economy. Paper presented at the National Conference of Catholic Bishops, Washington, D.C., 1986.

Edelman, Peter. *Budget and Policy Choices*. Washington, D.C.: Center for National Policy Press, 1983.

Ellis, Richard. "Rival Visions of Equality in American Political Culture." *The Review of Politics* 54 (1992).

Ellwood, David. "Political Science," in *The State of Public Management*, edited by Donald Kettl and H. Brinton Milward. Baltimore, Md.: The Johns Hopkins University Press, 1996.

———. *Poor Support: Poverty in the American Family*. New York: Basic Books, 1988.

Elster, Jon. *Making Sense of Marx*. Cambridge: Cambridge University Press, 1985.

Engels, Frederick. *Anti-Dühring*. New York: International Publishers, 1965 (1878).

————. *Ludwig Feuerbach and the Outcome of Classical German Philosophy.* New York: International Publishers, 1978.

————. *The Origin of Family, Private Property, and the State.* New York: International Publications, 1975.

————. *Socialism: Utopian and Scientific.* New York: International Publishers, 1975.

Etzioni, Amatai. *The Spirit of Community: Rights, Responsibilities, and the Communitarian Agenda.* New York: Crown Publishers, 1993.

Eyal, Gil, Ivan Szelenyi, and Eleanor Townsley. "The Theory of Post-Communist Managerialism." *New Left Review* 222 (March/April 1997): 60–92.

Foucault, Michel. *The Foucault Reader.* New York: Pantheon, 1984.

————. *Politics, Philosophy, Culture.* Edited by Lawrence Kritzman, translated by Alan Sheridan and others. New York: Routledge, 1988.

————. "Two Lectures." In *Power/Knowledge: Selected Writings and Other Interviews.* New York: Pantheon, 1980.

Frankel, Charles. "The Moral Framework of Welfare." In *Welfare and Wisdom.* Toronto: The University of Toronto Press, 1966.

Freire, Paulo. *Cultural Action for Freedom.* New York: Penguin Books, 1972.

————. *Education for Critical Consciousness.* New York: Sheed & Ward, 1974.

————. *Pedagogy of the Oppressed.* New York: Continuum Publishers, 1970.

Friedman, Milton. *Capitalism and Freedom.* Chicago: University of Chicago Press, 1962.

Gadamer, Hans-Georg. *Philosophical Hermeneutics.* Berkeley: University of California Press, 1976.

————. *Truth and Method.* New York: Seabury Press, 1975.

Galbraith, John Kenneth. *The Good Society: The Humane Agenda.* Boston: Houghton-Mifflin, 1996.

Gibson-Graham, J. K., Stephen Resnick, and Richard Wolff, eds. "Toward a Poststructuralist Political Economy." *Re/Presenting Class: Essays in Postmodern Marxism.* Durham, N.C.: Duke University Press, 2001.

Gilbert, Neil. *Capitalism and the Welfare State.* New Haven, Conn.: Yale University Press, 1983.

Gilder, George. *Wealth and Poverty.* New York: Bantam, 1982.

Gilens, Martin. *Why Americans Hate Welfare: Race, Media and the Politics of Antipoverty Policy.* Chicago: University of Chicago Press, 1999.

Gilligan, Carol. *In A Different Voice.* Cambridge, Mass.: Harvard University Press, 1982.

Goldberg, Gertrude, and Sheila Collins, eds. *Washington's New Poor Law: Welfare "Reform" and the Roads Not Taken, 1935 to the Present.* New York: The Apex Press, 2001.

Goodwin, Leonard. *Causes and Cures of Welfare: New Evidence on the Social Psychology of the Poor.* Lexington, Mass.: Lexington Books, 1983.

Gough, Ian. *Global Capital, Human Needs and Social Policies.* New York: Palgrave, 2000.

Govier, Trudy. "The Right to Eat and the Duty to Work." *Philosophy of the Social Sciences* 5 June 1975): 123–143.

Gramsci, Antonio. *The Modern Prince and Other Writings*. New York: International Publishers, 1978.

———. *Selections from the Prison Notebooks*. New York: International Publishers, 1971.

Green, Richard, and Lawrence Hubbell. "On Governance and Reinventing Government." In *Refounding Democratic Public Administration: Modern Paradoxes, Postmodern Challenges*, edited by Gary Wamsley and James Wolf. Thousand Oaks, Calif.: Sage Publications, 1996.

Gurr, Ted Robert. *Why Men Rebel*. Princeton, N.J.: Princeton University Press, 1970.

Habermas, Jürgen. *Communication and the Evolution of Society*. Boston: Beacon Press, 1979.

———. *Knowledge and Human Interests*. Boston: Beacon Press, 1971.

———. *Legitimation Crisis*. Boston: Beacon Press, 1975.

———. *The Philosophical Discourse of Modernity*. Cambridge, Mass.: MIT Press, 1987.

———. "Questions and Counter-Questions." In *Habermas and Modernity* edited by Richard Bernstein. Cambridge: Polity Press, 1985.

Handler, Joel and Yeheskel Hasenfeld. *The Moral Construction of Poverty*. Newbury Park, Calif.: Sage, 1991.

Harrington, Michael. *The New American Poverty*. New York: Holt, Rinehart and Winston, 1984.

———. *The Other America*. New York: The Macmillan Company, 1964.

———. *Socialism: Past and Future*. New York: A Mentor Book, 1992.

Harrison, Beverly. *Making the Connections: Essays in Feminist Social Ethics*. Edited by Carol Robb. Boston: Beacon Press, 1985.

Hart, Herbert Lionel Adolphus. "Rawls on Liberty and Equality." In *Reading Rawls: Critical Studies on Rawls' A Theory of Justice*, edited by Norman Daniels. New York: Basic Books, 1975.

Harvey, David. *The Condition of Postmodernity: An Enquiry into the Origins of Cultural Change*. Oxford: Blackwell, 1989.

———. *The Limits to Capital*. London: Verso, 1999.

Hayek, Friedrich von. *The Mirage of Social Justice*. Vol. 2, *Law, Legislation, and Liberty*. London: Routledge and Kegan Paul, 1982.

———. *The Road to Serfdom*. Chicago: University of Chicago Press, 1976.

———. *Rules and Order*. London: Routledge, 1973.

Heclo, Hugh. "The Social Question." In *Poverty, Inequality, and the Future of Social Policy*, edited by Katherine McFate, Roger Lawson, and William Wilson. New York: Russell Sage Foundation, 1995.

Hegel, Georg Wilhelm Friedrich. *The Philosophy of History*. New York: Dover Press, 1956.

Heilbroner, Robert. *Twenty-first Century Capitalism*. New York: Norton, 1993.

Held, Virginia. *Feminist Morality: Transforming Culture, Society, and Politics*. Chicago: University of Chicago Press, 1993.

Herman, Edward, and Noam Chomsky. *Manufacturing Consent: The Political Economy of the Mass Media*. New York: Pantheon Books, 1988.

Horkheimer, Max. *Eclipse of Reason.* New York: Seabury Press, 1974.

Hospers, John. *Libertarianism: A Political Philosophy for Tomorrow.* Los Angeles: Nash Publications, 1971.

Jameson, Fredric. "Marxism and Postmodernism." In *Postmodernism/Jameson/Critique*, edited by Douglas Kellner. Washington, D.C.: Maisonneuve Press, 1989.

———. "Postmodernism, or the Cultural Logic of Late Capitalism." *New Left Review* 146 (1984): 53–93.

———. *Postmodernism, or the Cultural Logic of Late Capitalism.* Durham, N.C.: Duke University Press, 1992.

Jencks, Christopher. "How Poor Are the Poor?" *The New York Review of Books*, May 9, 1985.

Jessop, Bob. *The Future of the Capitalist State.* Cambridge, U.K.: Polity Press, 2003.

Joe, Tom, and Cheryl C. Rogers. *By the Few for the Few: The Reagan Welfare Legacy.* Lexington, Mass.: Lexington Books, 1981.

Kaufman, Alexander. *Welfare in the Kantian State.* New York: Oxford University Press, 1999.

Kaus, Mickey. *The End of Equality.* New York: Basic Books, 1992.

Keynes, John Maynard. *The General Theory of Employment, Interest, and Money.* New York: Harcourt, Brace and Ward, 1964.

King, Cheryl, and Camilla Stivers, et al. *Government Is Us: Public Administration in an Anti-Government Era.* Thousand Oaks, Calif.: Sage Publications, 1998.

Kymlicka, William. *Contemporary Political Philosophy.* New York: Oxford University Press, 2001.

Lappé, Frances Moore, and Joseph Collins. *World Hunger: Twelve Myths.* New York: Grove Press, 1986.

Lekachman, Robert. *Greed Is Not Enough.* New York: Pantheon Books, 1982.

Lenin, Vladimir I. *Collected Works.* Moscow: Progress Publishers, 1964.

———. "Economics and Politics in the Era of the Dictatorship of the Proletariat." In *Collected Works*, vol. 30. Moscow: Progress Publishers, 1973.

———. *Marx, Engels, Marxism.* Moscow: Foreign Languages Publishing House, 1951.

———. *Selected Works.* New York: International Publishers, 1967.

Leonard, Peter. *Postmodern Welfare: Reconstructing an Emancipatory Project.* Thousand Oaks, Calif.: Sage Publications, 1997.

Locke, John. *The Second Treatise of Government: An Essay Concerning the True Original, Extent and End of Civil Government.* New York: Oxford University Press, 1947.

———. *Treatise on Civil Government.* New York: Appleton-Century-Croft, 1937.

Lowi, Ted J. "Why Is There No Socialism in the United States?" *Society* 22 (January/February 1985): 34–42.

Lyotard, Jean-Francois. "Defining the Postmodern." In *Postmodernism: ICA Documents*, edited by Lisa Appignanesi. London: Free Association Books, 1989.

MacIntyre, Alisdair. *After Virtue: A Study in Moral Theory.* South Bend, Ind.: University of Notre Dame Press, 1981.

Magdoff, Harry. *The Age of Imperialism: The Economics of United States Foreign Policy.* New York: Monthly Review Press, 1969.

Martin, Edward. *Welfare Policy, the Market, and Community.* Tempe: Arizona State University, 2000.

Martin, Randy. *On Your Marx: Rethinking Socialism and the Left.* Minneapolis: University of Minnesota Press, 2002.

Marx, Karl. *Capital.* Vol. 1. London: Penguin Books, 1976 (1867).

———. *Capital.* Vol. 1. Moscow: Foreign Language Publishing House Edition, 1959.

———. *Collected Works.* Moscow: Progress Publishers, 1971.

———. *Economic and Philosophic Manuscripts of 1844.* New York: International Publishers, 1974.

———. *The German Ideology.* New York: International Publishers, 1970 (1845).

———. *Karl Marx: Early Writings,* translated by T. B. Bottomore. New York: McGraw-Hill Book Company, 1964 (1844).

———. *Karl Marx: Selected Writings,* edited by Lawrence H. Simon. Indianapolis: Hackett Publishing Company, 1994 (1845).

———. *Selected Correspondence.* Moscow: Progress Publishers, 1965.

———. *Value, Price, and Profit.* New York: International Publishers, 1935.

Marx, Karl, and Friedrich Engels. *Collected Works.* Vol. 3. New York: International Publishers, 1975.

———. *The Communist Manifesto.* New York: Pathfinder Press, 1978 (1848).

McFate, Katherine, Roger Lawson, and William Julius Wilson. *Poverty, Inequality, and the Future of Social Policy.* New York: Russell Sage Foundation, 1995.

McGowan, John. *Postmodernism and Its Critics.* Ithaca, N.Y.: Cornell University Press, 1991.

McLaren, Peter, and Peter Leonard, eds. *Paulo Freire: A Critical Encounter.* London: Routledge, 1993.

Mead, Lawrence. *Beyond Entitlement: The Social Obligations of Citizenship.* New York: Free Press, 1986.

Merelman, Richard. "On the Neo-Elitist Critique of Community Power." *American Political Science Review* 62 (June 1968).

Miller, Richard W. "Marx and Morality." In *Canadian Journal of Philosophy 3*, Supplement, edited by Nielsen and Patten (1977).

Mills, C. Wright. *The Power Elite.* New York: Oxford University Press, 1956.

Moynihan, Daniel Patrick. *The Politics of a Guaranteed Income: The Nixon Administration and the Family Assistance Plan.* New York: Random House, 1973.

Murray, Michael. *". . . And Economic Injustice for All:" Welfare Reform for the 21st Century.* New York: M. E. Sharpe, 1997.

Navasky, Victor. *Naming Names.* New York: Viking Press, 1980.

Noble, Charles. *Welfare As We Knew It: A Political History of the American Welfare State.* New York: Oxford University Press, 1997.

Nozick, Robert. "Distributive Justice." *Philosophy and Public Affairs* (Fall 1973).

O'Connor, James. *The Fiscal Crisis of the State.* New York: St. Martin's Press, 1973.

Ollman, Bertell. *Dance of the Dialectic: Steps in Marx's Method.* Chicago: University of Illinois Press, 2003.

Parenti, Michael. *Democracy for the Few*. 6th ed. New York: St. Martin's Press, 1995.

Parsons, Talcott. *The Social System*. Glencoe, Ill.: Free Press, 1951.

Peffer, Rodney G. *Marxism, Morality, and Social Justice*. Princeton, N.J.: Princeton University Press, 1990.

Petras, James. "Latin America: The Resurgence of the Left." *New Left Review* 223 (May/June 1997): 17–47.

Phillips, Ann. "From Inequality to Difference: A Severe Case of Displacement." *New Left Review* 224 (July/August 1997): 143–153.

Phillips, Derek L. *Toward a Just Social Order*. Princeton, N.J.: Princeton University Press, 1986.

Piven, Frances Fox, and Richard Cloward. *The New Class War: Reagan's Attack on the Welfare State and its Consequences*. New York: Random House Pantheon Books, 1982.

———. *Regulating the Poor*. New York: Pantheon, 1971.

Postman, Neil, and Carl Weingartner. *Teaching as a Subversive Activity*. New York: Penguin Books, 1971.

Poulantzas, Nicos. *Classes in Contemporary Capitalism*. London: New Left Books, 1975.

———. *Political Power and Social Classes*. London: New Left Books, 1973.

———. *Pre-Capitalist Economic Formations*. New York: New World Paperbacks International Publishers, 1965.

Rawls, John. "Fairness to Goodness." *Philosophical Review* 84 (October 1975), 564.

———. *A Theory of Justice*. Cambridge, Mass.: Harvard University Press, 1971.

Reich, Robert. "The Fracturing of the Middle Class." *New York Times*, August 31, 1994. 13.

Rescher, Nicholas. *Welfare: The Social Issues in Philosophical Perspective*. Pittsburgh: University of Pittsburgh Press, 1972.

Rochmore, Tom. *Marx after Marxism: The Philosophy of Karl Marx*. Malden, Mass.: Blackwell, 2002.

Rorty, Richard. *Consequences of Pragmatism: Essays 1972–1980*. Minneapolis: University of Minnesota Press, 1982.

Rossi, Peter. *Down and Out in America: The Origins of Homelessness*. Chicago: University of Chicago Press, 1989.

Russell, Bertrand. "Proposed Roads to Freedom." In *Selected Papers of Bertrand Russell*. New York: Random House, 1955.

Rustin, Michael. "The Politics of Post-Fordism: Or, the Trouble with 'New Times.'" *New Left Review* 175 (1989): 54–78.

Schmidtz, David, and Robert Goodin. *Social Welfare and Individual Responsibility*. New York: Cambridge University Press, 1988.

Sen, Amartya. "Justice: Means versus Freedoms." *Philosophy and Public Affairs* 19, no. 2 (Spring 1990): 111–121.

———. *On Economic Inequality*. New York: Oxford, 1973.

Seidman, Steven. *Contested Knowledge: Social Theory in the Postmodern Era*. 2nd ed. Malden, Mass.: Blackwell Publishers, 1998.

———. *Postmodernism and Social Theory*. Oxford: Blackwell, 1992.

Shaw, Martin. "The State of Globalization: Towards a Theory of State Transformation." In *State/Space: A Reader*, edited by Neil Brenner, Bob Jessop, Martin Jones, and Gordon MacLeod. Oxford: Blackwell, 2003.

Shulman, Beth. *The Betrayal of Work: How Low-Wage Jobs Fail Thirty Million Americans*. New York: New Press, 2003.

Smith, Adam. *An Inquiry into the Nature and Causes of the Wealth of Nations (1776)*. Chicago: Encyclopedia Britannica, 1952 (1776).

Soros, George. *Open Society: Reforming Global Capitalism*. New York: Public Affairs, 2000.

Stalin, Joseph V. "Report to the Eighteenth Congress of the C.P.S.U. (B)." In *Problems of Leninism*. Peking: Foreign Languages Press, 1976.

Sterba, James. *The Demands of Justice*. South Bend, Ind.: University of Notre Dame Press, 1980.

———. *Morality and Social Justice*. Lanham, Md.: Rowman & Littlefield, 1996.

———. "The Welfare Rights of Distant Peoples and Future Generations: Moral Side-Constraints on Social Policy." *Social Theory and Practice* 7 (Spring 1981).

Stroesz, David, and Howard Karger. *Reconstructing the American Welfare State*. Lanham, Md.: Rowman & Littlefield, 1992.

Sullivan, William. *Reconstructing Public Philosophy*. Berkeley: University of California Press, 1982.

Swank, Duane. *Global Capital, Political Institutions, and Policy Change in Developed Welfare States*. New York: Cambridge University Press, 2002.

Sweezy, Paul. "Capitalism and Democracy." *Monthly Review* 32, no. 2 (June 1980).

Taylor, Charles. "On Social Justice." *Canadian Journal of Political and Social Theory* 1 (Fall 1977).

Thompson, Edward P. *The Poverty of Theory and Other Essays*. New York: International Publishers, 1978.

Thurow, Lester. "The Rich: Why Their World Might Crumble." *The New York Times Magazine*, November 19, 1995: 78.

———. *The Future of Capitalism*. New York: William Morrow, 1996.

Toqueville, Alexis de. *Democracy in America*. New York: Harper and Row, 1988.

Torres, Rodolfo, Louis Miron, and Jonathan Xavier Inda, eds. *Race, Identity, and Citizenship: A Reader*. Oxford: Blackwell Publishers, 1999.

Tullock, Gordon. *Private Wants, Public Needs*. New York: Basic Books, 1970.

Tyrrell, R. Emmett. *The Liberal Crack-Up*. New York: Simon and Shuster, 1984.

Van Parijs, Philippe. *Politics and Society*. Vol. 32 no. 1 March 2004.

Veblen, Thorstein. *The Theory of the Leisure Class*. New York: Random House, 1931.

Venakhi, Shenhar, ed. *Welfare Reform in America*. New York: Nova Science Publishers, 1996.

Verba, Sidney. *Elites and the Idea of Equality: A Comparison of Japan, Sweden and the United States*. Cambridge, Mass.: Harvard University Press, 1987.

Waligorski, Conrad. *The Political Theory of Conservative Economics*. Lawrence, Kans.: University Press of Kansas, 1990.

Wainwright, Hilary. *Reclaim the State: Experiments in Popular Democracy*. New York: Verso, 2003.

Waters, Malcolm. *Globalization*. New York: Routledge, 1995.

Weber, Max. *The Protestant Ethic and the Spirit of Capitalism*. London: Unwin, 1930.

———. *The Theory of Economic and Social Organization*. Edited by Alexander Morell Henderson and Talcott Parsons, translated by Talcott Parsons. New York: Oxford University Press, 1947.

White, Jay. "On the Growth of Knowledge in Public Administration." *Public Administration Review* 46 (January/February 1986).

White, John Kenneth. *The New Politics of Old Values*. 2nd ed. Hanover, N.H.: University Press of New England, 1990.

Wing, Adrien Katherine, ed. *Critical Race Feminism: A Reader*. New York: New York University Press, 1997.

Wolin, Sheldon. "Why Democracy?" *Democracy* (January 1981).

Wood, Allen. "Historical Materialism and Functional Explanation." *Inquiry* 29 (March 1986).

Zweig, Michael. *The Working Class Majority: America's Best Kept Secret*. Ithaca, N.Y.: Cornell University Press, 2000.

Index

About the Authors

Edward J. Martin teaches at the Graduate Center for Public Policy and Administration at California State University at Long Beach.

Rodolfo D. Torres is associate professor of Chicano-Latino studies, political science, and planning, policy, and design at the University of California at Irvine. Previous books include *Latino Metropolis* and *After Race: Racism after Multiculturalism*.